007

HAZLITT'S CRITICISM
OF SHAKESPEARE

A Selection

Edited By

R.S. White

Studies in British Literature
Volume 18

The Edwin Mellen Press
Lewiston/Queenston/Lampeter

Library of Congress Cataloging-in-Publication Data

Hazlitt, William, 1778-1830.
    Hazlitt's criticism of Shakespeare : a selection / edited by R.S.
White.
        p.   cm. -- (Studies in British literature ; v. 18)
    Includes bibliographical references (p.   ) and index.
    ISBN 0-7734-8917-7 (hard)
    1. Shakespeare, William, 1564-1616--Criticism and interpretation.
I. White, R. S., 1948- . II. Series.
PR2976.H395 1996
822.3'3--dc20   95-23495
                                               CIP

This is volume 18 in the continuing series
Studies in British Literature
Volume 18 ISBN 0-7734-8917-7
SBL Series ISBN 0-88946-927-X

A CIP catalog record for this book is available from the British Library.

Copyright © 1996 The Edwin Mellen Press

All rights reserved. For information contact

The Edwin Mellen Press
Box 450
Lewiston, New York
USA 14092-0450

The Edwin Mellen Press
Box 67
Queenston, Ontario
CANADA L0S 1L0

The Edwin Mellen Press, Ltd.
Lampeter, Dyfed, Wales
UNITED KINGDOM SA48 7DY

Printed in the United States of America

'By my hatred of tyrants I knew what their
hatred of the free-born spirit of man must be,
of the semblance, of the very name
of Liberty and Humanity'

(William Hazlitt, *The Plain Speaker*)

Contents

INTRODUCTION

The Making of a Shakespearian Critic

There is little in William Hazlitt's background or early training to mark him out even as a man of letters let alone a Shakespearean critic of distinction. His interests lay in political philosophy and painting, and his occupation emerged as a columnist in journals. His longest book was a three-volume biography of Napoleon Buonaparte. Hazlitt's intellectually circuitous route to Shakespeare, however, fitted him with a distinctive set of interests and attitudes which in their maturity inform his essays on Shakespeare's characters and his large body of theatre reviews. In order to appreciate his particular contribution to Shakespeare studies, which is becoming more significant with the emergence of new literary theories, we must first pay some attention to the formation of his general attitudes.

Hazlitt's public stance was always one of embattled independence. He must have acquired at least a part of his outlook on life from his father, a Unitarian minister who was too radical to find acceptance even amongst rational Dissenters in England and North America where the family spent a nomadic and impecunious four years from 1783 to 1787 (William was born in 1778). William's ambitious independence of mind emerged at the age of fourteen when he began to form in his head 'a system of political rights and general jurisprudence',[1] a moment which he later declared to be the first time he ever attempted to think. The project was to occupy him obsessively through his schooldays at Hackney College, from which he left at the end of his second year 'an avowed infidel', and beyond, emerging eventually in *An Essay on the Principles of Human Action: Being an Argument in Favour of the Natural Disinterestedness of the Human Mind* (1804). Although the book hardly makes for light reading and is not as original as Hazlitt believed, it is an important statement of attitudes, formed partly through rational enquiry and partly through prior beliefs. It lies behind not only his political writings but his literary criticism. On the many occasions when he was to praise Shakespeare for his 'disinterestedness', for example (the word was to be picked up by John Keats from Hazlitt),[2] he did not mean that Shakespeare maintains a poetic stance of 'aloofness',[3] he was not returning to eighteenth-century commonplaces about the way in which Shakespeare imitates nature, nor did he primarily mean the 'ventriloquial'[4] capacity of the dramatist to 'inhabit' his characters' beings. He was in fact conducting a debate which has moral and political dimensions, coming down on the side asserting that humanity is actively altruistic and sympathetic rather than passively selfish and self-seeking. As a radical Dissenter, friend of the anarchist Godwin and other political radicals, and an ally of Leigh Hunt the anti-monarchist, the argument was fundamental to Hazlitt. His firm stance accounts for the trenchant opposition he aroused when he wrote for the radical *Examiner* while Hunt was editor, and for his own pugnacity in responding to attacks from Tory reviewers in *Blackwood's*, *The Edinburgh Review* and *The Quarterly Review*. In *Free Thoughts on Public Affairs* (1806) and *Reply to Malthus* (1807) Hazlitt singled out his ideological enemies amongst his contemporaries. Burke, whose style he admired but whose politics he abhorred, argued for the privileges of a small aristocracy as the natural ruling class of England, and Malthus claimed that in a world of diminishing resources the existence of poverty can be justified as a necessary condition for the maintenance of an elite. In countering such justifications of inequality and illiberalism, Hazlitt had precedents. James Mackintosh supported the rights of all to participate in government of the country through elected representatives. William Godwin's monumental *Enquiry Concerning Political Justice* (1793)[5] expounded principles of natural rights and rational utopianism, arguing against Hobbes that people are naturally virtuous and selfless. Thomas Paine's rousing call for the American Revolution, *Rights of Man* (1791[6] and 1792), a direct attack on Burke, asserted social equality and attacked the corruption of a class system. From these writers Hazlitt forged his own scheme, defending personal liberty at a time when the British government was becoming increasingly repressive in fear of the French Revolution spilling over into England.

Hazlitt differed, however, from Mackintosh, Godwin and Paine in an important way, and it defines his own contribution. Whereas the others saw selflessness as either an intuitive or rational quality, Hazlitt traced its existence to the mental faculty which he prized and defended above all others, the sympathetic imagination, viewed as an active rather than passive or innate quality. In this he was opposing basic tenets advanced by Locke and Hartley that the mind is a mechanical, data-collecting and sponge-like faculty, depending solely on the sense experiences of the individual. He was also implicitly celebrating the power of the human imagination to make better worlds, an activity whose expression may lie through literature and drama. Hazlitt argues in the *Essay on the Principles of Human Action* that 'ideas are the offspring of the understanding, not of the senses', and he asserts the creative nature of the imagination. The 'mechanists of the mind' (among whom Hazlitt in crustier moods placed Wordsworth; see below, number 9[ii]), in Hazlitt's view, gave priority to the reason and a rationally conducted association of sense-impressions, conceding no more than memory as an exercise of individual, mental freedom.

It is tempting when dealing with writers of the Romantic age to lump them together in their belief in the imagination, as if it were created in literary circles and was a consistent programme. This is to underestimate the differences in emphasis and more particularly the varying sources for individual approaches, an intertextuality which stemmed in the Romantic age as much from friendships as from reading. Hazlitt's ideas were formed largely in political discourse. Perhaps the presence of Godwin explains the similarity between Hazlitt and Shelley on this issue, and Keats looked to Hazlitt himself for ideas. Meanwhile, Hazlitt saw other influential poets as ideological enemies. He never forgave Wordsworth, Coleridge and Southey for the 'long narrowing of the mind' which turned them from moderate radicals into 'egotistical' (self-centred or selfish) conservatives. In literary terms he recognised the great gifts of Wordsworth without accepting that he could be 'disinterested', and he could never really comprehend how Scott managed to transcend his politics to write novels of 'magnanimity'. All the time, his real model of disinterested selflessness, imaginative projection away from the self, was Shakespeare.

At the same time, Hazlitt takes pains to stress that in the context of drama, sympathy aroused by the playwright does not preclude conflict in his plays, and also that the quality he is talking about is not a vaguely benevolent outlook on life but a specific engagement with immediate problems through exercise of the feelings. In an important essay in The *London Magazine*, April, 1820, he argues that his own age is antithetical to drama. With his eye upon Coleridge and Godwin, and adverting to the significance of the French Revolution, he condemns his contemporaries' tendency to depersonalise, to 'abstract' conflicts from their immediate emotional contexts. 'We are more in love with a theory than a mistress'[7], he says of his age. The imaginative poet, and in particular the dramatist, 'can only act by sympathy with the public mind and manners of his age', and his own age, as Hazlitt sees it, is out of touch with 'passions ... worked up to the highest pitch of intensity'.[8] Using the age of Shakespeare as his implicit contrast, Hazlitt emphasises his own dearest preoccupations: that drama is not abstract but particular and concrete, that the kind of sympathy aroused by poetry is a commitment to strong feelings rather than thought, and that such sympathy is not irreconcilable with, but indeed necessarily includes, oppositions and contrasts:

> If a bias to abstraction is evidently, then, the reigning spirit of the age, dramatic poetry must be allowed to be most irreconcileable with this spirit; it is essentially individual and concrete, both in form and in power ... Within the circle of dramatic character and natural passion, each individual is to feel as keenly, as profoundly, as rapidly as possible, but he is not to feel beyond it, for others or for the whole. Each character, on the contrary, must be a kind of centre of repulsion to the rest; and it is their hostile interests, brought into collision, that must tug at the heartstrings, and call forth every faculty of thought, speech and action.[9]

This, Hazlitt argues, cannot occur in an age 'when the mind is turned habitually out of itself to general, speculative truth'. There is a paradox here: the poet displays sympathy by showing people in conflict. But the resolution comes through the involved feelings and sympathies of the audience, not 'recollected in tranquillity' but felt on the pulses. Unity is not 'organic' to the work of art, but is partially created by the audience's sympathy. Hazlitt's term for active sympathy in the writer and audience is 'gusto' (below, no. 2).

Hazlitt consistently developed the idea of the creativity of the imagination into the moral sphere, and it is here that Shakespeare becomes most relevant. Answering Hobbes's axiom that 'pity is only another name for self-love', Hazlitt argued for the existence of altruism as a function of the imagination:

> ... a sentiment of general benevolence can only arise from an habitual cultivation of the natural disposition of the mind to sympathise with the feelings of others by constantly taking an interest in those which we know, and imagining others that we do not know ... self-interest ... must be caused by a long narrowing of the mind to our own particular feelings and interests, and a voluntary insensibility to every thing which does not immediately concern ourselves.[10]

Hazlitt's application of this principle to Shakespeare's characters has both a superficial and a deeper aspect. It allows him simply to accept as axiomatic Shakespeare's capacity to create fictional personages which have a 'life' of their own, and he did not follow the profound path of Coleridge in analysing how this feat is achieved.[11] On the other hand, he does explore the consequences of the principle. He is sharply aware of the fact that both actors and readers are compelled to exercise the same active imagination of morals and emotions in order to recreate by a 'greeting of the Spirit' (Keats's phrase[12]) a process initiated by the dramatist. His famous celebration of 'gusto' ('power or passion defining any object'[13]) applies just as much to the reader or viewer of the work of art, as to the text of the work itself. Perhaps this explains why Hazlitt was able - so much more consistently and flexibly than any of his more literary contemporaries - both to write perceptively about literary works and to review Shakespeare in the theatre with critical understanding, for his underlying theory includes the active and mutual participation of readers, actors and audiences alike in the creation of meaning.[14] The process is fundamentally the same in the closet and in the theatre.

Moreover, Hazlitt's belief in the activity of the moral imagination makes him particularly strong where other 'moral' critics (such as Johnson, whom Hazlitt constantly maligns) can be reductive - in recognising first the 'mixed motives' of Shakespearean characters which makes easy judgment impossible, and secondly the moral complexity of 'outsider' characters. He constantly returned to Iago and Richard III as intriguingly complex figures, and he tried to understand the sources of their evil actions in diverse, often sympathetic ways. Shylock and Caliban are two others whom he treats with considerably more tolerance and psychological understanding than other critics of the day, without falling into the trap of sentimentality. On these characters Hazlitt is undogmatic, judicious and modern. Equally modern is his correlative suspicion of self-seeking egotism and power in general, which for example allows Hazlitt to be sceptical about the Duke in *Measure for Measure*, and deeply critical of Coriolanus (and *en passant*, Shakespeare himself for abandoning democratic openness in biasing audiences towards this character through the power of poetry and rhetoric). Even when he is writing on Shakespeare, Hazlitt peppers his essays with briefly ferocious attacks on self-seeking politicians and the insensitivity of those in power in his own day. All the accounts below of the history plays demonstrate this pugnacity. It is perhaps little wonder that in Hazlitt's hands the apparently harmless belle-lettrisme of Shakespearean criticism became a controversial medium provoking the wrath of political writers such as Gifford (see the essays on Coriolanus, below, numbers 19 and 48). Of Henry V Hazlitt wrote:

> Henry V. is a very favourite monarch with the English nation, and he appears to have been also a favourite with Shakespear, who labours hard to apologise for the actions of the king, by shewing us the character of the man, as 'the king of good fellows.' He scarcely deserves this honour. He was fond of war and low company: - we know little else of him. He was careless, dissolute, and ambitious; - idle, or doing mischief. In private, he seemed to have no idea of the common decencies of life, which he subjected to a kind of regal licence; in public affairs, he seemed to have no idea of any rule of right or wrong, but brute force, glossed over with a little religious hypocrisy and archiepiscopal advice...[No. 29 below]

And so on, for a paragraph. Hazlitt's contemptuous dismissal of monarchs and aristocrats surfaces frequently [see no. 13 below, for example], and ususally with devastating wit, in his Shakespearian criticism. It is the other side of disinterestedness: an ideological attack on those who perpetuate the inequalities that cause suffering. It is in this area (and this probably alone) that Hazlitt deserved the reputation of a 'good hater' (his phrase for Shylock).

Painting was second in importance to politics as an influence upon Hazlitt's literary work. He had always intended to become a professional painter and trained towards this end, but eventually came to the sad recognition that he had no talent. His most recent biographer, Stanley Jones, produces evidence that this negative opinion was Hazlitt's own, self-critical judgment and may not be fair.[15] Whether the reason was disappointed perfectionism or otherwise, he certainly never seemed able to finish paintings. As if anticipating Shaw's caustic observation about teaching, because he could not do, he became a critic, and many of his aesthetic principles were worked out through pictorial art before being applied to literature. 'Gusto' was a term, perhaps borrowed from the continental art critics,[16] applied mainly to painting:

> 'Gusto' is not a very helpful term in discussing Hazlitt's literary criticism, because he uses the term much more for painting than for poetry. It ought to be remembered that the examples developed in 'On Gusto' are from painters - Titian, Raphael, Corregio, Rembrandt and others. Only in the final paragraph does Hazlitt quickly speak of a properly literary

gusto, illustrated by examples from Milton only. For the rest, he simply ascribes gusto to Shakespeare, Pope, Dryden, Prior, Rabelais, Boccaccio, and The Beggar's Opera.[17]

To this list should be added the actor Edmund Kean. More central (and itself related to gusto) is the whole procedure of 'impressionistic' criticism, forged first as an instrument of art criticism and powerfully adapted to literary matters, which is arguably Hazlitt's most significant contribution to Shakespeare studies, at least in the Victorian age. When he says 'genuine criticism should reflect the colours, the light and shade, the soul and body of a work',[18] he is describing his practice as critic of art and literature alike. One sentence, taken from the essay on Othello in the *Characters of Shakespear's Plays* takes us close to the central constituents of the 'impressions' which Hazlitt tries to describe and convey as 'The picturesque contrasts of character in this play are almost as remarkable as the depth of passion'.[19] 'Picturesque contrasts' offers a clue to what links art and drama in Hazlitt's mind. Throughout his writing on Shakespeare we find 'Contrast' praised and pointed out, and 'depth of passion' is what makes the contrasts functional:

> *Lear* stands first for the profound intensity of the passion; *Macbeth* for the wildness of the imagination and the rapidity of the action; *Othello* for the progressive interest and powerful alternations of feeling; *Hamlet* for the refined development of thought and sentiment.[20]

Here we find the full repertoire of Hazlitt's critical vocabulary: intensity, passion, imagination, alternations of feeling, thought and sentiment - used as in his art criticism to capture the fleeting and the evanescent, the overall impression made on the reader who is actively participating in the experience of the plays through the exercise of the sympathetic imagination. What is also noticeable is Hazlitt's use of what Roy Park calls a 'kinetic vocabulary',[21] words denoting movement such as rapidity, progression, alternations, development. It is this emphasis that marks a distinction between the work of literature and the work of art - the former moves in a temporal dimension, and Hazlitt wishes to convey this. Whereas in his comments on painting he locates the impression in colours, textures and evocativeness (at least when speaking of still-lifes or landscapes), in drama he stresses the dynamic, momentary effects through time. In this conscious choice he avoids a danger implicit in impressionism as a critical practice (and one which twentieth-century thematic and imagistic critics have often succumbed to) - the tendency to represent the play as a static, immanent pattern. In choosing to dwell upon contrast as a central structural and emotional principle in Shakespeare's plays, Hazlitt is doing his best to avoid another pitfall of impressionistic criticism - the temptation to allow a consistent, single-noted set of responses to dominate.

.   .   .

In another area Hazlitt's training in pictorial art allows him a distinctive approach to Shakespeare. Ever since the minimal but none the less pioneering work of William Whiter,[22] the term 'imagery' has been used by critics. Coleridge in particular often points to imagery in Shakespeare as an important element of the poetic design. However, his understanding of poetic imagery is closely linked with his interest in symbolism and, one feels, a notion of the religious epiphany. When he agrees with Milton that poetry should be 'sensuous' and 'passionate' it is because he regards the image as numinous and emotionally charged - the 'truth' an image can convey is larger than just a picture: '*sensuous*, since it is only by sensuous images that we can elicit truth *as* at a flash; *passionate*, since images must be vivid in order to move our passions and awaken our affections'.[23] The function of the image is to display 'truth' and elicit feelings. Hazlitt, with his interest in art, is perhaps more interested in the momentary, pictorial effectiveness of an image rather than seeking for deeper significance. He often speaks of 'picturesque' language, images of 'exquisite beauty', as if what he primarily admires is the poet's skill in translating the visual into the verbal. When he implies that images can awaken the 'feelings' ('move our passions') he usually means that the image contributes to the impression of the play as a whole, rather than gesturing towards a symbolic dimension beyond the surface, or a level of platonic 'truth':

> The feelings of youth and of the spring are here blended together like the breath of opening flowers. Images of vernal beauty appear to have floated before the author's mind, in writing this poem [*Romeo and Juliet*], in profusion.[24]

(This comes in an essay in which Hazlitt scorns Wordsworth's tendency 'to indulge in the mystical visions of Platonism'.) Hazlitt's ideas on imagery come up against one interesting blind spot. Whereas Coleridge had essentially formed his approach in the context of Shakespeare's poems rather than his plays,[25] Hazlitt, despite calling *Romeo and Juliet* a 'poem', is more attuned to poetic drama (whether read or acted) as an accumulation of momentary effects, and he proves himself totally incapable of appreciating the Poems and Sonnets (see below, number 47), where imagery is always supporting ideas and thought rather than a dramatic impression or surface sensuousness. At the same time we should be wary of unfairly limiting Hazlitt. He was not so programmatic as to confuse the mediums of painting and drama for he criticised Shakespeare's early poetry for its 'attempt to substitute the language of painting for that of poetry'.[26] And on the other hand, he did not deny painting itself an extra-sensuous function for he could call it 'a language pointing to something beyond'.[27]

.   .   .

In attempting to lead the reader into a sympathetic understanding of Hazlitt's Shakespearean criticism I have stressed the importance of his individual and indeed unique combination of interests in radical political thought and in painting. However, it is necessary also to place him in the world of letters. He was, first, reacting against certain writers, and in particular Samuel Johnson. He reserves his most trenchant statements for Johnson, and his comments involuntarily reveal his own aims: 'he was to the poet what the painter of still life is to the painter of history'.

> It is the province of the didactic reasoner to take cognizance of those results of human nature which are constantly repeated and always the same, which follow one another in regular succession, which are acted upon by large classes of men, and embodied in received customs, laws, language, and institutions; and it was in arranging, comparing, and arguing on these kind of general results, that Johnson's excellence lay. But he could not quit his hold of the common-place and mechanical, and apply the general rule to the particular exception, or shew how the nature of man was modified by the workings of passion, or the infinite fluctuations of thought and accident.[28]

Johnson clearly emerges as a temperamental conservative, holding on to tradition and stability, whereas Hazlitt is the radical, impatient with ideas held 'by large classes of men', and interested in 'infinite fluctuations', uniquely unrepresentative characters, and change itself. However, it is impossible to avoid feeling that despite himself Hazlitt shares some quality of 'the didactic reasoner'. Much of his most searching criticism - his accounts of Iago, Caliban, Shylock and Coriolanus - has a moral intention, however flexible his judgements may be in expression. It would be surprising for him not to be often interested in the ethical questions posed by plays such as *Measure for Measure* and the tragedies, given his systematic assertion of the morality of the sympathetic imagination. What distinguishes Johnson is not really his 'didactic' emphasis but his ethical system itself, which is abhorrent to Hazlitt.

One would assume that by calling his book *Characters of Shakespear's Plays*, and by reviewing plays as if they are simply monologues by an actor like Kean, that Hazlitt is deeply indebted to eighteenth-century 'character criticism'. Closer inspection proves that he is not. He evidently did not read Maurice Morgann's *An Essay on the Dramatic Character of Sir John Falstaff*, a work which would probably have struck Hazlitt as speculative and not rooted in the drama itself. When he mentions a writer who drew parallels between Macbeth and Richard III (Thomas Whately), he gets the name wrong ('a gentleman of the name of Mason')[29] and anybody who has glanced at this dull and morally unsophisticated writer will conclude that the quick and unorthodox mind of Hazlitt took little more than the idea of comparing certain characters from the earlier book. William Richardson, another whom Hazlitt acknowledges, states as his aim 'to make poetry subservient to philosophy, and to employ it in tracing the principles of human conduct',[30] using Shakespeare's characters primarily as examples of moral conduct. Hazlitt was never interested in this kind of didacticism. On the other hand, Richardson may have given Romantic critics a word for Shakespeare, if not a spirit:

> [Shakespeare] the Proteus of the drama, changes himself into every character, and enters into every condition of human nature.[31]

The 'protean' quality of Shakespeare is praised by both Coleridge and Hazlitt,[32] and in this they may have Richardson to thank. For the rest, Hazlitt's acknowledgment to this writer is largely lip-service. There were indeed others writing in the late eighteenth century whose temper of thought is a little closer to Hazlitt's. Henry Mackenzie in 1786 saw, at least in the case of Falstaff, that character must be related to dramatic context,[33] a step towards Hazlitt's habit of seeing character against the 'impression' of the play.[34] Richard Stack in 1788, once again dwelling on Falstaff in the wake of Morgann, recognises the corollary of Mackenzie's approach, that character determines the design of the play as a whole.[35] There is no evidence that Hazlitt was aware of these writers, and his attack on Johnson is symptomatic of a more general rejection of the critical precepts of the eighteenth century. Despite the title of his book, Hazlitt's essays are not concerned with 'character' in the sense that his predecessors' books were, and his real subject is poetic drama rather than individual motivation of personages. His debate was with his contemporaries, with the greatest actor of his age, Kean, the greatest critic, Coleridge, and more generally the climate of opinion in the Romantic age in its belief in the primacy of imagination.

Hazlitt's most explicitly acknowledged debt (see number 7 below) is to August Schlegel, whom he quotes plentifully and with admiration. In this he was a true citizen of the Romantic society of poets, for the affinity existed between Coleridge and Schlegel as well, whatever the truth about whether the former borrowed from the latter early in his career. (Hazlitt was generous, even at a time when he could be forgiven for incriminating Coleridge, in exonerating the rival critic from the charge of plagiarism.)[36] Where Hazlitt differs fundamentally from the eighteenth-century critics is precisely in his impressionism as a critic. He does not see character in isolation, but instead as both cause and consequence of an overall spirit or dramatic effect which he locates in the poetic enterprise of a play. Indeed, the title of his book is misleading and it could easily have been called *Impressions of Shakespear's Poetic Drama* or even (borrowing from Schlegel) *On Dramatic Art and Literature*.[37] Undoubtedly there is a lot of attention paid to characters - unavoidable in the case of the tragic heroes, and certainly symptomatic of the individualism of the age of Byron's supermen among others, but Hazlitt does not regard characters as having an extra-dramatic existence and his emphasis is upon the way style and atmosphere of a play are intimately related to the central characters. He is certainly more adequate in his criticism of the tragedies overarched by one or two figures than of the comedies where relationships dominate, but this almost certainly results from his preference for plays which activate strong passions. He is not didactic in his readings, as were most eighteenth-century accounts, but he does show considerable interest in moral questions, for example expressing ethical doubts about the Duke in *Measure for Measture*, and in what we now call ideology.

As for his debts to contemporaries, it is salutary to keep in mind the words of Stanley Wells writing on Leigh Hunt's Shakespearian criticism:

> ... members of the literary circles of the romantic period held so many ideas in common that it is often impossible to determine who thought of what first.[38]

Hunt was himself Hazlitt's predecessor as theatre critic for *The Examiner* (of which Leigh Hunt was editor with his brother), and with the pride he took in being outspoken and remaining independent as reviewer he set a general tone which Hazlitt was only too happy to emulate. Hazlitt was lucky also to find an editor with congenial political attitudes. Hunt's criticism, written over a long period from 1808 to 1832, seems to have been taken as a model by Hazlitt, even down to the sharing of certain prejudices, such as a common dislike of Kemble's aristocratic style of acting. Hazlitt's reviews for various journals from 1813 until 1828 were, however, regarded as at least the equal of Hunt's for pungent readability, and they have certainly stood the test of time better. Despite his recognition that the actor's art is ephemeral ('one that perishes with him, and leaves no trace of itself, but in the faint descriptions of the pen or pencil'), Hazlitt immortalises through his own pen sharply described moments which demonstrate the multiple potential lying in Shakespeare's text awaiting realisation in the actor's performance.[39] Furthermore, his constant habit of referring back to the integrity of the text, and to his own imaginative understanding of the plays, adds a quality to his reviews which take them out of the category of historical curiosities and lends them an interest for the Shakespearean critic. His descriptions of the great Edmund Kean represented in Part Three demonstrate how much Hazlitt learned about the 'bye-play'[40] that can be pointed by the actor stimulated by his role, how readily he could acknowledge a 'new reading' made by the actor and, most important, how devastatingly critical he could be when this or another actor did not do justice to the humanity and common touch Hazlitt perceived in Shakespeare as writer. In terms of the text itself Hazlitt saw little reason to alter the words, and no reason to add anything. He shared with Hunt a contempt for the rewritings of Shakespeare carried out by Tate, Cibber, Davenant and Dryden and Garrick. At the same time, however much he learned from the theatre and from individual actors, he clearly agreed with, and probably discussed with Charles Lamb the general inferiority of stage representation to the imaginative recreation of the play in the mind.[41] In justifying the statement that 'THE MIDSUMMER NIGHT'S DREAM, when acted, is converted from a delightful fiction into a dull pantomime' (below, number 24) he draws, whether consciously or not, upon Lamb's careful distinction between illusions appropriate respectively to the stage and to reading, set out in the essay 'On the Tragedies of Shakespeare. Considered with reference to their Fitness for Stage

Representation'.[42] However, his uniquely extensive, first-hand knowledge of the theatre, gives Hazlitt many practical qualities not shared by his Romantic contemporaries. It is as an iconoclastic reader of Shakespeare, rather than as theatre reviewer, that Hazlitt is most accessible today although, more than any other critic of his day, he recognised the value of the stage as stimulus and testing ground for his interpretations of the text.

Undoubtedly the greatest critic of the Romantic age in England was Coleridge, and some comparison with Hazlitt is unavoidable. In order, however, for the comparison to be fair to each, the ground must be carefully chosen, and the assumption of Coleridge's superiority (adopted, for example, by M. H. Abrams)[43] would be a bar to reading either Hazlitt or Coleridge accurately. There were certain differences of principle between them which are apt to be overlooked. The relationship between the two men was a somewhat stormy one after a promising start. In 1798 (at the age of twenty), Hazlitt was entranced by the already famous Coleridge preaching a sermon, and a few days later they met when the great man visited Hazlitt's father. Coleridge did a great deal of talking and Hazlitt was sufficiently struck to be able to recall the flow of thought in 1823.[44] At Coleridge's invitation Hazlitt visited him several times, and on one occasion he met Wordsworth looking 'gaunt and Don Quixote-like'. Wordsworth was not impressed, but it is clear that in continuing to meet, Coleridge had taken to his young admirer. In recommending Hazlitt to Godwin he described Hazlitt, at that stage aspiring to be a painter, as 'a young man of profound Genius and original mind ...' and later wrote 'He sends well-headed & wellfeathered Thoughts straight forwards to the mark with a Twang of the bow-string'. The rift in the budding friendship came when Hazlitt stayed for a time in the Lake District when he was twenty-three. The actual occasion of Coleridge's withdrawal from friendship is shrouded in mystery. Both Wordsworth and Coleridge were for years to retail a story about a sexual peccadillo committed by Hazlitt (an incident which amused Haydon and Lamb) and in some ways the older poets used this story to try to damage Hazlitt's reputation at significant points of his career.[45] The incident seems far too trivial to account for the magnitude of Coleridge's distaste. More pertinently, I believe, Coleridge even before this was recording in his notebook some doubts about the Dissenter's open irreverence to 'the Divine Wisdom' of the orthodox Church. Friendship was never regained, and Hazlitt himself became increasingly bitter and disappointed with the group of Coleridge, Wordsworth and Southey for what he saw as their political backsliding into conservatism. In retrospect, it all seemed inevitable. Coleridge was starting to be lauded by the literary establishment, and retrenching into orthodox religion and politics. Hazlitt, then and always, was treated contemptuously, often in a very personal way, by Tory reviewers and literary cliques, and his outsider status was fundamentally caused by his refusal to budge on his stance as rational Dissenter and radical political thinker. With his upbringing and settled beliefs he could hardly do otherwise, and he regarded Coleridge as the traitor to his early beliefs. Intellectually, too, Hazlitt always stood in the shadow of the older men, and even his critically judicious criticism of Wordsworth's poetry was regarded with indignation by the ruling literary class of the day.

Consequently, until quite recently, commentators have tended to disregard Hazlitt's contributions to criticism as insubstantial. Luckily, he is now gaining more detached readers who are not so easily convinced of the negative opinions expressed in his own time. Roy Park, in a sympathetic and knowledgeable study, has drawn attention to a coherent 'philosophy of particularity' in Hazlitt's criticism,[46] John Kinnaird has encouraged us to see his critical temperament as consistent and developing through a critique of power,[47] W.P. Albrecht has taken seriously the coherence of his aesthetic[48] and Stanley Wells has called him one of our best theatre critics.[49] In a book which turned the tide of Hazlitt's critical fortunes, David Bromwich's *Hazlitt: The Mind of a Critic*,[50] we find a searching and admiring account of those strengths which have gone largely unnoticed. Bromwich is most detailed amongst those who sift through the intellectual relationship between Coleridge and Hazlitt. His general assessment of the doctrine of the active, sympathetic imagination, as applied in the fields of poetry, painting and literature, is that 'Hazlitt's discovery is sufficiently plain and sufficiently profound to attract and retain the allegiance of a subtle mind'.[51]

As critics of eighteenth-century taste, Coleridge and Hazlitt are often in agreement, with a depth of shared feeling that quotations can barely suggest; and the break with general nature, to which I have stressed Hazlitt's contribution, might by others be credited to Coleridge as the sole original. I remain convinced that Hazlitt, naturally a thinker for himself, had no need of Coleridge's guidance in a movement of revolt already alive on many fronts, but his own testimony here is partly in him. It affords the liveliest imaginable record of the way Coleridge's judgments took hold of anyone who once encountered them, and of their persuasiveness in revising the English poetic canon.[52]

While acknowledging the points of agreement between the critics, Bromwich stresses the differences: 'Coleridge had an idealizing temperament, Hazlitt a skeptical one.'[53] The fundamental aesthetic difference lies between Coleridge's notion of the work of art as an organic unity with its own inner laws that operate in 'aloof' fashion, independent of the reader, and Hazlitt's that the reader is involved in either creating, or being persuaded by, the rhetoric of the work of art through the active participation of the sympathetic imagination. Perhaps only Keats, with his own congenital understanding of reading as an active and creative process, fully grasped the significance of the distinction. As a general result of the differences, we may find Coleridge strong where Hazlitt is weak, but equally Hazlitt strong where Coleridge is weak. Coleridge can be deeply enquiring in his thoughts on Shakespeare where Hazlitt seems, consciously, to remain on the dramatic surface. The former is constantly looking 'behind' Shakespeare for a metaphysic, a set of ideas and philosophies that will explain the works as we have them in all their organic unity. But Hazlitt is looking directly at the texts, finding in the beliefs asserted on the surface a set of statements which can be tested against the reader's own convictions - even, in some cases, directly criticised for their bias (Coriolanus) or admired for their lack of narrow prejudice (Caliban, Shylock, Iago). Coleridge creates an inveigling labyrinth of speculation and metaphysical exploration which can be profound and intuitively revealing. Hazlitt is clear, concise and modest in his claims, asserting the values of a trustworthy fidelity to the literal meaning, involvement of the emotions rather than the abstracting intellect, and commonsense. Where the two writers meet on certain judgments of particular characters or scenes, Hazlitt may well be finding things of value in Coleridge's ideas - such intellectual impressionability and generosity is quite in character - but we should also note that time and again Hazlitt quotes and acknowledges carefully his debts to Schlegel, as if he is indicating that he may have found ideas in common between Coleridge and Schlegel but he finds the latter to be, for one reason or another, more quotable and more suitable for his own purposes. Since both Coleridge and Schlegel delivered their equally magisterial (though stylistically different) Lectures on Shakespeare in the same year, 1808, Hazlitt presumably felt the choice was open when deciding whom to acknowledge for a common thought.

In comparing Hazlitt and Coleridge, one must also bear in mind the differences of motivation and presentation between the two mens' publications. By profession, Hazlitt was a journalist and reviewer, or what we would now call a columnist for periodicals which were sympathetic to his radical, liberal views. So, for that matter, was Coleridge in his own *The Watchman* and later the *Morning Post* and *The Friend*, of which he was editor and proprietor. However (more is the pity, perhaps), Coleridge either did not need, or did not choose, to record his ideas on Shakespeare in the form of finished pieces such as theatrical reviews or sustained, discursive essays. Hazlitt did so need and so choose, and the form of the review clearly influenced his style, at once clear, crisp and concise. Similarly, Coleridge delivered lectures on Shakespeare but he did not seek to publish them, as Hazlitt published his *Characters of Shakespear's Plays*, and they are known only through reports by others (especially J.P. Collier)[54] or brief newspaper notices. We have jottings, notes, marginalia and fragments of sentences, but little published in systematic form on Shakespeare apart from the famous sections in *Biographia Literaria*. It may be more a matter of temperament than mode of publication, but the result in Coleridge's case is an often frustrating tendency to be opaque, self-contradictory and fragmentary. His gnomic comments beckon us towards some nugget of wisdom, but force the reader to work very hard in extracting the meaning or seeking to draw them into systematic unity with his other thoughts. Furthermore, even what purports to be a verbatim report of his lectures can never be proved to be exactly what Coleridge said, or intended to say, and his lectures at times were notoriously digressive and wandering so that what he would have said if forced to prepare copy for a publisher must remain in the realms of conjecture. Hazlitt, ironically, suffers from the liability of having published in essay form his ideas. We cannot give him the benefit of any doubt concerning the accuracy of a transcript when he (as he does) says things which are superficial. We can criticise his habit of repeating himself, two or more times, when we compare his reviews, his essays and his lectures. The fact remains, however, that Hazlitt's essays have the virtues of completion and ready comprehensibility. There is some evidence that the difference in this matter between the two men was symptomatic of diverging political attitudes. Coleridge's criticism has been described as perhaps calculatedly elitist, at least in his later writings:

His sentences tend to be laboured and tortuous: arguably they are appropriately so, since his meaning is complex and as time goes on he is more and more anxious to direct his message only to those qualified by education to understand him.[55]

Hazlitt, on the other hand, as the critic who praised Kean, implying a contrst with Kemble, for not being 'of the patrician order; he is one of the people, and what might be termed a radical performer' (below, number 58), and one who was disturbed by the discrepancy between Wordsworth's 'literary Jacobinism' and his actual political behaviour,[56] sought in his own writing to be consistent to his own beliefs. Admiring the journalism of William Cobbett (hurt when Cobbett fails to appreciate Shakespeare's democratic leanings - see below, number 12), Hazlitt attempted, within the constraints of conventions dominating the essay form in his day, to write with demotic clarity from the point of view of the "Plain Speaker". Many of his comments strongly imply that he would prefer to be understood than to be admired, appreciated more for clarity of thought and style than for profundity.

As an insurance for the lasting influence of his ideas, Hazlitt was lucky in having one young admirer in John Keats. It has been said that 'nearly all Keats's theories about poetry were developed from remarks of Hazlitt', with the following qualification:

Because [Keats] accepted nothing on trust, but proved his axioms on his pulses, Keats's borrowings were all transformed and individualised, so that they came to express not merely his tastes but his deepest convictions.[57]

Temperamentally there was a lot in common between the two men, signalled by the fact that Keats published his first poems in the radical *Examiner* when Hazlitt was writing for it, and they shared the fate of all Leigh Hunt's coterie in being damned by Tory critics. They met many times between 1816 and 1818, and Keats attended as many of Hazlitt's lectures as he could. Hazlitt gave him a copy of *Lectures on the English Poets* in manuscript. Keats was personally concerned that Hazlitt should know he had intellectual supporters in his time of greatest vilification in the press.[58] Since I have written in detail on the influence of Hazlitt upon Keats's critical understanding of Shakespeare,[59] I shall be summary here. Most of Keats's critical vocabulary came from Hazlitt. Words like 'intensity', 'passion', 'sympathy', 'disinterestedness' and 'egotism' are obviously not the prerogative of

Hazlitt alone, but in Keats's uses of them they bear the older critic's imprint. 'Gusto' and the concept of contrast in literature may be claimed as indisputable legacies from Hazlitt when Keats writes of Kean 'There is an indescribable gusto in his voice...'[60] and of his own feelings:

> ... and now - the knowledge of contrast, feeling for light and shade, all that information (primitive sense) necessary for a poem are great enemies to the recovery of the stomach.[61]

Hazlitt's crucial distinction, applied equally to writers and to political matters, between on the one hand disinterested sympathy, magnanimity as an act of imagination, and on the other selfishness, egotism and 'the long narrowing of the mind', have been given a sacred place in critical terminology in Keats's memorable rephrasings, 'Negative Capability' (with Shakespeare as exemplar) and the 'egotistical sublime' (Wordsworth and Milton).[62] Keats's interest in painting, fostered by Benjamin Haydon, led him to assess imagery along Hazlitt's lines, judging its sensuousness and palpability rather than its capacity to awaken 'thought' in the Coleridgean sense. Keats's famous comparison between Benjamin West's painting *Death on a White Horse* ('nothing to be intense upon') and *King Lear* (where 'all disagreeables evaporate, from their being in close relationship with Beauty and Truth')[63] owes as much to Hazlitt's essay on the painting in the *Edinburgh Magazine* as to the evidence of Keats's own mind and his critical insight.[64] Even the way in which Keats often makes *Lear* his touchstone of literary excellence is largely attributable to the high ranking of the play in Hazlitt's estimate. Similarly, like Hazlitt, Keats constantly uses tragedies to exemplify what he considers the greatest aspects of Shakespeare's art, comedy as a delightful, if lesser, bonus. One area in which we find disagreement, however, lies in Keats's admiration for the Sonnets and *Venus and Adonis* contrasting with Hazlitt's lesser estimate of their quality (see below, number 47). It may seem an odd conjunction of minds between the solitary, rather sombre Hazlitt and the young, infectiously enthusiastic poet (one is tempted to think of Armado and Moth), but undoubtedly Keats's respectful belief in Hazlitt's 'taste' has helped to perpetuate the latter's ideas.

Hazlitt's influence on Shakespearean criticism must remain a subject which demands a certain amount of speculation.[65] Very few modern critics have acknowledged, or apparently even read, his works, and yet there are certain areas in which his thought has been absorbed into the current. The reason for the indirectness of his impact is surely connected with the overt influence exerted by Keats. Many have absorbed Hazlitt's ideas through acquaintance with Keats's letters, and it is possible that without Keats more critics would trace certain ideas back to Hazlitt. (On the other hand, without Keats's appreciation of Hazlitt, the latter may have had even less influence.) However, it is fair to say that nineteenth-century criticism learned from his practice, and in its turn has affected that of the present century. Dowden quotes Hazlitt on Desdemona in approving fashion, and the whole enterprise of his *Shakspere: His Mind and Art*[66] follows in the mould of Hazlitt's *Characters*, concentrating upon overall 'impression' and treating characters as of a piece with the imaginative vision of the particular play. The comparison between the two is not to Hazlitt's discredit, for where Dowden is genially vague on points of atmosphere, Hazlitt is sharply observant and, with his 'philosophy of particularity'[67] and his emphasis upon contrast, he does not ignore the clashes of styles and tones in Shakespeare. Matthew Arnold, again perhaps through his thorough knowledge of Keats, assimilates some of Hazlitt's ideas, and although not specifically a Shakespearean critic he obviously contributed to the theoretical framework in which literary criticism was carried out up until at least the time of Leavis. His raising of 'Zeitgeist' to the level of critical terminology was anticipated by Hazlitt in *The Spirit of the Age*.[68] His usage of 'touchstone' passages of poetry is similar to Hazlitt's way of quoting a phrase or a passage and simply commenting on its exquisiteness, fineness or power (in cases where Coleridge would not be content to rest in the mystery of 'half-knowledge');[69] and more comprehensively, Arnold's general attitude to poetry, not only its social utility but its capacity to exercise the active imagination, is comparable to Hazlitt's:

> The grand power of poetry is its interpretative power; by which I mean, not a drawing out in black and white an explanation of the mystery of the universe, but the power of so dealing with things as to awaken in us a wonderfully full, new, and intimate sense of them, and our relations with them...[70]

The spirit behind such a statement, its emphasis upon poetry's 'power', its central capacity to awaken sympathy with the object, and its creative potential, bears comparison with, for example, the 'four things' that strike Hazlitt in reading *King Lear* (below, number 26). One could probably not prove a link between Hazlitt and

Arnold, but it is possible to see areas in which Hazlitt has, with Coleridge and Shelley as well as Keats, contributed to the setting up of certain emphases and priorities accepted by Arnold. There is an irony here, because the respective politcal stances of the two mmen could not have been further apart.

With A.C. Bradley we are on surer ground. As the greatest Victorian critic he in many ways sums up the critical movements of the century, and Hazlitt is an identifiable source. He refers several times in *Shakespearean Tragedy* to Hazlitt's account of Iago,[71] he takes Hazlitt's view as a starting point in arguing that King Lear is 'Shakespeare's greatest work, but it is not what Hazlitt called it, the best of his plays',[72] and he acknowledges Hazlitt on Falstaff.[73] Although some of these references are mildly critical of Hazlitt, the general design of Bradley's book on tragedy owes much to the earlier critic. We find the same concentration on character as an initiation into discussion of the play as a whole, and just as Hazlitt cannot be said to discuss character in isolation of other dramatic matters, so Bradley, when read as a whole, is found to be acutely aware of atmosphere, 'impression' and the contribution of imagery to general tone. He has the same habit of comparing plays by contrasting their heroes, and even using occasional references from art:

> There is in most of the later heroes something colossal, something which reminds us of Michael Angelo's figures. They are not merely exceptional men, they are huge men; as it were, survivors of the heroic age living in a later and smaller world. We do not receive this impression from Romeo or Brutus or Hamlet, nor did it lie in Shakespeare's design to allow more than touches of this trait to Julius Caesar himself; but it is strongly marked in Lear and Coriolanus, and quite distinct in Macbeth and even Antony. Othello is the first of these men, a being essentially large and grand, towering above his fellows, holding a volume of force which in repose ensures pre-eminence without an effort, and in commotion reminds us rather of the fury of the elements than of the tumult of common human passion.[74]

There is much in such a passage to remind us of Hazlitt's writing: the allusion to Michaelangelo, the hypnotic attention to power, the metaphor of 'the fury of the elements', the anchoring and central reference back to 'the tumult of common human passion'. In saying that 'Macbeth makes an impression quite different from that of Hamlet'[75] Bradley clears a space for himself to speak of 'impressions' in the fashion of Hazlitt:

In many parts of *Macbeth* there is in the language a peculiar compression, pregnancy, energy, even violence; the harmonious grace and even flow, often conspicuous in Hamlet, have almost disappeared. ... The other three tragedies all open with conversations which lead into the action: here the action bursts into wild life amidst the sounds of a thunderstorm and the echoes of a distant battle...[76]

Such an account need only be compared to the opening to Hazlitt's essay on Macbeth (below, number 15) to realise again a common vocabulary of kinesis, of the special rhythm of the play (as Bradley's paragraph continues), of contrast. Most important, we realise they are both using a common strategy in analysis - style, with its controlled rhythms, its imagery and metaphor, its heightened and often poetic tone, is used by both writers to 'enter' the work of literature under analysis, to participate in, and convey to the reader, the impression that the play itself is being recreated rather than critically distanced, in the commentator's attempt to mirror its movements of emotion. We notice such characteristics time and again throughout Bradley's book, and it is not too much to say that without the presence of Hazlitt (however percolated through his line of influence, Keats, Swinburne, Dowden and others), *Shakespearean Tragedy* would be a different book. Where Bradley differs, perhaps contaminated by facets of the writing of Lee, Boas, Carlyle and Dowden, is in his linking of Shakespeare's plays to an inner, autobiographical drama running through Shakespeare's own emotional life, and a tendency at times to treat characters as having an existence outside the context of drama. These may be dangers that lie implicit in Hazlitt's method, but he himself rarely confuses dramatic characters (existing in a text or situations or embodied through an actor) with 'real life'. The feelings evoked by the characters may be real enough to the reader or audience in the way the text stimulates the active participation of the sympathetic imagination, but the character remains a figure in a play.

In the twentieth century Hazlitt's Shakespearean criticism was at first ignored as its general style and approach fell out of fashion. With the rise of literary criticism as a profession, linked with the establishment of English as a subject for study in universities, a critical terminology including words like 'impression', 'sympathy' and 'passion' seems hopelessly vague and not susceptible to analytical treatment. In this climate, Coleridge's stock rose dramatically for he appears to offer the glimmerings of an analytical 'method', and a firm commitment to the literary work as an aesthetic object, obeying its own internal, 'organic' laws of structure and development, with a transcendent rather than mimetic significance for the reader. In his way, Coleridge was able to be father to modernists, Leavis, and New Critics alike. Hazlitt, meanwhile, was given a marginal and modest place as a witty and elegant essayist, surely a fate which he would have dreaded, given his implicit demand in his writing to be read as a serious thinker on matters contemporary, political and historical, and his personal tendency towards abrasiveness and political liberalism. We need to be reminded of the vast scope of his writing, the energy and clarity of his thought, the distinctiveness of his critical approach when his terms were new-forged with a weight of specific meaning which he fully explains and develops, the sureness of his taste. He was virtually alone in claiming *Lear* as not only the most painful play but the greatest work of literature by Shakespeare, a judgment which would now be accepted as almost axiomatic, but was in his own time made controversial if not treasonous by the fact that the play was banned between 1811 and 1820 because George III was mad.

What is needed to bring an old critic back into fashion is a new one revivifying his concepts and terms, and perhaps G. Wilson Knight - the greatest critic of this century even if oddly out of sympathy with it - took as his critical method a stance which is very close to Hazlitt's own:

> ... I would draw a distinction between the terms 'criticism' and 'interpretation' ... 'Criticism' to me suggests a certain process of deliberately objectifying the work under consideration; the comparison of it with other similar works in order especially to show in what respects it surpasses, or falls short of, those works; the dividing its 'good' from its 'bad'; and, finally, a formal judgement as to its lasting validity. 'Interpretation', on the contrary, tends to merge into the work it analyses; it attempts, as far as possible, to understand its subject in the light of its own nature, employing external reference, if at all, only as a preliminary to understanding ... Criticism is a judgement of vision, interpretation a reconstruction of vision.[77]

Even if the distinction is not so clear-cut as it sounds (in the best commentary, interpretation may precede or accompany criticism), it is one that Hazlitt would have recognised. His attack on Johnson was an attack on 'criticism' in Knight's sense:

... [Johnson] would be for setting up a foreign jurisdiction over poetry, and making criticism a kind of Procrustes' bed of genius, where he might cut down imagination to matter-of-fact, regulate the passions according to the reason, and translate the whole into logical diagrams and rhetorical declamation.[78]

Hazlitt's own enterprise, meanwhile, is unrepentantly committed to 'a reconstruction of vision', to exercise

that intenseness of passion, which, seeking to exaggerate whatever excites the feelings of pleasure or power in the mind, and moulding the impressions of natural objects according to the impulses of imagination, produces a genius and a taste for poetry.[79]

He readily admits that if one lowers 'Shakespeare's genius to the standard of common-place invention, it was easy to show that his faults were as great as his beauties', and was determined instead to admire the inspired ways in which Shakespeare broke the rules.

Now that critics are taking an interest in underlying political assumptions in works of literature and Shakespeare in particular,[80] Hazlitt can again come into his own. Theorists, rejecting the tyranny of the sacred text, are coming to see reading and performance as cooperative activities between reader and text, each exercising what Hazlitt called 'gusto',[81] and what our age more prosaically might call 'constructive practices'. Literary theorists who argue that Shakespeare's texts have been covertly appropriated for conservative causes, find a surprisingly modern ally in Hazlitt, who so often debunked the Tory critics' attempts to use Shakespeare in their cause, while himself using Shakespeare to illustrate and verify his own political stance. In this set of critical strategies, the intermediary between Hazlitt and recent critics is William Empson, who attacked institutions such as monarchy as strongly as Hazlitt, opening up, for example, a whole new approach to Falstaff forged in opposition to the conservative Dover Wilson. It is not surprising that Hazlitt is at last gaining recognition as a progressive critical force. Even postcolonial critics can look back to Hazlitt as a distant but pertinent forebear through his analysis of imperialism in *The Tempest* which in the 1980s became a celebrated test case for this approach. Indeed, the 1990s appear to be witnessing a genuine revaluation of Hazlitt, heralded in 1989 by a new, excellent biography,

Stanley Jones's *Hazlitt: A Life. From Winterslow to Frith Street* (Clarendon Press, Oxford, 1989), and by a critical book largely devoted to his Shakespeare criticism in the context of contemporary politics, Jonathan Bate's *Shakespearean Constitutions: Politics, Theatre, Criticism 1730-1830* (Oxford, 1989). Bate in his Penguin anthology *The Romantics on Shakespeare* (1992) has also elevated Hazlitt, placing him with Coleridge and August Schlegel as the one of 'three men [who] produced some of the finest Shakespearian criticism ever written'. I concur with this judgment, and hope that this book will help bring to new readers the best of Hazlitt's Shakespearian criticism and stage commentary.

...

The intention behind this volume is to present a generous selection from Hazlitt's criticism of Shakespeare, culled from his twenty-one volumes of prose as published today. *Characters of Shakespear's Plays* takes the lion's share of space as his most significant contribution to the subject and the selection represents over half that volume. Hazlitt's theatre criticism is presented not from the point of view of what it tells us about the stage in his day, but according to what he tells us about Shakespeare as his characters were played by Edmund Kean. The first part is made up of extracts from his many other essays, as they reflect upon Shakespeare. The exercise of selecting such fragments presents problems for the anthologist. Unlike (for example) Coleridge, it is often difficult to quote a passage or snippet from Hazlitt out of context without losing some of its force. Very often a comment on Shakespeare is expressed as an aside in the midst of an energetic argument about some facet of human behaviour. Equally a perception may take its place alongside references to the old Masters or contemporary poets, as a way of sharpening our understanding of their strengths and weaknesses. Or Shakespeare may be invoked at the climax of a relentlessly pursued theme. Given the aim of presenting a wide range of Hazlitt's insights into Shakespeare specifically within a short volume, there seemed no way of escaping this danger except by providing many of the essays on Shakespeare's plays themselves in full, and providing a generous selection from other essays. The selectivity defines both the uniqueness of this volume and also its limitations. An anthologist's greatest reward would come if some readers felt stimulated by the collection to go back to the essays in their totality, with a capacity to appreciate the diversity and energy of Hazlitt's structure of thought.

The text is reprinted from the great 'Centenary Edition' of Hazlitt's entire works edited by P.P. Howe. For permission to use the text I am grateful to the original publishers, Dent. The order in which the selection is presented attempts to maintain something of the integrity of the respective works in which they appear. In Hazlitt's case, chronological order would not reveal a lot, since he tended to repeat himself rather than rethinking when his judgment was settled; and to gather together his comments on each play would destroy the unity of *Characters of Shakespear's Plays* and detract from the cumulative sense of Hazlitt's power as theatre critic.

Quotations given in the text are exactly as Hazlitt wrote, with some of his errors pointed out in the Notes. He often quoted from memory, incorrectly. Even Howe cannot be sure which edition of Shakespeare was used by Hazlitt, though it appears to have been one published before the editorial work of Johnson and Steevens, or else ignoring such work. Howe writes that 'it was not one of those which has come down to us as primary'. Since readers of this selection will want to be able to find quotations in a handy edition rather than knowing the textual details of transmission, I refer in the Notes to *The Riverside Shakespeare*, edited by G. Blakemore Evans (Boston, 1974). When a lengthy quotation appears in the text, I signal it in square brackets, rather than quoting. This was a reluctant choice, but a necessary one if the book were not to have more quotations than text. For no particularly good reason I have reproduced Hazlitt's whimsical spellings of Shakespeare's name, since he does seem to have made definite decisions over these.

I offer a large debt of thanks to Dr Peter Regan for his scrupulous checking of my notes. At different stages Professor Jonathan Bate, Professor Reg Foakes, Michael Foot, Dr Hilary Fraser, Professor Paul Hamilton, Dr David Norbrook, Brian Southam, Professor Stanley Wells, and Jane Whiteley offered encouragement in the long haul to having Hazlitt's words republished in this form. At the University of Western Australia, Pauline Dugmore typed the script with painstaking care, and I am grateful to her for her patience and thoughtfulness.

R. S. White
University of Western Australia

NOTES

1. P.P. Howe (ed.), *The Complete Works of William Hazlitt*, 21 volumes (London, 1930), 19, 302.

2. See (for example), *The Letters of John Keats*, ed. Hyder E. Rollins, 2 volumes (Cambridge, Massachusetts, 1958), II, 80, where Keats cites Jesus and Socrates as examples of 'disinterested' men.

3. Coleridge uses the word in discussing 'Venus and Adonis' in *Biographia Literaria* (1817).

4. See headnote to 50 below.

5. *Enquiry Concerning Political Justice and its Influence on Modern Morals and Happiness* (1798). Hazlitt was interested in the ideas of Godwin, and wrote on him more than once, especially in *The Spirit of the Age* (1825).

6. *Rights of Man: Being an Answer to Mr Burke's Attack on the French Revolution.*

7. Howe, 18, 306.

8. Howe, 18, 305.

9. Ibid.

10. Howe, 1, 13-16.

11. Coleridge sought to analyse what he calls Shakespeare's 'profound insight into the constitution of the human soul': *Coleridge on Shakespeare*, ed. Terence Hawkes (Penguin edition, Harmondsworth, 1969), p. 92. Hazlitt's attention is more extroverted, appreciating the characters as dramatic creations who are designed for the stage. His understanding of 'secret motives' is not so much psychological as a matter of stage dynamics.

12. Keats, *Letters*, I, 243.

13. Howe, 4, 77.

14. To make a light comparison, Hazlitt sees conversation as a similarly collaborative enterprise: 'The soul of conversation is sympathy' (Howe, 12, 34) and 'The art of conversation is the art of hearing as well as of being heard' (Howe, 12, 39).

15. 'He who can, does. He who cannot, teaches' (*Man and Superman*, IV).

16. See John Kinnaird, *William Hazlitt: Critic of Power* (New York, 1978), p. 144.

17. Robert Ready, 'Hazlitt: In and Out of "Gusto"', *Studies in English Literature*, xiv (1974), pp. 537-46, 538-9.

18. Howe, 8, 217.

19. Below, no. 15.

20. Below, no. 25.

21. Roy Park, *Hazlitt and the Spirit of the Age* (Oxford, 1971), p. 154.

22. Walter Whiter, *A Specimen of a Commentary on Shakespeare* (1794), edited Alan Over and Mary Bell (London, 1974).

23. Coleridge, Hawkes, p. 108.

24. Below, no. 25.

25. Coleridge was among the pioneers in his high assessment of the Sonnets, as his annotated copy of them now in Dove Cottage Library shows, and his famous distinction between imagination and fancy in *Biographia Literaria* is based on a comparison between passages from 'Venus and Adonis' and 'The Rape of Lucrece' respectively. For Hazlitt's low estimate of the non-dramatic poetry, see below, no. 47. This is not to say that his interest in the plays was not essentially directed to the poetry.

26. Howe, 4, 359.

27. Howe, 17, 145.

28. Howe, 4, 175 (Preface to *Characters of Shakespear's Plays*).

29. Hazlitt makes this mistake in the Preface to *Characters of Shakespear's Plays*, and again in a footnote to a theatre review where he writes: 'See an admirable analysis of the two characters by the author of an Essay on Ornamental Gardens' (Howe, 5, 405). Whately's book was entitled *Remarks on Some of the Characters of Shakespeare* (published posthumously, 1785), reprinted in D. Nichol Smith (ed.), *Eighteenth Century Essays on Shakespeare* (Oxford, 1963), partially reprinted in Brian Vickers (ed.), *Shakespeare: The Critical Heritage*, volume 6, 1774-1801 (London, 1981).

30. *A Philosophical Analysis and Illustration of some of Shakespeare's Remarkable Characters* (1774), Vickers, p. 119.

31. Ibid.

32. Richardson himself may have found the term applied to Shakespeare in Edward Capell's introduction to his edition of the plays in 1768. See Jonathan Bate, *Shakespeare and the Romantic Imagination* (Oxford, 1986), pp. 14 ff., for fuller discussion. For a modern summary of 'protean' criticism, see Michel Grivelet, 'A Portrait of the Artist as Proteus', British Academy Shakespeare Lecture (London, 1975). Coleridge makes the claim in Chapter xv of *Biographia Literaria*, and Hazlitt in his essay 'On Genius and Common Sense' (*Table Talk*).

33. See Vickers, Numbers 264 and 287. Mackenzie's essays on Falstaff appeared in 1786, Morgann's in 1777. See also Brian Vickers, 'The Emergence of Character Criticism, 1774-1800', *Shakespeare Survey*, 34 (1981), pp. 11-20.

34. But only a short step. Mackenzie pays little attention to poetry or dramatic creation of

atmosphere, while Hazlitt always saw these as more important than character for its own sake.

35. 'Morgann on Falstaff Refuted' (1788), Vickers, No. 292.

36. Coleridge accused Hazlitt of plagiarising his ideas in an early letter to the *Morning Chronicle*, but Hazlitt, who generally spoke highly of Coleridge unless provoked, came to Coleridge's defence when the gibe was aimed at the poet. See P.P. Howe, *Life of William Hazlitt* (London, 1947), p. 141.

37. It is arguable, in fact that Hazlitt uses the word 'character' sometimes as a synonym for 'impression' (OED sense II.9: 'nature ..style...') in titles such as 'Characteristics: In the Manner of Rouchefoucault's Maxims' (Howe, vol. 9) and 'Character of Lord Bacon's Works - compared as to Style with Sir Thomas Browne and Jeremy Taylor' (Howe, 6, 326). Certainly, his use of the word itself is wider in connotation than the eighteenth century writers on Shakespeare who tend to follow the seventeenth century habit of speaking of 'the Character' as a genre, practised for example by John Earle. Even at this semantic level, let alone his general approach, Hazlitt belongs firmly among the Romantics rather than the eighteenth century critics.

38. Stanley Wells, 'Shakespeare in Leigh Hunt's Criticism', *Essays and Studies*, 33 (1980), pp. 119-38, p. 123.

39. See Stanley Wells, 'Shakespeare in Hazlitt's Theatre Criticism', *Shakespeare Survey*, 35 (1983), pp. 43-55.

40. See below, Number 53 and footnote 1 to that extract.

41. 'On the Tragedies of Shakespeare, Considered with Reference to Their Fitness for Stage Representation' (*Reflector*, No. IV, 1811). See the collection *Charles Lamb on Shakespeare*, ed. Joan Coldwell (Bucks, 1978) and Roy Park, 'Lamb, Shakespeare, and the Stage', *Shakespeare Quarterly*, 33 (1982), pp. 164-77. Despite the enthusiasm of some critics for the contribution of Lamb to Shakespeare studies, I believe a cool examination of the evidence does not sustain a high estimate. He wrote really only this one essay which could be hailed as significant, although clearly the *Tales from Shakespear* (1807) compiled with his sister Mary helped to present Shakespeare in an attractive manner to generations of children.

43. M.H. Abrams, The Mirror and the Lamp (New York, 1958), p. 154. Curiously, the general denigration of Hazlitt seems to infect one of his biographers: Herschel Baker, *William Hazlitt* (Cambridge, Massachusetts, 1962). One cannot avoid the impression that Baker is out of sympathy with his subject's fundamental political beliefs, and this fact colours his critical assessments.

44. See the essay on Coleridge in *The Spirit of the Age*.

45. All biographers of Hazlitt document this, but see the sympathetic account given by David Bromwich in his excellent book *Hazlitt: The Mind of a Critic* (New York and Oxford, 1983), pp.

266-7.

46. Park, above, p. 11 and passim.

47. Kinnaird, above.

48. W.P. Albrecht, *Hazlitt and the Creative Imagination* (Lawrence, Kansas, 1965).

49. Wells, 'Shakespeare in Hazlitt's Theatre Criticism', above.

50. Bromwich, above.

51. Bromwich, p. 230.

52. Ibid.

53. Ibid.

54. See R.A. Foakes (ed.), *Coleridge on Shakespeare: The Text of the Lectures of 1811-12* (London, 1971).

55. Marilyn Butler, *Romantics, Rebels and Reactionaries: English Literature and its Background* (Oxford, 1981), p. 69.

56. See Paul Hamilton, *Coleridge's Poetics* (Oxford, 1983), *passim.*

57. Kenneth Muir, 'Keats and Hazlitt' in Kenneth Muir (ed.), *John Keats: A Reassessment* (Liverpool, 1959), p. 158.

58. Keats, *Letters*, I, 166.

59. R.S. White, *Keats as a Reader of Shakespeare* (London, 1987).

60. Keats, Review of Kean's Richard III, *The Champion*, 21 December, 1817.

61. Keats, *Letters*, II, 360.

62. Keats, *Letters*, I, 193 and 387-8.

63. See Howe, 18, 135-40.

64. Keats, *Letters*, I. 192, letter to George and Tom Keats, 21 Dec., 1817.

65. There appears to be no published study of this subject, and the comments made here are by no means comprehensive. It would be valuable in particular to have a study of Hazlitt and Bradley.

66. *Shakspere: His Mind and Art* (London, 1875).

67. Park, above, and see White (above), pp. 33-7.

68. Matthew Arnold, *Essays in Criticism* (first series, 1889), 'The Function of Criticism at the Present Time'.

69. Keats, *Letters*, I, 193.

70. Arnold, above, pp. 81-2.

71. A.C. Bradley, *Shakespearean Tragedy* (London, 1904), pp. 171, 183, 186, 188.

72. Ibid., p. 202.

73. A.C. Bradley, *Oxford Lectures on Poetry* (London, second edition, 1909), p. 261.

74. *Shakespearean Tragedy*, pp. 142-3.

75. Ibid., p. 277.

76. Ibid., pp. 277-8.

77. G. Wilson Knight, *The Wheel of Fire* (fourth edition, London, 1949), p. 1.

78. Howe, 4, 176, from Preface to *Characters of Shakespear's Plays*.

79. Ibid.

80. See, for example, Jonathan Dollimore, *Radical Tragedy: Religion, Ideology and Power in the Drama of Shakespeare and his Contemporaries* (Brighton, 1984).

81. See, for example, Umberto Eco, *The Role of the Reader* and Roland Barthes, *The Rustle of Language*.

BIBLIOGRAPHY

Abrams, M.H.: *The Mirror and the Lamp: Romantic Theory and the Critical Tradition* (New York, 1953)

Albrecht, W. P.: *Hazlitt and the Creative Imagination* (Lawrence, Kansas, 1965)

-- 'Hazlitt, passion and King Lear', *Studies in English Literature*, xviii (1978), 610-24

Baker, Herschel: *William Hazlitt* (Cambridge, Massachusetts, 1962)

Bate, Jonathan: 'Hazlitt's Shakespearean Quotations', *Prose Studies*, vii (1984), 26-37

-- *Shakespeare and the English Romantic Imagination* (Oxford, 1986)

-- *Shakespearean Constitutions: Politics, Theatre, Criticism 1730-1830* (Oxford, 1989)

-- *The Romantics on Shakespeare*, Penguin Shakespeare Library (London, 1992)

Bate, W.J.: *John Keats* (Cambridge, Massachusetts, 1963)

Bradley, A.C: *Shakespearean Tragedy* (second edn., London, 1905)

-- *Oxford Lectures on Poetry* (second edn., London, 1909)

Bromwich, David: *Hazlitt: The Mind of a Critic* (Oxford and New York, 1983)

Bullitt, J.M.: 'Hazlitt and the Romantic Conception of the Imagination', *Philological Quarterly*, 24 (1945), 343-61

Butler, Marilyn: *Romantics, Rebels and Reactionaries: English Literature and its Background 1760-1830* (Oxford, 1981)

Coleridge, S.T.: *Biographia Literaria*, ed. George Watson (London, 1956)

-- *Coleridge on Shakespeare*, ed. Terence Hawkes (London, 1959, Harmondsworth, 1969)

-- *Coleridge on Shakespeare: The Text of the Lectures of 1811-12*, ed. R.A. Foakes (London, 1971)

-- *Coleridge's Criticism of Shakespeare*, ed. R.A. Foakes (London, 1990)

Donohue Jnr, Joseph W.: 'Hazlitt's Sense of the Dramatic Actor as Tragic Hero', *Studies in English Literature*, 5 (1965), 705-21

-- *Dramatic Character in the English Romantic Age* (Princeton, New Jersey, 1970)

-- *Theatre in the Age of Kean* (Oxford, 1975)

Dowden, Edward: *Shakspere: A Critical Study of His Mind and Art* (London, 1875)

Foot, Michael: *The Politics of Paradise: A Vindication of Byron* (London, 1988)

Foulkes, Richard (ed.): *Shakespeare and the Victorian Stage* (Cambridge, 1986)

Gifford, William, 'Hazlitt's *Characters of Shakespear's Plays*' *Quarterly Review*, 18 (1818), 458-66

Hamilton, Paul: *Coleridge's Poetics* (Oxford, 1983)

Harbage, Alfred: *Conceptions of Shakespeare* (Cambridge, Massachusetts, 1966)

Hazlitt, William: *Complete Works*, in 21 vols, ed. P.P. Howe (London, 1930-4)

Howe, P.P.: *The Life of William Hazlitt* (London, 1922)

Jeffrey, Francis: 'Hazlitt on Shakespeare', *Edinburgh Review*, 28 (1817), 472-88

Johnson, Dr Samuel: *Samuel Johnson on Shakespeare*, ed. H.R. Woudhuysen (Harmondsworth, 1989)

-- *Dr Johnson on Shakespeare*, ed. W.K. Wimsatt (Harmondsworth, 1969, first pub. 1960)

Jones, Stanley: *Hazlitt: A Life. From Winterslow to Frith Street* (Clarendon Press, Oxford, 1989)

Keats, John: *The Letters of John Keats*, ed. Hyder E. Rollins, in two vols (Cambridge, Massachusetts, 1958)

Kinnaird, John: *William Hazlitt: Critic of Power* (New York, 1978)

Klingopoulos, G. D.: 'Hazlitt as Critic', *Essays in Criticism*, vi (1956), 385-403

Lamb, Charles: *Charles Lamb on Shakespeare*, ed. Joan Coldwell (London, 1978)

McAleer, John J.: 'William Hazlitt--Shakespeare's "Advocate and Herald"', *Shakespeare Newsletter*, xxii (1972), 4

Miller, Perry Lou: 'William Hazlitt on the Genius of Shakespeare', *Shakespeare Quarterly*, v (1966), 64-71

Morgann, Maurice: *An Essay on the Dramatic Character of Sir John Falstaff* (London, 1777)

Muir, Kenneth: *John Keats: A Reassessment* (Liverpool, 1959)

Park, Roy: *Hazlitt and the Spirit of the Age* (Oxford, 1971)

-- 'Lamb, Shakespeare and the Stage', *Shakespeare Quarterly*, xxxiii (1982), 164-77

Raysor, T.M. (ed.): *Coleridge: Shakespearean Criticism*, in two vols (London, 1930)

Ready, Robert: 'Hazlitt: In and Out of "Gusto"', *Studies in English Literature*, xiv (1974), 537-46

Richardson, William: *A Philosophical Analysis and Illustration of Some of*

Shakespeare's Remarkable Characters (London, 1797)

Sauer, Thomas G.: *A.W. Schlegel's Shakespearean Criticism in England 1811-1846* (Bonn, 1981)

Shakespeare, William: *The Riverside Shakespeare*, ed. G. Blakemore Evans (Houghton Mifflin, Boston, 1974)

Sidney, Sir Philip: *Miscellaneous Prose of Sir Philip Sidney*, ed. Katherine Duncan-Jones and Jan van Dorsten (Oxford, 1973)

Vickers, Brian (ed.): *Shakespeare: The Critical Heritage*, in six vols, 6: 1774-1801 (London, 1981)

-- 'The Emergence of Character Criticism, 1774-1800', *Shakespeare Survey*, 34 (1981), 11-20

Wells, Stanley: 'Shakespeare in Leigh Hunt's Criticism', *Essays and Studies*, 33 (1980), 119-38

-- 'Shakespeare in Hazlitt's Theatre Criticism', *Shakespeare Survey*, 35 (1982), 43-55

Whately, Thomas: *Remarks on Some of the Characters of Shakespeare* (London, 1785)

White, R.S.: *Keats as a Reader of Shakespeare* (London, 1987)

Whiter, William: *A Specimen of a Commentary on Shakespeare* (1974), edited Alan Over and Mary Bell (London, 1974)

Whitley, Alvin: 'Hazlitt and the Theatre', *University of Texas Studies in English*, 34 (1955), 67-100

PART ONE

OF POETRY AND SHAKESPEARE

1. FROM 'ON IMITATION'

First published in *The Examiner*, March 3, 1816, reprinted in *The Round Table* (1817), a miscellaneous collection of Hazlitt's essays, many on literary topics. Although there is only one reference to Shakespeare in this essay ('The conceits in Shakespear were his greatest delight'), Hazlitt's definition of imitation is important to many of his comments on the poet's work. It leads him to admire 'a variety of details and distinctions' in the art or literature, in conscious reaction against Johnson's warning not to 'number the streaks of the tulip' (*Rasselas*).

Objects in themselves disagreeable or indifferent, often please in the imitation. A brick-floor, a pewter plate, an ugly cur barking, a Dutch boor smoking or playing at skittles, the inside of a shambles, a fishmonger's or a greengrocer's stall, have been made very interesting as pictures by the fidelity, skill, and spirit, with which they have been copied. One source of the pleasure thus received is undoubtedly the surprise or feeling of admiration, occasioned by the unexpected coincidence between the imitation and the object. The deception, however, not only pleases at first sight, or from mere novelty; but it continues to please upon farther acquaintance, and in proportion to the insight we acquire into the distinctions of nature and of art. By far the most numerous class of connoisseurs are the admirers of pictures of *still life*, which have nothing but the elaborateness of the execution to recommend them. One chief reason, it should seem then, why imitation pleases, is, because, by exciting curiosity, and inviting a comparison between the object and the representation, it opens a new field of inquiry, and leads the attention to a variety of details and distinctions not perceived before. This latter source of the pleasure derived from imitation has never been properly insisted on.

2. FROM 'ON GUSTO'

First published in *The Examiner*, 26 May, 1816, reprinted in *The Round Table*. Although not naming Shakespeare, the essay is a central reference point in Hazlitt's criticism, asserting his belief in the importance of feeling to the production and reception of the work of art.

GUSTO in art is power or passion defining any object. It is not so difficult to explain this term in what relates to expression (of which it may be said to be the highest degree) as in what relates to things without expression, to the natural appearances of objects, as mere colour or form. In one sense, however, there is hardly any object entirely devoid of expression, without some character of power belonging to it, some precise association with pleasure or pain: and it is in giving this truth of character from the truth of feeling, whether in the highest or the lowest degree, but always in the highest degree of which the subject is capable, that gusto consists.

3. FROM 'ON PEOPLE OF SENSE'

First published in *The London Magazine*, April, 1821, reprinted in *The Plain Speaker* (1826).

Poetry acts by sympathy with nature, that is, with the natural impulses, customs, and imaginations of men, and is, on that account, always popular, delightful, and at the same time instructive. It is nature moralizing and *idealizing* for us; inasmuch as, by shewing us things as they are, it implicitly teaches us what they ought to be; and the grosser feelings, by passing through the strainers of this imaginary, wide-extended experience, acquire an involuntary tendency to higher objects. Shakespear was, in this sense, not only one of the greatest poets, but one of the greatest moralists that we have. Those who read him are the happier, better, and wiser for it.[1]

4. FROM AN ESSAY ON MASSINGER'S *A NEW WAY TO PAY OLD DEBTS*

From *Prefatory Remarks to Oxberry's New English Drama*, a cumulative monthly anthology (1818-25) to which Hazlitt contributed many Prefaces, including ones on *As You Like It* and *Romeo and Juliet*.

All Shakespeare's characters act from mixed motives, and are made what they are by various circumstances. All Massinger's characters act from single motives, and become what they are, and remain so, by a pure effort of the will, in spite of circumstances.

5. FROM 'WHETHER GENIUS IS CONSCIOUS OF ITS POWERS'

Published in *The Plain Speaker* (1826).

The definition of genius is that it acts unconsciously; and those who have produced immortal works, have done so without knowing how or why. The greatest power operates unseen, and executes its appointed task with as little ostentation as difficulty. Whatever is done best, is done from the natural bent and disposition of the mind. It is only where our incapacity begins, that we begin to feel the obstacles, and to set an undue value on our triumph over them. Correggio, Michael Angelo, Rembrandt, did what they did without premeditation or effort - their works came from their minds as a natural birth - if you had asked them why they adopted this or that style, they would have answered, *because they could not help it,* and because they knew of no other. So Shakespear says:

> 'Our poesy is as a gum which issues
> From whence 'tis nourish'd. The fire i' th' flint
> Shows not till it be struck: our gentle flame
> Each bound it chafes.[1]

Shakespear himself was an example of his own rule, and appears to have owed almost every thing to chance, scarce any thing to industry or design. His poetry flashes from him, like the lightning from the summer-cloud, or the stroke from the sun-flower.

6. FROM 'ON POSTHUMOUS FAME, - WHETHER SHAKSPEARE WAS INFLUENCED BY LOVE OF IT?'

First published in *The Examiner*, May 22, 1814, reprinted in *The Round Table*. This extract introduces the distinction which was central to Hazlitt's thought, between the writer as one aware of his ego and after-fame and the writer as 'disinterested' and unaware of his own ego.

It has been much disputed whether Shakspeare was actuated by the love of fame, though the question has been thought by others not to admit of any doubt, on the ground that it was impossible for any man of great genius to be without this feeling. It was supposed, that that immortality, which was the natural inheritance of men of powerful genius, must be ever present to their minds, as the reward, the object, and the animating spring, of all their efforts. This conclusion does not appear to be well founded.

.   .   .

There is scarcely the slightest trace of any such feeling in his writings, nor any appearance of anxiety for their fate, or of a desire to perfect them or make them worthy of that immortality to which they were destined. And this indifference may be accounted for from the very circumstance, that he was almost entirely a man of genius, or that in him this faculty bore sway over every other: he was either not intimately conversant with the productions of the great writers who had gone before him, or at least was not much indebted to them: he revelled in the world of observation and of fancy; and perhaps his mind was of too prolific and active a kind to dwell with intense and continued interest on the images of beauty or of grandeur presented to it by the genius of others. He seemed scarcely to have an individual existence of his own, but to borrow that of others at will, and to pass successively through 'every variety of untried being,'[1] - to be now *Hamlet*, now *Othello*, now *Lear*, now *Falstaff*, now *Ariel*. In the mingled interests and feelings belonging to this wide range of imaginary reality, in the tumult and rapid transitions of this waking dream, the author could not easily find time to think of himself, nor wish to embody that personal identity in idle reputation after death, of which he was so little tenacious while living. To feel a strong desire that others should think highly of us, it is, in general, necessary that we should think highly of ourselves. There is something of egotism, and even pedantry, in this sentiment; and there is no author who was so little tinctured with these as Shakspeare. The passion for fame, like other passions, requires an exclusive and exaggerated admiration of its object, and attaches more consequence to literary attainments and pursuits than they really possess. Shakspeare had looked too much abroad into the world, and his views of things were of too universal and comprehensive a cast, not to have taught him to estimate the importance of posthumous fame according to its true value and relative proportions. Though he might have some conception of his future fame, he could not but feel the contrast between that and his actual situation; and, indeed, he complains bitterly of the latter in one of his sonnets.[2] He would perhaps think, that, to be the idol of posterity, when we are no more, was hardly a full compensation for being the object of the glance and scorn of fools while we are living; and that, in truth, this universal fame so much vaunted, was a vague phantom of blind enthusiasm; for what is the amount even of Shakspeare's fame? That, in that very country which boasts his genius and his birth, perhaps not one person in ten has ever heard of his name, or read a syllable of his writings!

7. FROM 'SCHLEGEL ON THE DRAMA'

Published in *The Edinburgh Review*, February 1816. Hazlitt was, for his time, relatively scrupulous about acknowledging his sources, and this is his appreciative, but critical, review of his greatest influence, W.A. Schlegel, whose *Lectures on Dramatic Literature* Hazlitt read in John Black's translation in 1815. There is an unresolved debate about whether Coleridge took some of his ideas from Schlegel after a trip to Germany - a charge he vehemently denied. Whatever the outcome of this scholarly quarrel, Coleridge can at least be credited with having first-hand acquaintance with the German criticism of his day while Hazlitt had to wait for the translation. As is evident from the review, Hazlitt also maintains his own independent views of Shakespeare.

.   .   .

William Schlegel has long been celebrated on the Continent as a philosophical critic, and as the admirable translator of Shakespear and Calderon into his native tongue. Madame de Staël[1] acknowledges her obligations to him, for the insight which he had given her into the discriminating features of German genius: and M. Sismondi,[2] in his work on Southern literature, bears the most honourable testimony to his talents and learning. The present work contains a critical and historical account of the ancient and modern drama, - the Greek, the Latin, the Italian, the French, the English, the Spanish, and the German. The view which the author has taken of the standard productions, whether tragic or comic, in these different languages, is in general ingenious and just; and his speculative reasonings on the principles of taste, are often as satisfactory as they are profound. But he sometimes carries the love of theory, and the spirit of partisanship, farther than is at all allowable. His account of Shakespear is admirably characteristic, and must be highly gratifying to the English reader. It is indeed by far the best account which has been given of the plays of that great genius by any writer, either among ourselves, or abroad. It is only liable to one exception - he will allow Shakespear to have had no faults. Now, we think he had a great many, and that he could afford to have had as many more. It shows a distrust of his genius to be tenacious of his defects.

.　　　.　　　.

If Shakespear never found a thorough partisan before, he has found one now. We have not room for half of his praise. He defends him at all points. His puns, his conceits, his anachronisms, his broad allusions, all go, not indeed for nothing, but for so many beauties. They are not something to be excused by the age, or atoned for by other qualities; but they are worthy of all acceptation in themselves. This we do not think it necessary to say. It is no part of our poetical creed, that genius can do no wrong. As the French show their allegiance to their kings by crying *Quand méme!*[3] - so we think to show our respect for Shakespear by loving him in spite of his faults. Take the whole of these faults, throw them into one scale, heap them up double, and then double that, and we will throw into the opposite scale single excellences, single characters, or even single passages, that shall outweigh them all! All his faults have not prevented him from showing as much knowledge of human nature, in all possible shapes, as is to be found in all other poets put together; and that, we conceive, is quite enough for one writer. Compared with this magical power, his faults are of just as much consequence as his bad spelling, and to be accounted for in the same way.

.　　　.　　　.

That which distinguishes his dramatic productions from all others, is this wonderful variety and perfect individuality. Each of his characters is as much itself, and as absolutely independent of the rest, as if they were living persons, not fictions of the mind. The poet appears, for the time, to identify himself with the character he wishes to represent, and to pass from one to the other, like the same soul successively animating different bodies. By an art like that of the ventriloquist,[4] he throws his imagination out of himself, and makes every word appear to proceed from the mouth of the person in whose name it is spoken. His plays alone are expressions of the passions, not descriptions of them. His characters are real beings of flesh and blood: they speak like men, not like authors. One might suppose that he had stood by at the time, and overheard all that passed. As, in our dreams, we hold conversations with ourselves, make remarks or communicate intelligence, and have no idea of the answer which we shall receive, and which we ourselves are to make, till we hear it; so, the dialogues in Shakespear are carried on without any consciousness of what is to follow, without any appearance of preparation or premeditation. The gusts[5] of passion come and go like sounds of music borne on the wind. Nothing is made out by inference and analogy, by climax and antithesis; all comes immediately from nature. Each object and circumstance seems to exist in his mind, as it existed in nature; each several train of thought and feeling goes on of itself without confusion or effort. In the world of his imagination, every thing has a life, a place, and being of its own![6]

The observations on Shakespear's language and versification [which follow,] are excellent. We cannot, however, agree with the author in thinking his rhyme superior to Spenser's. His excellence is confined to his blank verse; and in that he is unrivalled by any dramatic writer. Milton's alone is equally fine in its way. The objection to Shakespear's mixed metaphors is not here fairly got over. They give us no pain from long custom. They have, in fact, become idioms in the language. We take the meaning and effect of a well known passage entire, and no more stop to scan and spell out the particular words and phrases than the syllables of which they are composed. If our critic's general observations on Shakespear are excellent, he has shown still greater acuteness and knowledge of his author in those which he makes on the particular plays. They ought, in future, to be annexed to every edition of Shakespear, to correct the errors of preceding critics. In his analysis of the historical plays, - of those founded on the Roman history, - of the romantic comedies, and the fanciful productions of Shakespear, such as, the Midsummer Night's Dream, the Tempest, &c., he has shown the most thorough insight into the spirit of the poet. His contrast between Ariel and Caliban; the one made up of all that is gross and earthly, the other of all that is airy and refined, 'ethereal mould, sky-tinctured,'[7] - is equally happy and profound. He does not, however, confound Caliban with the coarseness of common low life. He says of him with perfect truth - 'Caliban is malicious, cowardly, false and base in his inclinations; and yet he is essentially different from the vulgar knaves of a civilized world, as they are occasionally portrayed by Shakespear. He is rude, but not vulgar. He never falls into the prosaical and low familiarity of his drunken associates, for he is a poetical being in his way; he always, too, speaks in verse. But he has picked up every thing dissonant and thorny in language, of which he has composed his vocabulary.'

In his account of Cymbeline and other plays, he has done justice to the sweetness of Shakespear's female characters, and refuted the idle assertion made by a critic, who was also a poet and a man of genius, that

- 'stronger Shakespear felt for man alone.'[8]

Who, indeed, in recalling the names of Imogen, of Miranda, of Juliet, of Desdemona, of Ophelia and Perdita, does not feel that Shakespear has expressed the very perfection of the feminine character, existing only for others, and leaning for support on the strength of its affections? The only objection to his female characters is, that he has not made them masculine. They are indeed the very reverse of ordinary tragedy-queens. In speaking of Romeo and Juliet, he says, 'It was reserved for Shakespear to unite purity of heart, and the glow of imagination, sweetness and dignity of manners, and passionate violence, in one ideal picture.' The character of Juliet was not to be mistaken by our author. It is one of perfect unconsciousness. It has nothing forward, nothing coy, nothing affected, nothing coquettish about it: - It is a pure effusion of nature.

8.   FROM 'SHAKESPEAR'S FEMALE CHARACTERS'

Published in *The Examiner*, July 26, 1816, anonymously. Since Hazlitt freely pillages the essay in his *Characters*, only the opening section is reproduced.

Shakespear's women (we mean those who were his favourites, and whom he intended to be the favourites of the reader) exist almost entirely in the relations and charities of domestic life. They are nothing in themselves, but every thing in their attachment to others. We think as little of their persons as they do themselves, because we are let into the secrets of their hearts, which are more important. We are too much interested in their affairs to stop to look at their faces, except by stealth and at intervals. We catch their beauties only sideways as in a glass, but we everywhere meet their hearts coming at us, - *full butt*....

No one ever hit the true perfection of the female character, the sense of weakness leaning on the strength of its affections for support, so well as Shakespear - no one ever so well painted natural tenderness free from all affectation and disguise, that

'Calls true love acted simple modesty'[1] -

no one else ever so well shewed how delicacy and timidity, urged to an extremity, grow romantic and extravagant, for the romance of his heroines (in which they abound) is only an excess of the common prejudices of their sex, scrupulous of being false to their vows, truant to their affections, and taught by the force of their feelings when to forego the forms of propriety for the essence of it. His women are in this respect exquisite logicians, for they argue from what they feel, and that is a sure game, when the stake is deep. They know their own minds exactly. High imagination springs from deep habit; and Shakespear's women only followed up the idea of what they liked, of what they had sworn to with their tongues, and what was engraven on their hearts, into its untoward consequences. They were the prettiest little set of martyrs and confessors on record.

9.   FROM *LECTURES ON THE ENGLISH POETS*

A compilation of comments from these Lectures could well have stood as an introduction to *Characters of Shakespear's Plays* instead of the disappointing Preface to that volume. As it was, the *Lectures* were published later, in 1818 and again in 1819, and the activity of writing the *Characters* may have given Hazlitt the confidence to range so widely and hazard generalisations that he would not have attempted earlier. The lectures on which the publication was built were delivered at the Surrey Institute, Great Surrey Street in London, during January and February of 1818. John Keats arrived at the first lecture an hour late, 'got there just as they were coming out' (Keats, *Letters*, I, 214), but he attended regularly thereafter, mentioning some of the lectures in his letters though not the ones printed below. The series was repeated in April and May at the Crown and Anchor Tavern in the Strand, a fact which Howe says was taken at the time as proof of the exceptional success of the first rendering. As published, the *Lectures* deal with poets from Chaucer to Wordsworth and other contemporaries. Of Wordsworth Hazlitt says 'His egotism is in some respect a madness' (v.163), and it is clear that in many of his writings he uses Shakespeare to exemplify the opposite quality of selfless sympathy. Keats encapsulated the distinction in coining the phrases 'egotistical sublime' and 'Negative Capability' (Keats, *Letters*, I, 387 and 193). Both Hazlitt and Keats were appreciative of Wordsworth's poetic gifts, but for moral and political reasons preferred the Shakespearean mode. In the extracts which follow, Hazlitt first lays down some of his general thoughts on the nature of poetry, and then concentrates on Shakespeare in particular.

(i) FROM LECTURE ONE, 'INTRODUCTORY - ON POETRY IN GENERAL'

The best general notion which I can give of poetry is, that it is the natural impression of any object or event, by its vividness exciting an involuntary movement of imagination and passion, and producing, by sympathy, a certain modulation of the voice, or sounds, expressing it.

In treating of poetry, I shall speak first of the subject-matter of it, next of the forms of expression to which it gives birth, and afterwards of its connection with harmony of sound.

Poetry is the language of the imagination and the passions. It relates to whatever gives immediate pleasure or pain to the human mind. It comes home to the bosoms and businesses of men; for nothing but what so comes home to them in the most general and intelligible shape, can be a subject for poetry. Poetry is the universal language which the heart holds with nature and itself. He who has a contempt for poetry, cannot have much respect for himself, or for any thing else.

. . .

It is strictly the language of the imagination; and the imagination is that faculty which represents objects, not as they are in themselves, but as they are moulded by other thoughts and feelings, into an infinite variety of shapes and combinations of power. This language is not the less true to nature, because it is false in point of fact;[1] but so much the more true and natural, if it conveys the impression which the object under the influence of passion makes on the mind. Let an object, for instance, be presented to the senses in a state of agitation or fear - and the imagination will distort or magnify the object, and convert it into the likeness of whatever is most proper to encourage the fear. 'Our eyes are made the fools'[2] of our other faculties. This is the universal law of the imagination,

> That if it would but apprehend some joy,
>
> It comprehends some bringer of that joy:
>
> Or in the night imagining some fear,
>
> How easy is each bush suppos'd a bear!'[3]

When Iachimo says of Imogen,

> '- The flame o' th'taper
>
> Bows toward her, and would under-peep her lids
>
> To see the enclosed lights'[4] -

this passionate interpretation of the motion of the flame to accord with the speaker's own feelings, is true poetry. The lover, equally with the poet, speaks of the auburn tresses of his mistress as locks of shining gold, because the last tinge of yellow in the hair has, from novelty and a sense of personal beauty, a more lustrous effect to the imagination than the purest gold. We compare a man of gigantic stature to a tower: not that he is any thing like so large, but because the excess of his size beyond what we are accustomed to expect, or the usual size of things of the same class, produces by contrast a greater feeling of magnitude and ponderous strength than another object of ten times the same dimensions. The intensity of the feeling makes up for the disproportion of the objects. Things are equal to the imagination, which have the power of affecting the mind with an equal degree of terror, admiration, delight, or love. When Lear calls upon the heavens to avenge his cause, 'for they are old like him,'[5] there is nothing extravagant or impious in this sublime identification of his age with theirs; for there is no other image which could do justice to the agonising sense of his wrongs and his despair!

Poetry is the high-wrought enthusiasm of fancy and feeling. As of describing natural objects, it impregnates sensible impressions with the forms of fancy, so it describes the feelings of pleasure or pain, by blending them with the strongest movements of passion, and the most striking forms of nature. Tragic poetry, which is the most impassioned species of it, strives to carry on the feeling to the utmost point of sublimity or pathos, by all the force of comparison or contrast; loses the sense of present suffering in the imaginary exaggeration of it; exhausts the terror or pity by an unlimited indulgence of it; grapples with impossibilities in its desperate impatience of restraint; throws us back upon the past, forward into the future; brings every moment of our being or object of nature in startling review before us; and in the rapid whirl of events, lifts us from the depths of woe to the highest contemplations on human life. When Lear says of Edgar, 'Nothing but his unkind daughters could have brought him to this;'[6] what a bewildered amazement, what a wrench of the imagination, that cannot be brought to conceive of any other cause of misery than that which has bowed it down, and absorbs all other sorrow in its own! His sorrow, like a flood, supplies the sources of all other sorrow. Again, when he exclaims in the mad scene, 'The little dogs and all, Tray, Blanche, and Sweetheart, see, they bark at me!'[7] it is passion lending occasion to imagination to make every creature in league against him, conjuring up ingratitude and insult in their least looked-for and most galling shapes, searching every thread of fibre of his heart, and finding out the last remaining image of respect or attachment to the bottom of his breast, only to torture and kill it! In like manner, the 'So I am'[8] of Cordelia gushes from her heart like a torrent of tears, relieving it of a weight of love and of supposed ingratitude, which had pressed upon it for years. What a fine return of the passion upon itself is that in Othello - with what a mingled agony of regret and despair he clings to the last traces of departed happiness - when he exclaims,

Oh now, for ever
Farewel the tranquil mind. Farewel content;
Farewel the plumed troops and the big war,
That make ambition virtue! Oh farewel!
Farewel the neighing steed, and the shrill trump,
The spirit-stirring drum, th'ear-piercing fife,
The royal banner, and all quality,
And O you mortal engines, whose rude throats
Th'immortal Jove's dread clamours conterfeit,
Farewel! Othello's occupation's gone!'

How his passion lashes itself up and swells and rages like a tide in its sounding course, when in answer to the doubts expressed of his returning love, he says,

'Never, Iago. Like to the Pontic sea,
Whose icy current and compulsive course
Ne'er feels retiring ebb, but keeps due on

> To the Propontic and the Hellespont:
> Even so my bloody thoughts, with violent pace,
> Shall ne'er look back, ne'er ebb to humble love,
> Till that a capable and wide revenge
> Swallow them up.'[10] .

The climax of his expostulation afterwards with Desdemona is at that line,

> 'But there where I had garner'd up my heart,
> To be discarded thence!'[11]

One mode in which the dramatic exhibition of passion excites our sympathy without raising our disgust is, that in proportion as it sharpens the edge of calamity and disappointment, it strengthens the desire of good.[12] It enhances our consciousness of the blessing, by making us sensible of the magnitude of the loss. The storm of passion lays bare and shews us the rich depths of the human soul: the whole of our existence, the sum total of our passions and pursuits, of that which we desire and that which we dread, is brought before us by contrast; the action and re-action are equal; the keenness of immediate suffering only gives us a more intense aspiration after, and a more intimate participation with the antagonist world of good; makes us drink deeper of the cup of human life; tugs at the heartstrings; loosens the pressure about them; and calls the springs of thought and feeling into play with tenfold force.

Impassioned poetry is an emanation of the moral and intellectual part of our nature, as well as of the sensitive - of the desire to know, the will to act, and the power to feel; and ought to appeal to these different parts of our constitution, in order to be perfect. The domestic or prose tragedy, which is thought to be the most natural, is in this sense the least so, because it appeals almost exclusively to one of these faculties, our sensibility. The tragedies of Moore and Lillo,[13] for this reason, however affecting at the time, oppress and lie like a dead weight upon the mind, a load of misery which it is unable to throw off: the tragedy of Shakspeare, which is true poetry, stirs our inmost affections; abstracts evil from itself by combining it with all the forms of imagination, and with the deepest workings of the heart, and rouses the whole man within us.

(ii) FROM LECTURE THREE, 'ON SHAKESPEARE AND MILTON'

The arts of painting and poetry are conversant with the world of thought within us, and with the world of sense around us - with what we know, and see, and feel intimately. They flow from the sacred shrine of our own breasts, and are kindled at the living lamp of nature. But the pulse of the passions assuredly beat as high, the depths and soundings of the human heart were as well understood three thousand, or three hundred years ago, as they are at present: the face of nature, and 'the human face divine'[1] shone as bright then as they have ever done. But it is *their* light, reflected by true genius on art, that marks out its path before it, and sheds a glory round the Muses' feet, like that which

> 'Circled Una's angel face,
> And made a sunshine in the shady place.'[2]

.   .   .

The striking peculiarity of Shakspeare's mind was its generic quality, its power of communication with all other minds - so that it contained a universe of thought and feeling within itself, and had no one peculiar bias, or exclusive excellence more than another. He was just like any other man, but that he was like all other men. He was the least of an egotist that it was possible to be. He was nothing in himself; but he was all that others were, or that they could become. He not only had in himself the germs of every faculty and feeling, but he could follow them any anticipation, intuitively, into all their conceivable ramifications, through every change of fortune or conflict of passion, or turn of thought. He had 'a mind reflecting ages past,'[3] and present: - all the people that ever lived are there. There was no respect of persons with him. His genius shone equally on the evil and on the good,[4] on the wise and the foolish, the monarch and the beggar: 'All corners of the earth, kings, queens, and states, maids, matrons, nay, the secrets of the grave,'[5] are hardly hid from his searching glance. He was like the genius of humanity, changing places with all of us at pleasure, and playing with our purposes as with his own. He turned the globe round for his amusement, and surveyed the generations of men, and the individuals as they passed, with their different concerns, passions, follies, vices, virtues, actions, and motives - as well those that they knew, as those which they did not know, or acknowledge to themselves. The dreams of childhood, the ravings of despair, were the toys of his fancy. Airy beings waited at his call, and came at his bidding. Harmless fairies 'nodded to him, and did him courtesies':[6] and the night-hag bestrode the blast at the command of 'his so potent art.'[7] The world of spirits lay open to him, like the world of real men and women: and there is the same truth in his delineations of the one as of the other; for if the preternatural characters he describes could be supposed to exist, they would speak, and feel, and act, as he makes them. He had only to think of any thing in order to become that thing, with all the circumstances belonging to it. When he conceived of a character, whether real or imaginary, he not only entered into all its thoughts and feelings, but seemed instantly, and as if by touching a secret spring, to be surrounded with all the same objects, 'subject to the same skyey influences,'[8] the same local, outward, and unforeseen accidents which would occur in reality.

. . .

Chaucer's characters are sufficiently distinct from one another, but they are too little varied in themselves, too much like identical propositions. They are consistent, but uniform; we get no new idea of them from first to last; they are not placed in different lights, nor are their subordinate *traits* brought out in new situations; they are like portraits or physiognomical studies, with the distinguishing features marked with inconceivable truth and precision, but that preserve the same unaltered air and attitude. Shakspeare's are historical figures, equally true and correct, but put into action, where every nerve and muscle is displayed in the struggle with others, with all the effect of collision and contrast, with every variety of light and shade. Chaucer's characters are narrative, Shakspeare's dramatic, Milton's epic. That is, Chaucer told only as much of his story as he pleased, as was required for a particular purpose. He answered for his characters himself. In Shakspeare they are introduced upon the stage, are liable to be asked all sorts of questions, and are forced to answer for themselves. In Chaucer we perceive a fixed essence of character. In Shakspeare there is a continual composition and decomposition of its elements, a fermentation of every particle in the whole mass, by its alternate affinity or antipathy to other principles which are brought in contact with it. Till the experiment is tried, we do not know the result, the turn which the character will take in its new circumstances. Milton took only a few simple principles of character, and raised them to the utmost conceivable grandeur, and refined them from every base alloy. His imagination, 'nigh sphered in Heaven,'[9] claimed kindred only with what he saw from that height, and could raise to the same elevation with itself. He sat retired and kept his state alone, 'playing with wisdom';[10] while Shakspeare mingled with the crowd, and played the host, 'to make society the sweeter welcome.'[11]

The passion in Shakspeare is of the same nature as his delineation of character. It is not some one habitual feeling or sentiment preying upon itself, growing out of itself, and moulding every thing to itself; it is passion modified by passion, by all the other feelings to which the individual is liable, and to which others are liable with him; subject to all the fluctuations of caprice and accident; calling into play all the resources of the understanding and all the energies of the will; irritated by obstacles or yielding to them; rising from small beginnings to its utmost height; now drunk with hope, now stung to madness, now sunk to despair, now blown to air with a breath, now raging like a torrent. The human soul is made the sport of fortune, the prey of adversity: it is stretched on the wheel of destiny, in restless ecstacy. The passions are in a state of projection. Years are melted down to moments, and every instant teems with fate. We know the results, we see the process.

The great fault of a modern school of poetry is,[12] that it is an experiment to reduce poetry to a mere effusion of natural sensibility; or what is worse, to divest it both of imaginary splendour and human passion, to surround the meanest objects with the morbid feelings and devouring egotism of the writers' own minds. Milton and Shakspeare did not so understand poetry. They gave a more liberal interpretation both to nature and art. They did not do all they could to get rid of the one and the other, to fill up the dreary void with the Moods of their own Minds. They owe their power over the human mind to their having had a deeper sense than others of what was grand in the objects of nature, or affecting in the events of human life. But to the men I speak of there is nothing interesting, nothing heroical, but themselves. To them the fall of gods or of great men is the same. They do not enter into the feeling. They cannot understand the terms. They are even debarred from the last poor, paltry consolation of an unmanly triumph over fallen greatness; for their minds reject, with a convulsive effort and intolerable loathing, the very idea that there ever was, or was thought to be, any thing superior to themselves. All that has ever excited the attention or admiration of the world, they look upon with the most perfect indifference; and they are surprised to find that the world repays their indifference with scorn. 'With what measure they mete, it has been meted to them again.'[13] -

Shakespeare's imagination is of the same plastic kind as his conception of character or passion. 'It glances from heaven to earth, from earth to heaven.'[14] Its movement is rapid and devious. It unites the most opposite extremes: or, as Puck says, in boasting of his own feats, 'puts a girdle round about the earth in forty minutes.'[15]

.   .   .

Shakspeare's language and versification are like the rest of him. He has a magic power over words: they come winged at his bidding; and seem to know their places. They are struck out at a heat, on the spur of the occasion, and have all the truth and vividness which arise from an actual impression of the objects. His epithets and single phrases are like sparkles, thrown off from an imagination, fired by the whirling rapidity of its own motion. His language is hieroglyphical.[16] It abounds in sudden transitions and elliptical expressions. This is the source of his mixed metaphors, which are only abbreviated forms of speech. These, however, give no pain from long custom. The have in fact, become idioms in the language. They are the building, and not the scaffolding to thought. We take the meaning and effect of a well-known passage entire, and no more stop to scan and spell out the particular words and phrases, than the syllables of which they are composed. In trying to recollect any other author, one sometimes stumbles, in case of failure, on a word as good. In Shakspeare, any other word but the true one, is sure to be wrong. If any body, for instance, could not recollect the words of the following description,

'- Light thickens,
And the crow makes wing to the rooky wood,'[17]

he would be greatly at a loss to substitute others for them equally expressive of the feeling. These remarks, however, are strictly applicable only to the impassioned parts of Shakspeare's language, which flowed from the warmth and originality of his imagination, and were of his own. The language used for prose conversation and ordinary business is sometimes technical, and involved in the affectation of the time. Compare, for example, Othello's apology to the senate, relating 'his whole course of love,'[18] with some of the preceding parts relating to his appointment, and the official dispatches from Cyprus. In this respect, 'the business of the state does him offence.'[19] His versification is no less powerful, sweet, and varied. It has every occasional excellence, of sullen intricacy, crabbed and perplexed, or of the smoothest and loftiest expansion - from the ease and familiarity of measured conversation to the lyrical sounds

> '- Of ditties highly penned,
> Sung by a fair queen in a summer's bower,
> With ravishing division to her lute.'[20]

It is the only blank verse in the language, except Milton's, that for itself is readable. It is not stately and uniformly swelling like his, but varied and broken by the inequalities of the ground it has to pass over in its uncertain course,

> 'And so by many winding nooks it strays,
> With willing sport to the wild ocean.'[21]

It remains to speak of the faults of Shakspeare. They are not so many or so great as they have been represented; what there are, are chiefly owing to the following causes:- The universality of his genius was perhaps, a disadvantage to his single works; the variety of his resources, sometimes diverting him from applying them to the most effectual purposes. He might be said to combine the powers of Æschylus and Aristophanes, of Dante and Rabelais, in his own mind. If he had been only half what he was, he would perhaps have appeared greater. The natural ease and indifference of his temper made him sometimes less scrupulous than he might have been. He is relaxed and careless in critical places; he is in earnest throughout only in Timon, Macbeth, and Lear. Again, he had no models of acknowledged excellence constantly in view to stimulate his efforts, and by all that appears, no love of fame. He wrote for the 'great vulgar and the small,'[22] in his time, not for posterity. If Queen Elizabeth and the maids of honour laughed heartily at his worst jokes, and the catcalls in the gallery were silent at his best passages, he went home satisfied, and slept the next night well. He did not trouble himself about Voltaire's criticisms.[23] He was willing to take advantage of the ignorance of the age in many things; and if his plays pleased others, not to quarrel with them himself. His very facility of production would make him set less value on his own excellences, and not care to distinguish nicely between what he did well or ill. His blunders in chronology and geography do not amount to above half a dozen, and they are offences against chronology and geography, not against poetry. As to the unities, he was right in setting them at defiance. He was fonder of puns than became so great a man.[24] His barbarisms were those of his age. His genius was his own. He had no objection to float down with the stream of common taste and opinion: he rose above it by his own buoyancy, and an impulse which he could not keep under, in spite of himself or others, and 'his delights did shew most dolphin-like.'[25]

He had an equal genius for comedy and tragedy; and his tragedies are better than his comedies, because tragedy is better than comedy. His female characters, which have been found fault with as insipid, are the finest in the world. Lastly, Shakspeare was the least of a coxcomb of any one that ever lived, and much of a gentleman.

·　　·　　·

10. FROM *LECTURES ON THE ENGLISH COMIC WRITERS*

These lectures were delivered at the Surrey Institute in 1818, repeated between January and March of 1819 at the Crown and Anchor, and published in the same year. The volume begins with an introductory essay, 'On Wit and Humour', which is full of epigrammatic descriptions of different kinds of comedy, particularly on humour which is mixed with sadness: '[the *Thousand and One Nights*] is the gaiety of despair, the mirth and laughter of a respite during pleasure from death' (Howe, vi.14); 'Wit is, in fact, the eloquence of indifference' (Howe, vi.15); 'Punch is not merry in himself' but 'he is the cause of heartfelt mirth in other men' (Howe, vi.25, the quotation significantly being an adaptation of Falstaff's 'I am not only witty in myself, but the cause that wit is in other men' in *2 Henry IV*, I.ii.9-10). Hazlitt's preference for the graver kind of humour, lined with melancholy, lies behind his more general assessment that Shakespeare's tragedies are greater than his comedies, and also his recognition of Shakespeare's comic 'magnanimity'. The other lectures cover poets, dramatists, novelists and painters (especially Hogarth) up to Gay's *The Beggars' Opera*.

(i)   FROM 'LECTURE ONE: INTRODUCTORY: ON WIT AND HUMOUR'

Lear and the Fool are the sublimest instance I know of passion and wit united, or of imagination unfolding the most tremendous sufferings, and of burlesque on passion playing with it, aiding and relieving its intensity by the most pointed, but familiar and indifferent illustrations of the same thing in different objects, and on a meaner scale.   The Fool's reproaching Lear with 'making his daughters his mothers,'[1] his snatches of proverbs and old ballads, 'The hedge-sparrow fed the cuckoo so long, that it had its head bit off by its young,'[2] and 'Whoop jug, I know when the horse follows the cart,'[3] are a running commentary of trite truisms, pointing out the extreme folly of the infatuated old monarch, and in a manner reconciling us to its inevitable consequences.

(ii)   FROM 'LECTURE TWO: ON SHAKESPEAR AND BEN JONSON'

This lecture is important to the theorist of the comic, for its distinctions between various types of humour, satire and comedy of manners.   It opens, however, with a paean of praise for Shakespeare's tragedies.

Dr JOHNSON thought Shakspeare's comedies better than his tragedies, and gives as a reason, that he was more at home in the one than in the other.[1] That comedies should be written in a more easy and careless vein than tragedies, is but natural. This is only saying that a comedy is not so serious a thing as a tragedy.   But that he shewed a greater mastery in the one than the other, I cannot allow, nor is it generally felt.   The labour which the Doctor thought it cost Shakspeare to write his tragedies, only shewed the labour which it cost the critic in reading them, that is, his general indisposition to sympathise heartily and spontaneously with works of high-wrought passion or imagination.

.   .   .

It is in fact the established rule at present, in these cases, to speak highly of the Doctor's authority, and to dissent from almost every one of his critical decisions. For my own part, I so far consider this preference given to the comic genius of the poet as erroneous and unfounded, that I should say that he is the only tragic poet in the world in the highest sense, as being on a par with, and the same as Nature, in her greatest heights and depths of action and suffering. There is but one who durst walk within that mighty circle, treading the utmost bound of nature and passion, shewing us the dread abyss of woe in all its ghastly shapes and colours, and laying open all the faculties of the human soul to act, to think and suffer, in direst extremities; whereas I think, on the other hand, that in comedy, though his talents there too were as wonderful as they were delightful, yet that there were some before him, others on a level with him, and many close behind him. I cannot help thinking, for instance, that Moliere was as great, or a greater comic genius than Shakspeare, though assuredly I do not think that Racine was as great, or a greater tragic genius.

.   .   .

He put his strength into his tragedies, and played with comedy. He was greatest in what was greatest; and his *forte* was not trifling, according to the opinion here combated, even though he might do that as well as any body else, unless he could do it better than any body else. - I would not be understood to say that there are not scenes or whole characters in Shakspeare equal in wit and drollery to any thing upon record. Falstaff alone is an instance which, if I would, I could not get over. 'He is the leviathan of all the creatures of the author's comic genius, and tumbles about his unwieldy bulk in an ocean of wit and humour.'[2] But in general it will be found (if I am not mistaken) that even in the very best of these, the spirit of humanity and the fancy of the poet greatly prevail over the mere wit and satire, and that we sympathise with his characters oftener than we laugh at them. His ridicule wants the sting of ill-nature. He had hardly such a thing as spleen in his composition. Falstaff himself is so great a joke, rather from his being so huge a mass of enjoyment than of absurdity. His re-appearance in the Merry Wives of Windsor is not 'a consummation devoutly to be wished,'[3] for we do not take pleasure in the repeated triumphs over him. - Mercutio's quips and banter upon his friends shew amazing gaiety, frankness, and volubility of tongue, but we think no more of them when the poet takes the words out of his mouth, and gives the description of Queen Mab.[4] Touchstone, again, he is a shrewd biting fellow, a lively mischievous wag: but still what are his gibing sentences and chopped logic to the fine moralising vein of the fantastical Jacques, stretched beneath 'the shade of melancholy boughs?'[5] Nothing. That is, Shakspeare was a greater poet than wit: his imagination was the leading and master-quality of his mind, which was always ready to soar into its native element: the ludicrous was only secondary and subordinate. In the comedies of gallantry and intrigue, with what freshness and delight we come to the serious and romantic parts! What a relief they are to the mind, after those of mere ribaldry or mirth! Those in Twelfth Night, for instance, and Much Ado about Nothing, where Olivia and Hero are concerned, throw even Malvolio and Sir Toby, and Benedick and Beatrice, into the shade. They 'give a very echo to the seat where love is throned.'6 What he has said of music might be said of his own poetry -

> 'Oh! it came o'er the ear like the sweet south
> Breathing upon a bank of violets,
> Stealing and giving odour.'7

How poor, in general, what a falling off, these parts seem in mere comic authors; how ashamed we are of them; and how fast we hurry the blank verse over, that we may get upon safe ground again, and recover our good opinion of the author! A striking and lamentable instance of this may be found (by any one who chooses) in the high-flown speeches in Sir Richard Steele's Conscious Lovers.8 - As good an example as any of this informing and redeeming power in our author's genius might be taken from the comic scenes in both parts of Henry IV. Nothing can go much lower in intellect or morals than many of the characters. Here are knaves and fools in abundance, of the meanest order, and stripped stark-naked. But genius, like charity, 'covers a multitude of sins:'9 we pity as much as we despise them; in spite of our disgust we like them, because they like themselves, and because we are made to sympathise with them; and the ligament, fine as it is, which links them to humanity, is never broken. Who would quarrel with Wart or Feeble, or Mouldy or Bull-calf, or even with Pistol, Nym, or Bardolph?10 None but a hypocrite. The severe censurers of the morals of imaginary characters can generally find a hole for their own vices to creep out at; and yet do not perceive how it is that the imperfect and even deformed characters in Shakspeare's plays, as done to the life, by forming a part of our personal consciousness, claim our personal forgiveness, and suspend or evade our moral judgment, by bribing our self-love to side with them. Not to do so, is not morality, but affectation, stupidity, or ill-nature. I have more sympathy with one of Shakspeare's pick-purses, Gadshill or Peto, than I can possibly have with any member of the Society for the Suppression of Vice,[11] and would by no means assist to deliver the one into the hands of the other. Those who cannot be persuaded to draw a veil over the foibles of ideal characters, may be suspected of wearing a mask over their own! Again, in point of understanding and attainments, Shallow sinks low enough; and yet his cousin Silence is a foil to him; he is the shadow of a shade, glimmers on the very verge of downright imbecility, and totters on the brink of nothing. 'He has been merry twice or once ere now,'[12] and is hardly persuaded to break his silence in a song. Shallow has 'heard the chimes at midnight,'[13] and roared out glees and catches at taverns and inns of court, when he was young. So, at least, he tells his cousin Silence, and Falstaff encourages the loftiness of his pretensions. Shallow would be thought a great man among his dependents and followers; Silence is nobody - not even in his own opinion: yet he sits in the orchard, and eats his carraways and pippins among the rest. Shakspeare takes up the meanest subjects with the same tenderness that we do an insect's wing, and would not kill a fly. To give a more particular instance of what I mean, I will take the inimitable and affecting, though most absurd and ludicrous dialogue, between Shallow and Silence, on the death of old Double:

[Quotes *2 Henry IV*, III.ii.1-52]

There is not any thing more characteristic than this in all Shakspeare. A finer sermon on mortality was never preached. We see the frail condition of human life, and the weakness of the human understanding in Shallow's reflections on it; who, while the past is sliding from beneath his feet, still clings to the present. The meanest circumstances are shewn through an atmosphere of abstraction that dignifies them: their very insignificance makes them more affecting, for they instantly put a check on our aspiring thoughts, and remind us that, seen through that dim perspective, the difference between the great and little, the wise and foolish, is not much. 'One touch of nature makes the whole world kin:'[14] and old Double, though his exploits had been greater, could but have had his day. There is a pathetic *naiveté* mixed up with Shallow's common-place reflections and impertinent digressions. The reader laughs (as well he may) in reading the passage, but he lays down the book to think. The wit, however, diverting, is social and humane. But this is not the distinguishing characteristic of wit, which is generally provoked by folly, and spends its venom upon vice.

The fault, then, of Shakspeare's comic Muse is, in my opinion, that it is too good-natured and magnanimous. It mounts above its quarry. It is 'apprehensive, quick, forgetive, full of nimble, fiery, and delectable shapes:'[15] but it does not take the highest pleasure in making human nature look as mean, as ridiculous, and contemptible as possible. It is in this respect, chiefly, that it differs from the comedy of a later, and (what is called) a more refined period. Genteel comedy is the comedy of fashionable life, and of artificial character and manners. The most pungent ridicule, is that which is directed to mortify vanity, and to expose affectation; but vanity and affectation, in their most exorbitant and studied excesses, are the ruling principles of society, only in a highly advanced state of civilisation and manners. Men can hardly be said to be a truly contemptible animal, till, from the facilities of general intercourse, and the progress of example and opinion, he becomes the ape of the extravagances of other men. The keenest edge of satire is required to distinguish between the true and false pretensions to taste and elegance; its lash is laid on with the utmost severity, to drive before it the common herd of knaves and fools, not to lacerate and terrify the single stragglers. In a word, it is when folly is epidemic, and vice worn as a mark of distinction, that all the malice of wit and humour is called out and justified to detect the imposture, and prevent the contagion from spreading. The fools in Wycherley and Congreve are of their own, or one another's making, and deserve to be well scourged into common sense and decency: the fools in Shakspeare are of his own or nature's making; and it would be unfair to probe to the quick, or hold up to unqualified derision, the faults which are involuntary and incorrigible, or those which you yourself encourage and exaggerate, from the pleasure you take in witnessing them. Our later comic writers represent a state of manners, in which to be a man of wit and pleasure about town was become the fashion, and in which the swarms of egregious pretenders in both kinds openly kept one another in countenance, and were become a public nuisance. Shakspeare, living in a state of greater rudeness and simplicity, chiefly gave certain characters which were a kind of *grotesques*, or solitary excrescences growing up out of their native soil without affectation, and which he undertook kindly to pamper for the public entertainment. For instance, Sir Andrew Aguecheek is evidently a creature of the poet's own fancy. The author lends occasion to his absurdity to shew itself as much as he pleases, devises antics for him which would not enter into his own head, makes him 'go to church in a galliard, and return home in a coranto;'[16] adds fuel to his folly, or throws cold water on his courage; makes his puny extravagances venture out or slink into corners without asking his leave; encourages them into indiscreet luxuriance, or checks them in the bud, just as it suits him for the jest's sake. The gratification of the fancy, 'and furnishing matter for innocent mirth,' are, therefore, the chief object of this and other characters like it, rather than reforming the moral sense, or indulging our personal spleen. ... - We find that the scenes of Shakspeare's comedies are mostly laid in the country, or are transferable there at pleasure. The genteel comedy exists only in towns, and crowds of borrowed characters, who copy others as the satirist copies them, and who are only seen to be despised. 'All beyond Hyde Park is a desart to it:'[17] while there the pastoral and poetic comedy begins to vegetate and flourish, unpruned, idle, and fantastic. It is hard to 'lay waste a country gentleman'[18] in a state of nature, whose humours may have run a little wild or to seed, or to lay violent hands on a young booby 'squire, whose absurdities have not yet arrived at years of discretion: but my Lord Foppington, who is 'the prince of coxcombs,' and 'proud of being at the head of so prevailing a party,'[19] deserves his fate. I am not for going so far as to pronounce Shakspeare's 'manners damnable, because he had not seen the court;'[20] but I think that comedy does not find its richest harvest till individual infirmities have passed into general manners, and it is the example of courts, chiefly, that stamps folly with credit and currency, or glosses over vice with meretricious lustre. I conceive, therefore, that the golden period of our comedy was just after the age of Charles II when the town first became tainted with the affectation of the manners and conversation of fashionable life, and before the distinction between rusticity and elegance, art and nature, was lost (as it afterwards was) in a general diffusion of knowledge, and the reciprocal advantages of civil intercourse. ...

In another point of view, or with respect to that part of comedy which relates to gallantry and intrigue, the difference between Shakspeare's comic heroines and those of a later period may be referred to the same distinction between natural and artificial life, between the world of fancy and the world of fashion. The refinements of romantic passion arise out of the imagination brooding over 'airy nothing,'[21] or over a favourite object, where 'love's golden shaft hath killed the flock of all affections else:'[22] whereas the refinements of this passion in genteel comedy, or in every day life, may be said to arise out of repeated observation and experience, diverting and frittering away the first impressions of things by a multiplicity of objects, and producing, not enthusiasm, but fastidiousness or giddy dissipation. For the one a comparatively rude age and strong feelings are best fitted; for 'there the mind must minister to itself:'[23] to the other, the progress of society and a knowledge of the world are essential; for here the effect does not depend on leaving the mind concentred in itself, but on the wear and tear of the heart, amidst the complex and rapid movements of the artificial machinery of society, and on the arbitrary subjection of the natural course of the affections to every the slightest fluctuation of fashion, caprice, or opinion. Thus Olivia, in Twelfth Night, has but one admirer of equal rank with herself, and but one love, to whom she innocently plights her hand and heart; or if she had a thousand lovers, she would be the sole object of their adoration and burning vows, without a rival. The heroine of romance and poetry sits secluded in the bowers of fancy, sole queen and arbitress of all hearts; and as the character is one of imagination, 'of solitude and melancholy musing born,' so it may be best drawn from the imagination.

.   .   .

There are people who cannot taste olives - and I cannot much relish Ben Jonson, though I have taken some pains to do it, and went to the task with every sort of good will. I do not deny his power or his merit; far from it: but it is to me of a repulsive and unamiable kind. He was a great man in himself, but one cannot readily sympathise with him. Jonson chiefly gives the *humours* of men, as connected with certain arbitrary or conventional modes of dress, action, and expression, which are intelligible only while they last, and not very interesting at any time. Shakspeare's characters are men; Ben Jonson's are more like machines, governed by mere routine, or by the convenience of the poet, whose property they are. In reading the one, we are let into the minds of his characters, we see the play of their thoughts, how their humours flow and work: the author takes a range over nature, and has an eye to every object or occasion that presents itself to set off and heighten the ludicrous character he is describing. His humour (so to speak) bubbles, sparkles, and finds its way in all directions, like a natural spring. In Ben Jonson it is, as it were, confined in a leaden cistern, where it stagnates and corrupts; or directed only through certain artificial pipes and conduits, to answer a given purpose. The comedy of this author is far from being 'lively, audible, and full of vent:'[24] it is for the most part obtuse, obscure, forced, and tedious. He wears out a jest to the last shred and coarsest grain.

11.   FROM 'SIR WALTER SCOTT, RACINE AND SHAKESPEAR'

Published in *The Plain Speaker* (1826). Hazlitt's attitude towards Scott was ambiguous, since he admired some qualities of the writing but detested Scott's Tory politics. He uses Shakespeare as a touchstone to clarify his feelings about Scott's novels.

No one admires or delights in the Scotch Novels more than I do; but at the same time when I hear it asserted that his mind is of the same class with Shakespear's, or that he imitates nature in the same way, I confess I cannot assent to it. No two things appear to me more different. Sir Walter is an imitator of nature and nothing more; but I think Shakespear is infinitely more than this. The creative principle is every where restless and redundant in Shakespear, both as it relates to the invention of feeling and imagery; in the Author of Waverley it lies for the most part dormant, sluggish, and unused. Sir Walter's mind is full of information, but the *'o'er-informing power'*[1] is not there. Shakespear's spirit, like fire, shines through him: Sir Walter's, like a stream, reflects surrounding objects. It is true, he has shifted the scene from Scotland into England and France, and the manners and characters are strikingly English and French; but this does not prove that they are not local, and that they are not borrowed, as well as the scenery and costume, from comparatively obvious and mechanical sources. Nobody from reading Shakespear would know (except from the *Dramatis Persona*) that Lear was an English king. He is merely a king and a father. The ground is common: but what a well of tears has he dug out of it! The tradition is nothing, or a foolish one. There are no data in history to go upon; no advantage is taken of costume, no acquaintance with geography or architecture or dialect is necessary: but there is an old tradition, human nature - an old temple, the human mind - and Shakespear walks into it and looks about him with a lordly eye, and seizes on the sacred spoils as his own. The story is a thousand or two years old, and yet the tragedy has no smack of antiquarianism in it.

.   .   .

All nature was, as [Lear] supposed, in a conspiracy against him, and the most trivial and insignificant creatures concerned in it were the most striking proofs of its malignity and extent. It is the depth of passion, however, or of the poet's sympathy with it, that distinguishes this character of torturing familiarity in them, invests them with corresponding importance, and suggests them by the force of contrast. It is not that certain images are surcharged with a prescriptive influence over the imagination from known and existing prejudices, so that to approach or even mention them is sure to excite a pleasing awe and horror in the mind (the effect in this case is mostly mechanical) - the whole sublimity of the passage is from the weight of passion thrown into it, and this is the poet's own doing. This is not trick, but genius.

This finding out a parallel between the most unlike objects, because the individual would wish to find one to support the sense of his own misery and helplessness, is truly Shakespearian; it is an instinctive law of our nature, and the genuine inspiration of the Muse. Racine (but let me not anticipate) would make him pour out three hundred verses of lamentation for his loss of kingdom, his feebleness, and his old age, coming to the same conclusion at the end of every third couplet, instead of making him grasp at once at the Heavens for support. The witches in Macbeth are traditional, preternatural personages; and there Sir Walter would have left them after making what use of them he pleased as a sort of Gothic machinery. Shakespear makes something more of them, and adds to the mystery by explaining it.

> 'The earth hath bubbles as the water hath,
> And these are of them.'[2]

We have their physiognomy too -

> - 'and enjoin'd silence,
> By each at once her choppy finger laying
> Upon her skinny lip.'[3]

And the mode of their disappearance is thus described -

> 'And then they melted into thin air.'[4]

What an idea is here conveyed of silence and vacancy!

.   .   .

Shakespear's witches are nearly exploded on the stage. Their broomsticks are left; their metaphysics are gone, buried five editions deep in Captain Medwin's Conversations![5] The passion in Othello is made out of nothing but itself; there is no external machinery to help it on; its highest intermediate agent is an old-fashioned pocket-handerchief. Yet 'there's magic in the web'[6] of thoughts and feelings, done after the commonest pattern of human life. The power displayed in it is that of intense passion and powerful intellect, wielding every-day events, and imparting its force to them, not swayed or carried along by them as in a go-cart. The splendour is that of genius darting out its forked flame on whatever comes in its way, and kindling and melting it in the furnace of affection, whether it be flax or iron. The colouring, the form, the motion, the combination of objects depend on the pre-disposition of the mind, moulding nature to its own purposes; in Sir Walter the mind is as wax to circumstances, and owns no other impress. Shakespear is a half-worker with nature. Sir Walter is like a man who has got a romantic spinning-jenny, which he has only to set a going, and it does his work for him much better and faster than he can do it for himself. He lays an embargo on 'all appliances and means to boot,'[7] on history, tradition, local scenery, costume and manners, and makes his characters chiefly up of these. Shakespear seizes only on the ruling passion, and miraculously evolves all the rest from it.

To return to Othello. Take the celebrated dialogue in the third act. "Tis common.'[8] There is nothing but the writhings and contortions of the heart, probed by affliction's point, as the flesh shrinks under the surgeon's knife. All its starts and flaws are but the conflicts and misgivings of hope and fear, in the most ordinary but trying circumstances. The 'Not a jot, not a jot,'[9] has nothing to do with any old legend or prophecy. It is only the last poor effort of human hope, taking refuge on the lips. When after being infected with jealousy by Iago, he retires apparently comforted and resigned, and then without any thing having happened in the interim, returns stung to madness, crowned with his wrongs, and raging for revenge, the effect is like that of poison inflaming the blood, or like fire inclosed in a furnace. The sole principle of invention is the sympathy with the natural revulsion of the human mind, and its involuntary transition from false security to uncontrollable fury. The springs of mental passion are fretted and wrought to madness, and produce this explosion in the poet's breast. So when Othello swears 'By yon *marble* heaven,'[10] the epithet is suggested by the hardness of his heart from the sense of injury: the texture of the outward object is borrowed from that of the thoughts: and that noble simile, 'Like the Propontic,'[11] &c. seems only an echo of the sounding tide of passion, and to roll from the same source, the heart. The dialogue between Hubert and Arthur,[12] and that between Brutus and Cassius[13] are among the finest illustrations of the same principle, which indeed is every where predominant (perhaps to a fault) in Shakespear. His genius is like the Nile overflowing and enriching its banks; that of Sir Walter is like a mountain-stream rendered interesting by the picturesqueness of the surrounding scenery. Shakespear produces his most striking dramatic effects out of the workings of the finest and most intense passions; Sir Walter places his *dramatis persona* in romantic situations, and subjects them to extraordinary occurrences, and narrates the results. The one gives us what we see and hear; the other what we *are*. Hamlet is not a person whose nativity is cast, or whose death is foretold by portents: he weaves the web of his destiny out of his own thoughts, and a very quaint and singular one it is. We have, I think, a stronger fellow-feeling with him than we have with Bertram or Waverley.[14] All men feel and think, more or less: but we are not all foundlings, Jacobites, or astrologers. We might have been overturned with these gentlemen in a stage-coach: we seem to have been school-fellows with Hamlet at Wittenberg.

I will not press this argument farther, lest I should make it tedious, and run into questions I have no intention to meddle with. All I mean to insist upon is, that Sir Walter's *forte* is in the richness and variety of his materials, and Shakespear's in the working them up.

.   .   .

12.   FROM 'COBBETT AND SHAKESPEAR: A POSTSCRIPT'

Published in *The Examiner*, November 26, 1815. It was a reply to the unlikely sounding article by Cobbett, 'On the Subject of Potatoes' (*Weekly Political Register*, November 18, 1815). Hazlitt was used to dealing with what he considered false criticism of Shakespeare from Tory critics, but it came as a surprise to have to defend the poet against a radical whom Hazlitt admired.

He does so by drawing attention to the populist potential in the plays, but the tone is largely tongue in cheek.

We had just concluded our ramble with Puck and Bottom, and were beginning to indulge in some less airy recreations, when in came the last week's *Cobbett*, and with one blow overset our Round Table,[1] and marred all our good things. If while Mr C. and his lady are sitting in their garden at Botley, like Adam and Eve in Paradise, the delight of one another, the envy of their neighbours, and the admiration of the rest of the world, suddenly a large fat hog from the wilds of Hampshire should bolt right through the hedge, and with snorting menaces and foaming tusks, proceed to lay waste the flower-pots and root up the potatoes, such as the surprise and indignation of so economical a couple would be on this occasion, was the consternation at our Table when Mr Cobbett himself made his appearance among us, vowing vengeance against Milton and Shakespear, Sir Hugh Evans and Justice Shallow, and all the delights of human life. We were not prepared for such an onset. More barbarous than Mr Wordsworth's calling Voltaire dull, or than Voltaire's calling Cato the only English tragedy; more barbarous than Mr Locke's admiration of Sir Richard Blackmore;[2] more barbarous than the declaration of a German Elector - afterwards made into an English king - that he hated poets and painters; more barbarous than the Duke of Wellington's letter to Lord Castlereagh,[3] or than the *Catalogue Raisonnée* of the Flemish Masters published in the *Morning Chronicle*,[4] or than the Latin style of the second Greek scholar of the age,[5] or the English style of the first: - more barbarous than any or all of these is Mr Cobbett's attack on our two great poets. As to Milton, except the fine egotism of the situation of Adam and Eve, which Mr Cobbett has applied to himself, there is not much in him to touch our politician: but we cannot understand his attack upon Shakespear, which is cutting his own throat. If Mr Cobbett is for getting rid of his kings and queens, his fops and his courtiers, if he is for pelting Sir Hugh and Falstaff off the stage, yet what will he say to Jack Cade and First and Second Mob? If we are to scout the Roman rabble, where will the *Register* find English readers? Has the author never found himself out in Shakespear? He may depend upon it he is there, for all the people that ever lived are there! Has he never been struck with the valour of Ancient Pistol, who 'would not swagger in any shew of resistance to a Barbary-hen'?[6] Can he not, upon occasion, 'aggravate his voice'[7] like Bottom in the play? In absolute insensibility, he is a fool to Master

Barnardine;[8] and there is enough of gross animal instinct in Caliban to make a whole herd of Cobbetts. Mr Cobbett admires Bonaparte; and yet there is nothing finer in any of his addresses to the French people than what Coriolanus says to the Romans when they banish him. He abuses the Allies in good set terms; yet one speech of Constance describes them and their magnanimity better than all the columns of the *Political Register*. Mr Cobbett's address to the people of England on the alarm of an invasion, which was stuck on all the church-doors in Great Britain, was not more eloquent than Henry V.'s address to his soldiers before the battle of Agincourt;[9] nor do we think Mr Cobbett was ever a better specimen of the common English character than the two soldiers in the same play. After all, there is something so droll in his falling foul of Shakespear for want of delicacy, with his desperate lounges and bear-garden dexterity, snorting, fuming, and grunting, that we cannot help laughing at the affair, now that our surprise is over; as we suppose Mr Cobbett does, if he can only keep him out of his premises by hallooing and hooting or dry blows, to see his old friend, Grill,[10] trudging along the high-road in search of his acorns and pignuts.

13. FROM *THE PLAIN SPEAKER* (1826)

This rather sad and angry piece is included here to show that the continuing strain in the *Characters* of anti-royalism and populism (particularly in the essays on the History Plays), was quite conscious and deliberate on Hazlitt's part. It shows that he conceived his book on Shakespeare as partly a contribution to political debate of the time. As he indicates, critics of other persuasions recognised this motivation, and attacked him for it. The piece should be read alongside the 'Letter to Gifford', reproduced in part below, after the *Characters*. It appears in 'Whether Genius is Conscious of its Powers' (above, no. 5).

.   .   .

Here too I have written *Table-Talks* without number, and as yet without a falling-off, till now that they are nearly done, or I should not make this boast. I could swear (were they not mine) the thoughts in many of them are founded as the rock, free as air,[1] the tone like an Italian picture. What then? Had the style been like polished steel, as firm and as bright, it would have availed me nothing, for I am not a government tool! I had endeavoured to guide the taste of the English people to the best old English writers; but I had said that English kings did not reign by right divine, and that his present majesty was descended from an elector of Hanover in a right line; and no loyal subject would after this look into Webster or Deckar because I had pointed them out. I had done something (more than any one except Schlegel) to vindicate the *Characters of Shakespear's Plays* from the stigma of French criticism: but our Anti-Jacobin and Anti-Gallican writers soon found out that I had said and written that Frenchmen, Englishmen, men were not slaves by birth-right. This was enough to *damn* the work. Such has been the head and front of my offending. While my friend Leigh Hunt was writing the *Descent of Liberty*,[2] and strewing the march of the Allied Sovereigns with flowers, I sat by the waters of Babylon and hung my harp upon the willows. I knew all along there was but one alternative - the cause of kings or of mankind. This I foresaw, this I feared; the world see it now, when it is too late. Therefore I lamented, and would take no comfort when the Mighty fell, because we, all men, fell with him, like lightning from heaven, to grovel in the grave of Liberty, in the stye of Legitimacy! There is but one question in the hearts of monarchs, whether mankind are their property or not. There was but this one question in mine. I had made an abstract, metaphysical principle of this question. I was not the dupe of the voice of the charmers. By my hatred of tyrants I knew what their hatred of the free-born spirit of man must be, of the semblance, of the very name of Liberty and Humanity. And while others bowed their heads to the image of the BEAST, I spit upon it and buffetted it, and made mouths at it, and pointed at it, and drew aside the veil that then half concealed it, but has been since thrown off, and named it by its right name; and it is not to be supposed that my having penetrated their mystery would go unrequited by those whose darling and whose delight the idol, half-brute, half-demon, was, and who were ashamed to acknowledge the image and superscription as their own!

PART TWO

CHARACTERS OF SHAKESPEAR'S PLAYS

A SELECTION FROM *CHARACTERS OF SHAKESPEAR'S PLAYS*

Characters of Shakespear's Plays was first published in 1817, then again in 1818, the latter edition, with its few changes, providing the text for the present selection. The volume is, by common consent, among Hazlitt's most complete and rounded works of literature, and certainly he afforded himself the opportunity of giving his most sustained and detailed impressions of Shakespeare's plays, unhampered by the necessity of the reviewer to address a particular performance. He writes unashamedly as an 'enthusiast': 'An overstrained enthusiasm is more pardonable with respect to Shakespear than the want of it; for our admiration cannot easily surpass his genius' (Preface). Accordingly, he spends some time at the outset excoriating what he saw as the temperate detachment of Doctor Johnson, a 'didactic reasoner' who 'retained the regular, habitual impressions of actual objects, but he could not follow the rapid flights of fancy, or the strong movements of passion' (Preface). Because of the title of the book, it is tempting - and common - for critics to place Hazlitt's work in the line of eighteenth-century character criticism as practised by Whateley and Richardson (whom Hazlitt read) and Morgann (whom he probably did not read). However, even the most superficial reading indicates the book reacts against this tradition which was closely allied to the particular kind of moral or didactic approach so condemned in the case of Johnson. Instead, Hazlitt places himself directly in the romantic school of critics by acknowledging warmly the work of Schlegel. In every essay we find that it is the diversity, uniqueness and even eccentricity of Shakespeare's characters which are valued over the representative or exemplary qualities. Character is never seen as something independent of impression, 'atmosphere', the rhythm of a particular play, and the mesh of imagery presented in the poetry. The book is dedicated to another 'impressionist', Charles Lamb, 'as a mark of old friendship and lasting esteem'.

Most of the essays in the book were newly written for the occasion, although those on *Cymbeline, Coriolanus, A Midsummer Night's Dream* and the *Henry VI* plays were previously published in *The Examiner* and Hazlitt freely lifts sentences from his reviews on performances. The indications are, then, that *Characters* was conceived as a complete volume rather than as a collection of essays. It has its own unity which stems as much from Hazlitt's projected personality - his elegance of expression, his wit and his occasional flashes of social outrage - as from the application of a consistent set of literary values. A general inability (or unwillingness) to deal with matters of structure or unity in a play are compensated for by his energetic commitment to the dramatic and poetic force of a moment. His demand for the exercise of the feelings and the moral conscience in reading are amply vindicated by the amount of local insight generated in the circumstances of his own readings.

Some of the essays are reproduced in full, while the signal 'From' in the headnotes indicates the editor's selection. It has to be admitted that, from the Shakespearean critic's point of view (as distinct from that of the reader primarily interested in Hazlitt) not everything he wrote on the subject is worth conserving. Certainly some of the essays are more important than others, and one could pick out those on 'Macbeth', 'Othello', 'Coriolanus', 'Hamlet' and 'Lear' as containing Hazlitt's most complete statements. His essays on the comedies seek to maintain a light touch, but he often praises the 'serious' side of these plays as his special interest. The Preface is not quoted, since it consists largely of quotations from Johnson (whom Hazlitt attacks) and Schlegel and Pope (whom he praises). The order of the essays is Hazlitt's.

14.   FROM 'CYMBELINE'

Cymbeline was a 'favourite play' for Hazlitt, although this does not fully explain why he begins the collection of essays with it. He admired the skill with which the plot is conducted and its intricacies resolved, the 'striking and powerful contrasts', and above all he was enchanted by the character of Imogen. Hazlitt sets the tone for other 'Imogen-idolators' like Swinburne and Dowden. In the essay he speculates upon the reasons for the fineness of Shakespeare's heroines, a subject he had already written upon in 'Shakespear's Female Characters' (above, no. 8). He freely draws from that essay in the present chapter. Garrick had popularised *Cymbeline* in his revivals of the play from 1761 to 1776, but until Macready's performances in 1843 it was played only occasionally (see Foulkes, pp.138-52). Nor was it a favourite among critics, who in the eighteenth century used it mainly as a quarry for discovering 'defective' lines. Hazlitt has the honour of being the first, and still among the best, of critics who have written seriously on this neglected play. Elizabeth Griffith in 1775 had praised Shakespeare's depiction of Imogen (Vickers, vi, 144).

.   .   .

CYMBELINE is one of the most delightful of Shakespear's historical plays. It may be considered as a dramatic romance, in which the most striking parts of the story are thrown into the form of a dialogue, and the intermediate circumstances are explained by the different speakers, as occasion renders it necessary. The action is less concentrated in consequence; but the interest becomes more aerial and refined from the principle of perspective introduced into the subject by the imaginary changes of scene, as well as by the length of time it occupies. The reading of this play is like going a journey with some uncertain object at the end of it, and in which the suspense is kept up and heightened by the long intervals between each action. Though the events are scattered over such an extent of surface, and relate to such a variety of characters, yet the links which bind the different interests of the story together are never entirely broken. The most straggling and seemingly casual incidents are contrived in such a manner as to lead at last to the most complete development of the catastrophe. The ease and conscious unconcern with which this is affected only makes the skill more wonderful. The business of the plot evidently thickens in the last act: the story moves forward with increasing rapidity at every step; its various ramifications are drawn from the most distant points to the same centre; the principal characters are brought together, and placed in very critical situations; and the fate of almost every person in the drama is made to depend on the solution of a single circumstance - the answer of Iachimo to the question of Imogen respecting the obtaining of the ring from Posthumus. Dr Johnson is of opinion that Shakespear was generally inattentive to the winding-up of his plots.[1] We think the contrary is true; and we might cite in proof of this remark not only the present play, but the conclusion of *Lear*, of *Romeo and Juliet*, of *Macbeth*, of *Othello*, even of *Hamlet*, and of other plays of less moment, in which the last act is crowded with decisive events brought about by natural and striking means.

The pathos in CYMBELINE is not violent or tragical, but of the most pleasing amiable kind. A certain tender gloom overspreads the whole. Posthumus is the ostensible hero of the piece, but its greatest charm is the character of Imogen. Posthumus is only interesting from the interest she takes in him; and she is only interesting herself from her tenderness and constancy to her husband. It is the peculiar excellence of Shakespear's heroines, that they seem to exist only in their attachment to others. They are pure abstractions of the affections. We think as little of their persons as they do themselves, because we are let into the secrets of their hearts, which are more important. We are too much interested in their affairs to stop to look at their faces, except by stealth and at intervals. No one ever hit the true perfection of the female character, the sense of weakness leaning on the strength of its affections for support, so well as Shakespear - no one ever so well painted natural tenderness free from affectation and disguise - no one else ever so well shewed how delicacy and timidity, when driven to extremity, grow romantic and extravagant; for the romance of his heroines (in which they abound) is only an excess of the habitual prejudices of their sex, scrupulous of being false to their vows, truant to their affections, and taught by the force of feeling when to forego the forms of propriety for the essence of it. His women were in this respect exquisite logicians; for there is nothing so logical as passion. They knew their own minds exactly; and only followed up a favourite purpose, which they had sworn to with their tongues, and which was engraven on their hearts, into its untoward consequences. They were the prettiest little set of martyrs and confessors on record. - Cibber, in speaking of the early English stage, accounts for the want of prominence and theatrical display in Shakespear's female characters from the circumstance, that women in those days were not allowed to play the parts of women, which made it necessary to keep them a good deal in the back-ground.[2] Does not this state of manners itself, which prevented their exhibiting themselves in public, and confined them to the relations and charities of domestic life, afford a truer explanation of the matter? His women are certainly very unlike stage-heroines; the reverse of tragedy-queens.

We have almost as great an affection for Imogen as she had for Posthumus; and she deserves it better. Of all Shakespear's women she is perhaps the most tender and the most artless. Her incredulity in the opening scene with Iachimo, as to her husband's infidelity, is much the same as Desdemona's backwardness to believe Othello's jealousy. Her answer to the most distressing part of the picture is only, 'My lord, I fear, has forgot Britain.'[3] Her readiness to pardon Iachimo's false imputations and his designs against herself, is a good lesson to prudes; and may shew that where there is a real attachment to virtue, it has no need to bolster itself up with an outrageous or affected antipathy to vice. The scene in which Pisanio gives Imogen his master's letter, accusing her of incontinency on the treacherous suggestions of Iachimo, is as touching as it is possible for anything to be...

[Hazlitt quotes at length from III.ii]

She all along relies little on her personal charms, which she fears may have been eclipsed by some painted Jay of Italy; she relies on her merit, and her merit is in the depth of her love, her truth and constancy. Our admiration of her beauty is excited with as little consciousness as possible on her part. There are two delicious descriptions given of her, one when she is asleep, and one when she is supposed dead. Arviragus thus addresses her -

> - 'With fairest flowers,
> While summer lasts, and I live here, Fidele
> I'll sweeten thy sad grave; thou shalt not lack
> The flow'r that's like thy face, pale primrose, nor
> The asur'd hare-bell, like thy veins, no, nor
> The leaf of eglantine, which not to slander,
> Out-sweeten'd not thy breath.'[4]

The yellow Iachimo gives another thus, when he steals into her bedchamber:-

> - 'Cytherea,
> How bravely thou becom'st thy bed! Fresh lily,
> And whiter than the sheets! That I might touch -
> But kiss, one kiss - 'Tis her breathing that
> Perfumes the chamber thus: the flame o' th' taper
> Bows toward her, and would under-peep her lids
> To see th' enclosed lights now canopied
> Under the windows, white and azure, laced
> With blue of Heav'n's own tint - on her left breast
> A mole cinque-spotted, like the crimson drops
> I' th' bottom of a cowslip.'[5]

There is a moral sense in the proud beauty of this last image, a rich surfeit of the fancy, - as that well-known passage beginning, 'Me of my lawful pleasure she restrained, and prayed me oft forbearance,'[6] sets a keener edge upon it by the inimitable picture of modesty and self-denial.

The character of Cloten, the conceited, booby lord, and rejected lover of Imogen, though not very agreeable in itself, and at present obsolete, is drawn with much humour and quaint extravagance. The description which Imogen gives of his unwelcome addresses to her - 'Whose love-suit hath been to me as fearful as a siege' - is enough to cure the most ridiculous lover of his folly. It is remarkable that though Cloten makes so poor a figure in love, he is described as assuming an air of consequence as the Queen's son in a council of state, and with all the absurdity of his person and manners, is not without shrewdness in his observations. So true is it that folly is as often owing to a want of proper sentiments as to a want of understanding! The exclamation of the ancient critic - Oh Menander and Nature, which of you copied from the other! would not be misapplied to Shakespear.

The other characters in this play are represented with great truth and accuracy, and as it happens in most of the author's works, there is not only the utmost keeping in each separate character; but in the casting of the different parts, and their relation to one another, there is an affinity and harmony, like what we may observe in the gradations of colour in a picture. The striking and powerful contrasts in which Shakespear abounds could not escape observation; but the use he makes of the principle of analogy to reconcile the greatest diversities of character and to maintain a continuity of feeling throughout, has not been sufficiently attended to. In CYMBELINE, for instance, the principal interest arises out of the unalterable fidelity of Imogen to her husband under the most trying circumstances. Now the other parts of the picture are filled up with subordinate examples of the same feeling, variously modified by different situations, and applied to the purposes of virtue or vice. The plot is aided by the amorous importunities of Cloten, by the persevering determination of Iachimo to conceal the defeat of his project by a daring imposture: the faithful attachment of Pisanio to his mistress is an affecting accompaniment to the whole; the obstinate adherence to his purpose in Bellarius, who keeps the fate of the young princes so long a secret in resentment for the ungrateful return to his former services, the incorrigible wickedness of the Queen, and even the blind uxorious confidence of Cymbeline, are all so many lines of the same story, tending to the same point. The effect of this coincidence is rather felt than observed; and as the impression exists unconsciously in the mind of the reader, so it probably arose in the same manner in the mind of the author, not from design, but from the force of natural association, a particular train of thought suggesting different inflections of the same predominant feeling, melting into, and strengthening one another, like chords in music.

[Hazlitt next speaks, rather uncritically, of the characters of Bellarius, Guiderius and Arviragus.]

The forest of Arden in *As You Like It* can alone compare with the mountain scenes in CYMBELINE: yet how different the contemplative quiet of the one from the enterprising boldness and precarious mode of subsistence in the other! Shakespear not only lets us into the minds of his characters, but gives a tone and colour to the scenes he describes from the feelings of their supposed inhabitants. He at the same time preserves the utmost propriety of action and passion, and gives all their local accompaniments. If he was equal to the greatest things, he was not above an attention to the smallest. Thus the gallant sportsmen in CYMBELINE have to encounter the abrupt declivities of hill and valley: Touchstone and Audrey jog along a level path. The deer in CYMBELINE are only regarded as objects of prey, 'The game's a-foot,'[7] etc. - with Jaques they are fine subjects to moralise upon at leisure, 'under the shade of melancholy boughs.'[8]

We cannot take leave of this play, which is a favourite with us, without noticing some occasional touches of natural piety and morality. We may allude here to the opening of the scene in which Bellarius instructs the young princes to pay their orisons to heaven:

> - 'See, boys! this gate
> Instructs you how t' adore the Heav'ns; and bows you
> To morning's holy office.
> *Guiderius.* Hail, Heav'n!
> *Arviragus.* Hail, Heav'n!
> *Bellarius.* Now for our mountain-sport, up to yon hill.'[9]

What a grace and unaffected spirit of piety breathes in this passage! In like manner, one of the brothers says to the other, when about to perform the funeral rites to Fidele,

> 'Nay, Cadwall, we must lay his head to the east;
> My Father hath a reason for 't' [10]

- as if some allusion to the doctrines of the Christian faith had been casually dropped in conversation by the old man, and had been no farther inquired into.

Shakespear's morality is introduced in the same simple, unobtrusive manner. Imogen will not let her companions stay away from the chase to attend her when sick, and gives her reason for it -

> 'Stick to your journal course; the breach of custom
> Is breach of all!'[11]

When the Queen attempts to disguise her motives for procuring the poison from Cornelius, by saying she means to try its effects on 'creatures not worth the hanging,'[12] his answer conveys at once a tacit reproof of her hyprocisy, and a useful lesson of humanity -

> - Your Highness
> Shall from this practice but make hard your heart.'[13]

15. 'MACBETH'

This essay is an important one for the study of Hazlitt's understanding of Shakespeare, and it is quoted in full except for an endpiece on the Witches written by Lamb (acknowledged by Hazlitt). The opening of the essay shows Hazlitt's 'impressionistic criticism' at its most powerful. He attempts to evoke the atmosphere of the play, and his analysis shows that he considered character to be both affected by and causing a more general impression of the play as a whole. Later, he investigates more closely the 'principle of contrast' which underlies the impression, a principle which Hazlitt sees as Shakespearian and at its most systematic in this play. While Hazlitt owes something to Coleridge in the latter's analysis of Lady Macbeth as 'a class individualized', revealing womanliness even 'in the very moment of dark and bloody imagination' (Hawkes, pp. 213 and 219), yet the interpretation goes further than Coleridge in enquiring into the sources for her actions. In speaking of Lady Macbeth and Macbeth, Hazlitt achieves a relatively complex analysis by suspending moral judgment, and by referring his imaginative conception of the play to actual performances he has seen. He is, for the time, unusually attentive to Lady Macbeth, and the analysis is subtle. The opening passage gives us Hazlitt's general assessment of the distinctiveness of each tragedy, and later in the essay he contrasts Richard III and Macbeth as studies in evil, a comparison which had been drawn by Steevens, Whately and others, and had become something of a commonplace by Hazlitt's time (see e.g. Vickers, vi, 407-29 and 462-5). This is not to say that Hazlitt's treatment of the subject is not individual.

> The poet's eye in a fine frenzy rolling
>
> Doth glance from heaven to earth, from earth to heaven;
>
> And as imagination bodies forth
>
> The forms of things unknown, the poet's pen
>
> Turns them to shape, and gives to airy nothing
>
> A local habitation and a name.'[1]

MACBETH and *Lear, Othello* and *Hamlet*, are usually reckoned Shakespeare's four principal tragedies. *Lear* stands first for the profound intensity of the passion; MACBETH for the wildness of the imagination and the rapidity of the action; *Othello* for the progressive interest and powerful alternations of feeling; *Hamlet* for the refined development of thought and sentiment. If the force of genius shewn in each of these works is astonishing, their variety is not less so. They are like different creations of the same mind, not one of which has the slightest reference to the rest. This distinctness and originality is indeed the necessary consequence of truth and nature. Shakespear's genius alone appeared to possess the resources of nature. He is 'your only *tragedy-maker.*'[2] His plays have the force of things upon the mind. What he represents is brought home to the bosom as a part of our experience, implanted in the memory as if we had known the places, persons, and things of which he treats. MACBETH is like a record of a preternatural and tragical event. It has the rugged severity of an old chronicle with all that the imagination of the poet can engraft upon traditional belief. The castle of Macbeth, round which 'the air smells wooingly,' and where 'the temple-haunting martlet builds,'[3] has a real subsistence in the mind; the Weird Sisters meet us in person on 'the blasted heath';[4] the 'air-drawn dagger'[5] moves slowly before our eyes; the 'gracious Duncan,' the 'blood-boultered Banquo'[6] stand before us; all that passed through the mind of Macbeth passes, without the loss of a title, through ours. All that could actually take place, and all that is only possible to be conceived, what was said and what was done, the workings of passion, the spells of magic, are brought before us with the same absolute truth and vividness. - Shakespear excelled in the openings of his plays: that of MACBETH is the most striking of any. The wildness of the scenery, the sudden shifting of the situations and characters, the bustle, the expectations excited, are equally extraordinary. From the first entrance of the Witches and the description of them when they meet Macbeth,

> - 'What are these
> So wither'd and so wild in their attire,
> That look not like the inhabitants of th' earth
> And yet are on 't?'[7]

the mind is prepared for all that follows.

This tragedy is alike distinguished for the lofty imagination it displays, and for the tumultuous vehemence of the action; and the one is made the moving principle of the other. The overwhelming pressure of preternatural agency urges on the tide of human passion with redoubled force. Macbeth himself appears driven along by the violence of his fate like a vessel drifting before a storm: he reels to and fro like a drunken man; he staggers under the weight of his own purposes and the suggestions of others; he stands at bay with his situation; and from the superstitious awe and breathless suspense into which the communications of the Weird Sisters throw him, is hurried on with daring impatience to verify their predictions, and with impious and bloody hand to tear aside the veil which hides the uncertainty of the future. He is not equal to the struggle with fate and conscience. He now 'bends up each corporal instrument to the terrible feat';[8] at other times his heart misgives him, and he is cowed and abashed by his success. 'The deed, no less than the attempt, confounds him.'[9] His mind is assailed by the stings of remorse, and full of 'preternatural solicitings.'[10] His speeches and soliloquies are dark riddles on human life, baffling solution, and entangling him in their labyrinths. In thought he is absent and perplexed, sudden and desperate in act, from a distrust of his own resolution. His energy springs from the anxiety and agitation of his mind. His blindly rushing forward on the objects of his ambition and revenge, or his recoiling from them, equally betrays the harassed state of his feelings. - This part of his character is admirably set off by being brought in connection with that of Lady Macbeth, whose obdurate strength of will and masculine firmness give her the ascendancy over her husband's faultering virtue. She at once seizes on the opportunity that offers for the accomplishment of all their wished-for greatness, and never flinches from her object till all is over. The magnitude of her resolution almost covers the magnitude of her guilt. She is a great bad woman, whom we hate, but whom we fear more than we hate. She does not excite our loathing and abhorrence like Regan and Gonerill. She is only wicked to gain a great end; and is perhaps more distinguished by her commanding presence of mind and inexorable self-will, which do not suffer her to be diverted from a bad purpose, when once formed, by weak and womanly regrets, than by the hardness of her heart or want of natural affections. The impression which her lofty determination of character makes on the mind of Macbeth is well described where he exclaims,

> - 'Bring forth men children only;
> For thy undaunted mettle should compose
> Nothing but males!'[11]

Nor do the pains she is at to 'screw his courage to the sticking-place,'[12] the reproach to him, not to be 'lost so poorly in himself,'[13] the assurance that 'a little water clears them of this deed,'[14] show anything but her greater consistency in depravity. Her strong-nerved ambition furnishes ribs of steel to 'the sides of his intent';[15] and she is herself wound up to the execution of her baneful project with the same unshrinking fortitude in crime, that in other circumstances she would probably have shown patience in suffering. The deliberate sacrifice of all other considerations to the gaining 'for their future days and nights sole sovereign sway and masterdom,'[16] by the murder of Duncan, is gorgeously expressed in her invocation on hearing of 'his fatal entrance under her battlements':[17]

> - 'Come all you spirits
> That tend on mortal thoughts, unsex me here:
> And fill me, from the crown to th' toe, top-full
> Of direst cruelty; make thick my blood,
> Stop up the access and passage to remorse,
> That no compunctious visitings of nature
> Shake my fell purpose, nor keep peace between
> The effect and it. Come to my woman's breasts,
> And take my milk for gall, you murthering ministers,
> Wherever in your sightless substances
> You wait on nature's mischief. Come, thick night!
> And pall thee in the dunnest smoke of hell,

That my keen knife see not the wound it makes,

Nor heav'n peep through the blanket of the dark,

To cry, hold, hold! - '[18]

When she first hears that 'Duncan comes there to sleep' she is so overcome by the news, which is beyond her utmost expectations, that she answers the messenger, 'Thou'rt mad to say it':[19] and on receiving her husband's account of the predictions of the Witches, conscious of his instability of purpose, and that her presence is necessary to goad him on to the consummation of his promised greatness, she exclaims -

- 'Hie thee hither,

That I may pour my spirits in thine ear,

And chastise with the valour of my tongue

All that impedes thee from the golden round,

Which fate and metaphysical aid doth seem

To have thee crowned withal.'[20]

This swelling exultation and keen spirit of triumph, this uncontroulable eagerness of anticipation, which seems to dilate her form and take possession of all her faculties, this solid, substantial flesh and blood display of passion, exhibit a striking contrast to the cold, abstracted, gratuitous, servile malignity of the Witches, who are equally instrumental in urging Macbeth to his fate for the mere love of mischief, and from a disinterested delight in deformity and cruelty. They are hags of mischief, obscene panders to iniquity, malicious from their impotence of enjoyment, enamoured of destruction, because they are themselves unreal, abortive, half-existences - who become sublime from their exemption from all human sympathies and contempt for all human affairs, as Lady Macbeth does by the force of passion! Her fault seems to have been an excess of that strong principle of self-interest and family aggrandisement, not amenable to the common feelings of compassion and justice, which is so marked a feature in barbarous nations and times. A passing reflection of this kind, on the resemblance of the sleeping king to her father, alone prevents her from slaying Duncan with her own hand.

In speaking of the character of Lady Macbeth, we ought not to pass over Mrs Siddons's manner of acting that part.[21] We can conceive of nothing grander It was something above nature. It seemed almost as if a being of a superior order had dropped from a higher sphere to awe the world with the majesty of her appearance. Power was seated on her brow, passion emanated from her breast as from a shrine; she was tragedy personified. In coming on in the sleeping-scene, her eyes were open, but their sense was shut. She was like a person bewildered and unconscious of what she did. Her lips moved involuntarily - all her gestures were involuntary and mechanical. She glided on and off the stage like an apparition. To have seen her in that character was an event in every one's life, not to be forgotten.

The dramatic beauty of the character of Duncan, which excites the respect and pity even of his murderers, has been often pointed out. It forms a picture of itself. An instance of the author's power of giving a striking effect to a common reflection, by the manner of introducing it, occurs in a speech of Duncan, complaining of his having been deceived in his opinion of the Thane of Cawdor, at the very moment that he is expressing the most unbounded confidence in the loyalty and services of Macbeth.

> 'There is no art
> To find the mind's construction in the face:
> He was a gentleman, on whom I built
> An absolute trust.
> O worthiest cousin, *(addressing himself to Macbeth.)*
> The sin of my ingratitude e'en now
> Was great upon me,' etc.[22]

Another passage to show that Shakespear lost sight of nothing that could in any way give relief or heightening to his subject, is the conversation which takes place between Banquo and Fleance immediately before the murder-scene of Duncan.

> '*Banquo.*   How goes the night, boy?
>
> *Fleance.*   The moon is down: I have not heard the clock.
>
> *Banquo.*   And she goes down at twelve.
>
> *Fleance.*   I take't, 'tis later, Sir.
>
> *Banquo.*   Hold, take my sword. There's husbandry in heav'n,
> Their candles are all out.
>
> -A heavy summons lies like lead upon me,

And yet I would not sleep: Merciful Powers,
Restrain in me the cursed thoughts that nature
Gives way to in repose.'[23]

In like manner, a fine idea is given of the gloomy coming on of evening, just as
Banquo is going to be assassinated.

'Light thickens and the crow
Makes wing to the rooky wood.'[24]

.   .   .

Now spurs the lated traveller apace
To gain the timely inn.'[25]

MACBETH (generally speaking) is done upon a stronger and more systematic
principle of contrast than any other of Shakespear's plays. It moves upon the
verge of an abyss, and is a constant struggle between life and death. The action is
desperate and the reaction is dreadful. It is a huddling together of fierce extremes,
a war of opposite natures which of them shall destroy the other. There is nothing
but what has a violent end or violent beginnings. The lights and shades are laid on
with a determined hand; the transitions from triumph to despair, from the height of
terror to the repose of death, are sudden and startling; every passion brings in its
fellow-contrary, and the thoughts pitch and jostle against each other as in the dark.
The whole play is an unruly chaos of strange and forbidden things, where the
ground rocks under our feet. Shakespear's genius here took its full swing, and
trod upon the farthest bounds of nature and passion. This circumstance will
account for the abruptness and violent antitheses of the style, the throes and labour
which run through the expression, and from defects will turn them into beauties.
'So fair and foul a day I have not seen,'[26] etc. 'Such welcome and unwelcome
news together.'[27] 'Men's lives are like the flowers in their caps, dying or ere they
sicken.'[28] 'Look like the innocent flower, but be the serpent under it.'[29] The
scene before the castle gate follows the appearance of the Witches on the heath, and
is followed by a midnight murder. Duncan is cut off betimes by treason leagued
with witchcraft, and Macduff is ripped untimely from his mother's womb to
avenge his death. Macbeth, after the death of Banquo, wishes for his presence in
extravagant terms, 'To him and all we thirst,'[30] and when his ghost appears, cries
out, 'Avaunt and quit my sight,'[31] and being gone, he is 'himself again.'[32]

Macbeth resolves to get rid of Macduff, that 'he may sleep in spite of thunder';[33] and cheers his wife on the doubtful intelligence of Banquo's taking-off with the encouragement - 'Then be thou jocund: ere the bat has flown his cloistered flight; ere to black Hecate's summons the shard-born beetle has rung night's yawning peal, there shall be done - a deed of dreadful note.'[34] In Lady Macbeth's speech 'Had he not resembled my father as he slept, I had done't,'[35] there is murder and filial piety together; and in urging him to fulfil his vengeance against the defenceless king, her thoughts spare the blood neither of infants nor old age. The description of the Witches is full of the same contradictory principle; they 'rejoice when good kings bleed,'[36] they are neither of the earth nor the air, but both; 'they should be women, but their beards forbid it';[37] they take all the pains possible to lead Macbeth on to the height of his ambition, only to betray him 'in deeper consequence,'[38] and after showing him all the pomp of their art, discover their malignant delight in his disappointed hopes, by that bitter taunt, 'Why stands Macbeth thus amazedly?'[39] We might multiply such instances every where.

The leading features in the character of Macbeth are striking enough, and they form what may be thought at first only a bold, rude, Gothic outline. By comparing it with other characters of the same author[40] we shall perceive the absolute truth and identity which is observed in the midst of the giddy whirl and rapid career of events. Macbeth in Shakespear no more loses his identity of character in the fluctuations of fortune or the storm of passion, than Macbeth in himself would have lost the identity of his person. Thus he is as distinct a being from Richard III as it is possible to imagine, though these two characters in common hands, and indeed in the hands of any other poet, would have been a repetition of the same general idea, more or less exaggerated. For both are tyrants, usurpers, murderers, both aspiring and ambitious, both courageous, cruel, treacherous. But Richard is cruel from nature and constitution. Macbeth becomes so from accidental circumstances. Richard is from his birth deformed in body and mind, and naturally incapable of good. Macbeth is full of 'the milk of human kindness,'[41] is frank, sociable, generous. He is tempted to the commission of guilt by golden opportunities, by the instigations of his wife, and by prophetic warnings. Fate and metaphysical aid conspire against his virtue and his loyalty. Richard on the contrary needs no prompter, but wades through a series of crimes to the height of his ambition from the ungovernable violence of his temper and a reckless love of mischief. He is never gay but in the prospect or in the success of his villainies: Macbeth is full of horror at the thoughts of the murder of Duncan, which he is with difficulty prevailed on to commit, and of remorse after its perpetration. Richard has no mixture of common humanity in his composition, no regard to kindred or posterity, he owns no fellowship with others, he is 'himself alone.'[42] Macbeth is not destitute of feelings of sympathy, is accessible to pity, is even made in some measure the dupe of his uxoriousness, ranks the loss of friends, of the cordial love of his followers, and of his good name, among the causes which have made him weary of life, and regrets that he has ever seized the crown by unjust means, since he cannot transmit it to his posterity -

> 'For Banquo's issue have I fil'd my mind -
> For them the gracious Duncan have I murther'd,
> To make them kings, the seed of Banquo kings.'[43]

In the agitation of his mind, he envies those whom he has sent to peace. 'Duncan is in his grave; after life's fitful fever he sleeps well.'[44] - It is true, he becomes more callous as he plunges deeper in guilt, 'direness is thus rendered familiar to his slaughterous thoughts,'[45] and he in the end anticipates his wife in the boldness and bloodiness of his enterprises, while she for want of the same stimulus of action, 'is troubled with thick-coming fancies that rob her of her rest,'[46] goes mad and dies. Macbeth endeavours to escape from reflection on his crimes by repelling their consequences, and banishes remorse for the past by the meditation of future mischief. This is not the principle of Richard's cruelty, which displays the wanton malice of a fiend as much as the frailty of human passion. Macbeth is goaded on to acts of violence and retaliation by necessity; to Richard, blood is a pastime. - There are other decisive differences inherent in the two characters. Richard may be regarded as a man of the world, a plotting, hardened knave, wholly regardless of everything but his own ends, and the means to secure them. - Not so Macbeth. The superstitions of the age, the rude state of society, the local scenery and customs, all give a wildness and imaginary grandeur to his character. From the strangeness of the events that surround him, he is full of amazement and fear; and stands in doubt between the world of reality and the world of fancy. He sees sights not shown to mortal eye, and hears unearthly music. All is tumult and disorder within and without his mind; his purposes recoil upon himself, are broken and disjointed; he is the double thrall of his passions and his evil destiny. Richard is not a character either of imagination or pathos, but of pure self-will. There is no conflict of opposite feelings in his breast. The apparitions which he sees only haunt him in his sleep; nor does he live like Macbeth in a waking dream. Macbeth has considerable energy and manliness of character; but then he is 'subject to all the skyey influences.'[47] He is sure of nothing but the present moment. Richard in the busy turbulence of his projects never loses his self-possession, and makes use of every circumstance that happens as an instrument of his long-reaching designs. In his last extremity we can only regard him as a wild beast taken in the toils: while we never entirely lose our concern for Macbeth; and he calls back all our sympathy by that fine close of thoughtful melancholy -

> 'My way of life is fallen into the sear,
>
> The yellow leaf; and that which should accompany old age,
>
> As honour, troops of friends, I must not look to have;
>
> But in their stead, curses not loud but deep,
>
> Mouth-honour, breath, which the poor heart
>
> Would fain deny, and dare not.'[48]

We can conceive a common actor to play Richard tolerably well; we can conceive no one to play Macbeth properly, or to look like a man that had encountered the Weird Sisters. All the actors that we have ever seen, appear as if they had encountered them on the boards of Covent-garden or Drury-lane, but not on the heath at Fores, and as if they did not believe what they had seen. The Witches of MACBETH indeed are ridiculous on the modern stage, and we doubt if the Furies of Æschylus would be more respected. The progress of manners and knowledge has an influence on the stage, and will in time perhaps destroy both tragedy and comedy.

16.   FROM 'JULIUS CAESAR'

The prime interest of this essay is Hazlitt's commentary upon 'political character'. In Shakespeare's design Hazlitt sees reflected his own republicanism, a reading which makes him blind to Brutus's faults. Hazlitt's reference to some of 'those careless and natural digressions which occur so frequently and beautifully in Shakespeare' is a valuable perception, although the language is not what we would use today.

Shakespear's JULIUS CÆSAR is not equal as a whole, to either of his other plays taken from the Roman history. It is inferior in interest to *Coriolanus*, and both in interest and power to *Antony and Cleopatra*. It however abounds in admirable and affecting passages, and is remarkable for the profound knowledge of character, in which Shakespear could scarcely fail. If there is any exception to this remark, it is in the hero of the piece himself. We do not much admire the representation here given of Julius Cæsar, nor do we think it answers to the portrait given of him in his Commentaries. He makes several vapouring and rather pedantic speeches, and does nothing. Indeed, he has nothing to do. So far, the fault of the character is the fault of the plot.

The spirit with which the poet has entered at once into the manners of the common people, and the jealousies and heart-burnings of the different factions, is shown in the first scene, where Flavius and Marullus, tribunes of the people, and some citizens of Rome, appear upon the stage.

> '*Flavius.*   Thou art a cobbler, art thou?
>
> *Cobbler.*   Truly, Sir, *all* that I live by, is the *awl*: I meddle
> with no trades-man's matters, nor woman's
> matters, but *with-al*, I am indeed, Sir, a surgeon to
> old shoes; when they are in great danger, I recover
> them.
>
> *Flavius.*   But wherefore art not in thy shop to-day?
> Why dost thou lead these men about the streets?
>
> *Cobbler.*   Truly, Sir, to wear out their shoes, to get myself
> into more work. But indeed, Sir, we make holiday
> to see Caesar, and rejoice in his triumph.'[1]

Shakespear has in this play and elsewhere shown the same penetration into political character and the springs of public events as into those of every-day life. For instance, the whole design of the conspirators to liberate their country fails from the generous temper and overweening confidence of Brutus in the goodness of their cause and the assistance of others. Thus it has always been. Those who mean well themselves think well of others, and fall a prey to their security. That humanity and honesty which dispose men to resist injustice and tyranny render them unfit to cope with the cunning and power of those who are opposed to them. The friends of liberty trust to the professions of others, because they are themselves sincere, and endeavour to reconcile the public good with the least possible hurt to its enemies, who have no regard to any thing but their own unprincipled ends, and stick at nothing to accomplish them. Cassius was better cut out for a conspirator. His heart prompted his head. His watchful jealousy made him fear the worst that might happen, and his irritability of temper added to his inveteracy of purpose, and sharpened his patriotism. The mixed nature of his motives made him fitter to contend with bad men. The vices are never so well employed as in combating one another. Tyranny and servility are to be dealt with after their own fashion: otherwise, they will triumph over those who spare them, and finally pronounce their funeral panegyric, as Antony did that of Brutus.

> 'All the conspirators, save only he,
> Did that they did in envy of great Cæsar:
> He only in a general honest thought
> And common good to all, made one of them.'[2]

The quarrel between Brutus and Cassius is managed in a masterly way. The dramatic fluctuation of passion, the calmness of Brutus, the heat of Cassius, are admirably described; and the exclamation of Cassius on hearing of the death of Portia, which he does not learn till after their reconciliation, 'How 'scaped I killing when I crost you so?'[3] gives double force to all that has gone before. The scene between Brutus and Portia, where she endeavours to extort the secret of the conspiracy from him, is conceived in the most heroical spirit, and the burst of tenderness in Brutus -

> 'You are my true and honourable wife;
> As dear to me as are the ruddy drops
> That visit my sad heart'[4]

is justified by her whole behaviour. Portia's breathless impatience to learn the event of the conspiracy, in the dialogue with Lucius, is full of passion. The interest which Portia takes in Brutus and that which Calphurnia takes in the fate of Cæsar are discriminated with the nicest precision. Mark Antony's speech over the dead body of Cæsar has been justly admired for the mixture of pathos and artifice in it: that of Brutus certainly is not so good.

The entrance of the conspirators to the house of Brutus at midnight is rendered very impressive. In the midst of this scene, we meet with one of those careless and natural digressions which occur so frequently and beautifully in Shakespear. After Cassius has introduced his friends one by one, Brutus says -

> 'They are all welcome.
> What watchful cares do interpose themselves
> Betwixt your eyes and night?
>
> *Cassius,* Shall I entreat a word? *(They whisper.)*
> *Decius.* Here lies the east: doth not the day break here?
> *Casca.* No.
> *Cinna.* O Pardon, Sir, it doth; and yon grey lines,
> That fret the clouds, are messengers of day.
> *Casca.* You shall confess, that you are both deceiv'd:
> Here, as I point my sword, the sun arises,
> Which is a great way growing on the south,
> Weighing the youthful season of the year.
> Some two months hence, up higher toward the north
> He first presents his fire, and the high east.
> Stands as the Capitol, directly here.'[5]

We cannot help thinking this graceful familiarity better than all the fustian in the world. - The truth of history in JULIUS CÆSAR is very ably worked up with dramatic effect. The councils of generals, the doubtful turns of battles, are represented to the life. The death of Brutus is worthy of him - it has the dignity of the Roman senator with the firmness of the Stoic philosopher. But what is perhaps better than either, is the little incident of his boy, Lucius, falling asleep over his instrument, as he is playing to his master in his tent, the night before the battle. Nature has played him the same forgetful trick once before on the night of the conspiracy. The humanity of Brutus is the same on both occasions.

> - 'It is no matter:
> Enjoy the honey-heavy dew of slumber.

Thou hast no figures nor no fantasies,
Which busy care draws in the brains of men.
Therefore though sleep'st so sound.'[6]

17.   'OTHELLO'

This essay is quoted in full, since the play is one that Hazlitt analyses time and again in his theatrical reviews and it is clearly important to him. The general remarks on tragedy at the beginning supplement the many remarks made by Hazlitt in which he stresses that literature (and especially tragedy) is instructive mainly because it involves the exercise of 'the passions', demanding 'the power of the imagination' in sympathetic projection on the reader's part. This idea is constantly found in Hazlitt, and it owes something to Sidney's view of poetry as both instructive and emotionally absorbing, in *The Defence of Poetry*. The 'balance of the affections' is Hazlitt's romantic equivalent for Aristotelian *catharsis*. In this and his other pieces on Iago, Hazlitt implicitly questions Coleridge's notion of Iago's 'motiveless malignity'. A.C. Bradley was to find Hazlitt's ideas useful in his own section on Iago in *Shakespearian Tragedy*. There is an emphasis, as in Hazlitt's other essays, upon contrast, which here he sees as operating through strongly opposed characters and through 'the alternate ascendancy of different passions'. See below, numbers 51 and 52 for Hazlitt's impressions of Kean playing the role of Iago, which deeply influenced his criticism. Hazlitt's image is haunting when he describes Iago as one 'who thinks a fatal experiment on the peace of a family a better thing than watching the palpitations in the heart of a flea in a microscope...'

It has been said that tragedy purifies the affections by terror and pity.[1] That is, it substitutes imaginary sympathy for mere selfishness. It gives us a high and permanent interest, beyond ourselves, in humanity as such. It raises the great, the remote, and the possible to an equality with the real, the little and the near. It makes man a partaker with his kind. It subdues and softens the stubbornness of his will. It teaches him that there are and have been others like himself, by showing him as in a glass what they have felt, thought, and done. It opens the chambers of the human heart. It leaves nothing indifferent to us that can affect our common nature. It excites our sensibility by exhibiting the passions wound up to the utmost pitch by the power of imagination or the temptation of circumstances; and corrects their fatal excesses in ourselves by pointing to the greater extent of sufferings and of crimes to which they have led others. Tragedy creates a balance of the affections. It makes us thoughtful spectators in the lists of life. It is the refiner of the species; a discipline of humanity. The habitual study of poetry and works of imagination is one chief part of a well-grounded education. A taste for liberal art is necessary to complete the character of a gentleman. Science alone is hard and mechanical. It exercises the understanding upon things out of ourselves, while it leaves the affections unemployed, or engrossed with our own immediate, narrow interests. - OTHELLO furnishes an illustration of those remarks. It excites our sympathy in an extraordinary degree. The moral it conveys has a closer application to the concerns of human life than that of almost any other of Shakespear's plays. 'It comes directly home to the bosoms and business of men.'2 The pathos in *Lear* is indeed more dreadful and overpowering: but it is less natural, and less of every day's occurrence. We have not the same degree of sympathy with the passions described in *Macbeth*. The interest in *Hamlet* is more remote and reflex. That of OTHELLO is at once equally profound and affecting.

The picturesque contrasts of character in this play are almost as remarkable as the depth of the passion. The Moor Othello, the gentle Desdemona, the villain Iago, the good-natured Cassio, the fool Roderigo, present a range and variety of characters as striking and palpable as that produced by the opposition of costume in a picture. Their distinguishing qualities stand out to the mind's eye, so that even when we are not thinking of their actions or sentiments, the idea of their persons is still as present to us as ever.3 These characters and the images they stamp upon the mind are the farthest asunder possible, the distance between them is immense: yet the compass of knowledge and invention which the poet has shown in embodying these extreme creations of his genius is only greater than the truth and felicity with which he has identified each character with itself, or blended their different qualities together in the same story. What a contrast the character of Othello forms to that of Iago! At the same time, the force of conception with which these two figures are opposed to each other is rendered still more intense by the complete consistency with which the traits of each character are brought out in a state of the highest finishing. The making one black and the other white, the one unprincipled, the other unfortunate in the extreme, would have answered the common purposes of effect, and satisfied the ambition of an ordinary painter of character. Shakespear has laboured the finer shades of difference in both with as much care and skill as if he had had to depend on the execution alone for the success of his design. On the other hand, Desdemona and Æmilia are not meant to be opposed with anything like strong contrast to each other. Both are, to outward appearance, characters of common life, not more distinguished than women usually are, by difference of rank and situation. The difference of their thoughts and sentiments is however laid open, their minds are separated from each other by signs as plain and as little to be mistaken as the complexions of their husbands.

The movement of the passion in Othello is exceedingly different from that of Macbeth. In Macbeth there is a violent struggle between opposite feelings, between ambition and the stings of conscience, almost from first to last: in Othello, the doubtful conflict between contrary passions, though dreadful, continues only for a short time, and the chief interest is excited by the alternate ascendancy of different passions, by the entire and unforeseen change from the fondest love and most unbounded confidence to the tortures of jealousy and the madness of hatred. The revenge of Othello, after it has once taken thorough possession of his mind, never quits it, but grows stronger and stronger at every moment of its delay. The nature of the Moor is noble, confiding, tender, and generous; but his blood is the most inflammable kind; and being once roused by a sense of his wrongs, he is stopped by no considerations of remorse or pity till he has given a loose to all the dictates of his rage and his despair. It is in working his noble nature up to this extremity through rapid but gradual transitions, in raising passion to its height from the smallest beginnings and in spite of all obstacles, in painting the expiring conflict between love and hatred, tenderness and resentment, jealousy and remorse, in unfolding the strength and the weakness of our nature, in uniting sublimity of thought with the anguish of the keenest woe, in putting in motion the various impulses that agitate this our mortal being, and at last blending them in that noble tide of deep and sustained passion, impetuous but majestic, that 'flows on to the Propontic, and knows no ebb,'[4] that Shakespear has shown the mastery of his genius and of his power over the human heart. The third act of OTHELLO is his finest display, not of knowledge or passion separately, but of the two combined, of the knowledge of character with the expression of passion, of consummate art in the keeping up of appearances with the profound workings of nature, and the convulsive movements of uncontroulable agony, of the power of inflicting torture and of suffering it. Not only is the tumult of passion in Othello's mind heaved up from the very bottom of the soul, but every the slightest undulation of feeling is seen on the surface, as it arises from the impulses of imagination or the malicious suggestions of Iago. The progressive preparation for the catastrophe is wonderfully managed from the Moor's first gallant recital of the story of his love, of 'the spells and witchcraft he had used,'[5] from his unlooked-for and romantic success, the fond satisfaction with which he dotes on his own happiness, the unreserved tenderness of Desdemona and her innocent importunities in favour of Cassio, irritating the suspicions instilled into her husband's mind by the perfidy of Iago, and rankling there to poison, till he loses all command of himself, and his rage can only be appeased by blood. She is introduced, just before Iago begins to put his scheme in practice, pleading for Cassio with all the thoughtless gaiety of friendship and winning confidence in the love of Othello.

> 'What! Michael Cassio
> That came a wooing with you, and so many a time,
> When I have spoke of you dispraisingly,
> Hath ta'en your part, to have so much to do
> To bring him in? - Why this is not a boon:
> 'Tis as I should intreat you wear your gloves,
> Or feed on nourishing meats, or keep you warm;
> Or sue to you to do a peculiar profit
> To your person. Nay, when I have a suit,
> Wherein I mean to touch your love indeed,
> It shall be full of poise, and fearful to be granted.'[6]

Othello's confidence, at first only staggered by broken hints and insinuations, recovers itself at sight of Desdemona; and he exclaims

> 'If she be false, O then Heav'n mocks itself:
> I'll not believe it.'[7]

But presently after, on brooding over his suspicions by himself, and yielding to his apprehensions of the worst, his smothered jealousy breaks out into open fury, and he returns to demand satisfaction of Iago like a wild beast stung with the envenomed shaft of the hunters. 'Look where he comes,'[8] etc. In this state of exasperation and violence, after the first paroxysms of his grief and tenderness have had their vent in that passionate apostrophe, 'I felt not Cassio's kisses on her lips,'[9] Iago, by false aspersions, and by presenting the most revolting images to his mind,[10] easily turns the storm of passion from himself against Desdemona, and works him up into a trembling agony of doubt and fear, in which he abandons all his love and hopes in a breath.

> 'Now do I see 'tis true. Look here, Iago,
> All my fond love thus do I blow to Heav'n. 'Tis gone.
> Arise black vengeance from the hollow hell;
> Yield up, O love, thy crown and hearted throne
> To tyrannous hate! Swell bosom with thy fraught;
> For 'tis of aspicks' tongues.'[11]

From this time, his raging thoughts 'never look back, ne'er ebb to humble love,' till his revenge is sure of its object, the painful regrets and involuntary recollections of past circumstances which cross his mind amidst the dim trances of passion, aggravating the sense of his wrongs, but not shaking his purpose. Once indeed, where Iago shows him Cassio with the handkerchief in his hand, and making sport (as he thinks) of his misfortunes, the intolerable bitterness of his feelings, the extreme sense of shame, makes him fall to praising her accomplishments and relapse into a momentary fit of weakness, 'Yet, oh the pity of it, Iago, the pity of it!'[12] This returning fondness however only serves, as it is managed by Iago, to whet his revenge, and set his heart more against her. In his conversations with Desdemona, the persuasion of her guilt and the immediate proofs of her duplicity seem to irritate his resentment and aversion to her; but in the scene immediately preceding her death, the recollection of his love returns upon him in all its tenderness and force; and after her death, he all at once forgets his wrongs in the sudden and irreparable sense of his loss.

> 'My wife! My wife! What wife? I have no wife.
> Oh insupportable! Oh heavy hour!'[13]

This happens before he is assured of her innocence; but afterwards his remorse is as dreadful as his revenge has been, and yields only to fixed and death-like despair. His farewell speech, before he kills himself, in which he conveys his reasons to the senate for the murder of his wife, is equal to the first speech in which he gave them an account of his courtship of her, and 'his whole course of love.'[14] Such an ending was alone worthy of such a commencement.

If any thing could add to the force of our sympathy with Othello, or compassion for his fate, it would be the frankness and generosity of his nature, which so little deserve it. When Iago first begins to practise upon his unsuspecting friendship, he answers -

> - ' 'Tis not to make me jealous,
> To say my wife is fair, feeds well, loves company,
> Is free of speech, sings, plays, and dances well;
> Where virtue is, these are most virtuous.
> Nor from my own weak merits will I draw
> The smallest fear or doubt of her revolt,
> For she had eyes and chose me.'[15]

This character is beautifully (and with affecting simplicity) confirmed by what Desdemona herself says of him to Æmilia after she has lost the handkerchief, the first pledge of his love to her.

> 'Believe me, I had rather have lost my purse
> Full of cruzadoes. And but my noble Moor
> Is true of mind, and made of no such baseness,
> As jealous creatures are, it were enough
> To put him to ill thinking.
> *Æmilia.*   Is he not jealous?
> *Desdemona.*   Who he? I think the sun where he was born
> Drew all such humours from him.'[16]

In a short speech of Æmilia's, there occurs one of those side-imitations of the fluctuations of passion which we seldom meet with but in Shakespear. After Othello has resolved upon the death of his wife, and bids her dismiss her attendant for the night, she answers,

> 'I will, my Lord.
> *Æmilia.*   How goes it now? *He looks gentler than he did.*'[17]

Shakespear has here put into half a line what some authors would have spun out into ten set speeches.

The character of Desdemona is inimitable both in itself, and as it appears in contrast with Othello's groundless jealousy, and with the foul conspiracy of which she is the innocent victim. Her beauty and external graces are only indirectly glanced at: we see 'her visage in her mind';[18] her character every where predominates over her person.

> 'A maiden never bold:
> Of spirit so still and quiet, that her motion
> Blush'd at itself.'[1]

There is one fine compliment paid to her by Cassio, who exclaims triumphantly when she comes ashore at Cyprus after the storm,

> 'Tempests themselves, high seas, and howling winds,
> As having sense of beauty, do omit
> Their mortal natures, letting safe go by
> The divine Desdemona.'[20]

In general, as is the case with most of Shakespear's females, we lose sight of her personal charms in her attachment and devotedness to her husband.[21] 'She is subdued even to the very quality of her lord';[22] and to Othello's 'honours and his valiant parts her soul and fortunes consecrates.'[23] The lady protests so much herself, and she is as good as her word. The truth of conception, with which timidity and boldness are united in the same character, is marvellous. The extravagance of her resolutions, the pertinacity of her affections, may be said to arise out of the gentleness of her nature. They imply an unreserved reliance on the purity of her own intentions, an entire surrender of her fears to her love, a knitting of herself (heart and soul) to the fate of another. Bating the commencement of her passion, which is a little fantastical and headstrong (though even that may perhaps be consistently accounted for from her inability to resist a rising inclination)[24] her whole character consists in having no will of her own, no prompter but her obedience. Her romantic turn is only a consequence of the domestic and practical part of her disposition; and instead of following Othello to the wars, she would gladly have 'remained at home a moth of peace,'[25] if her husband could have staid with her. Her resignation and angelic sweetness of temper do not desert her at the last. The scenes in which she laments and tries to account for Othello's estrangement from her are exquisitely beautiful. After he has struck her, and called her names, she says,

> - 'Alas, Iago,What shall I do to win my lord again?
> Good friend, go to him; for by this light of heaven,
> I know not how I lost him.
> Here I kneel; If e'er my will did trespass 'gainst his love,
> Either in discourse, or thought, or actual deed,
> Or that mine eyes, mine ears, or any sense
> Delighted them on any other form;
> Or that I do not, and ever did,
> And ever will, though he do shake me off
> To beggarly divorcement, love him dearly,
> Comfort forswear me. Unkindness may do much,
> And his unkindness may defeat my life,
> But never taint my love.
> *Iago.*   I pray you be content: 'tis but his humour.
>   The business of the state does him offence.
> *Desdemona.*   If 'twere no other!' -[26]

The scene which follows with Æmilia and the song of the Willow, are equally beautiful, and show the author's extreme power of varying the expression of passion, in all its moods and in all circumstances.

> *'Æmilia.*   Would you had never seen him.
> *Desdemona.*   So would not I: my love doth so approve him,
>   That even his stubbornness, his checks, his frowns,
>   Have grace and favour in them,' etc.[27]

Not the unjust suspicions of Othello, not Iago's unprovoked treachery, place Desdemona in a more amiable or interesting light than the conversation (half earnest, half jest) between her and Æmilia on the common behaviour of women to their husbands. This dialogue takes place just before the last fatal scene. If Othello had overheard it, it would have prevented the whole catastrophe; but then it would have spoiled the play.

The character of Iago is one of the supererogations of Shakespear's genius.[28] Some persons, more nice than wise, have thought this whole character unnatural, because his villainy is *without a sufficient motive.*[29] Shakespear, who was as good a philosopher as he was a poet, thought otherwise. He knew that the love of power, which is another name for the love of mischief, is natural to man. He would know this as well or better than if it had been demonstrated to him by a logical diagram, merely from seeing children paddle in the dirt or kill flies for sport. Iago in fact belongs to a class of character, common to Shakespear and at the same time peculiar to him; whose heads are as acute and active as their hearts are hard and callous. Iago is to be sure an extreme instance of the kind; that is to say, of diseased intellectual activity, with the most perfect indifference to moral good or evil, or rather with a decided preference of the latter, because it falls more readily in with his favourite propensity, gives greater zest to his thoughts and scope to his actions. He is quite or nearly as indifferent to his own fate as to that of others; he runs all risks for a trifling and doubtful advantage; and is himself the dupe and victim of his ruling passion - an insatiable craving after action of the most difficult and dangerous kind. 'Our ancient' is a philosopher, who fancies that a lie that kills has more point in it than an alliteration or an antithesis; who thinks a fatal experiment on the peace of a family a better thing than watching the palpitations in the heart of a flea in a microscope; who plots the ruin of his friends as an exercise for his ingenuity, and stabs men in the dark to prevent *ennui*. His gaiety, such as it is, arises from the success of his treachery; his ease from the torture he has inflicted on others. He is an amateur of tragedy in real life; and instead of employing his invention on imaginary characters, or long-forgotten incidents, he takes the bolder and more desperate course of getting up his plot at home, casts the principal parts among his nearest friends and connections, and rehearses it in downright earnest, with steady nerves and unabated resolution. We will just give an illustration or two.

One of his most characteristic speeches is that immediately after the marriage of Othello.

> '*Roderigo.*   What a full fortune does the thick lips owe,
>   If he can carry her thus!
> *Iago.*   Call up her father:
>   Rouse him (*Othello*) make after him, poison his delight,

> Proclaim him in the streets, incense her kinsmen,
>
> And tho' he in a fertile climate dwell,
>
> Plague him with flies: tho' that his joy be joy,
>
> Yet throw such changes of vexation on it,
>
> As it may lose some colour.'[30]

In the next passage, his imagination runs riot in the mischief he is plotting, and breaks out into the wildness and impetuosity of real enthusiasm.

> '*Roderigo.* Here is her father's house: I'll call aloud.
>
> *Iago.*   Do, with like timourous accent and dire yell
>
> As when, by night and negligence, the fire
>
> Is spied in populous cities.'[31]

One of his most favourite topics, on which he is rich indeed, and is descanting on which his spleen serves him for a Muse, is the disproportionate match between Desdemona and the Moor. This is a clue to the character of the lady which he is by no means ready to part with. It is brought forward in the first scene, and he recurs to it, when in answer to his insinuations against Desdemona, Roderigo says,

> 'I cannot believe that in her - she's full of most blest conditions.
>
> *Iago.*   Bless'd fig's end. The wine she drinks is made of grapes.
>
> If she had been blest, she would never have married the Moor.'[32]

And again with still more spirit and fatal effect afterwards, when he turns this very suggestion arising in Othello's own breast to her prejudice.

> '*Othello.*   And yet how nature erring from itself -
>
> *Iago.*   Ay, there's the point; - as to be bold with you,
>
> Not to affect many proposed matches
>
> Of her own clime, complexion, and degree,' etc.[33]

This is probing to the quick. Iago here turns the character of poor Desdemona, as it were, inside out. It is certain that nothing but the genius of Shakespear could have preserved the entire interest and delicacy of the part, and have even drawn an additional elegance and dignity from the peculiar circumstances in which she is placed. - The habitual licentiousness of Iago's conversation is not to be traced to the pleasure he takes in gross or lascivious images, but to his desire of finding out the worst side of everything, and of proving himself an over-match for appearances. He has none of 'the milk of human kindness'[34] in his composition. His imagination rejects every thing that has not a strong infusion of the most unpalatable ingredients; his mind digests only poisons. Virtue or goodness or whatever has the least 'relish of salvation in it,'[35] is, to his depraved appetite, sickly and insipid: and he even resents the good opinion entertained of his own integrity, as if it were an affront cast on the masculine sense and spirit of his character. Thus at the meeting between Othello and Desdemona, he exclaims - 'Oh, you are well tuned now: but I'll set down the pegs that make this music, *as honest as I am*'[36] - his character of *bonhommie* not sitting at all easy upon him. In the scenes, where he tries to work Othello to his purpose, he is proportionably guarded, insidious, dark, and deliberate. We believe nothing ever came up to the profound dissimulation and dextrous artifice of the well-known dialogue in the third act, where he first enters upon the execution of his design.

> *'Iago.*   My noble lord.
>
> *Othello.*   What doest thou say, Iago?
>
> *Iago.*   Did Michael Cassio,
>
> When you woo'd my lady, know of your love?
>
> *Othello.*   He did from first to last.
>
> Why dost thou ask?
>
> *Iago.*   But for a satisfaction of my thought,
>
> No further harm.
>
> *Othello.*   Why of thy thought, Iago?
>
> *Iago.*   I did not think he had been acquainted with it.
>
> *Othello.*   O yes, and went between us very oft -
>
> *Iago.*   Indeed!
>
> *Othello.*   Indeed? Ay, indeed. Discern'st thou aught of that?
>
> Is he not honest?
>
> *Iago.*   Honest, my lord?
>
> *Othello.*   Honest? Ay, honest.
>
> *Iago.*   My lord, for aught I know.
>
> *Othello.*   What do'st thou think?
>
> *Iago.*   Think, my lord!

Othello.   Think, my lord! Alas, thou echo'st me,

As if there was some monster in thy thought

Too hideous to be shewn.' [37]

The stops and breaks, the deep workings of treachery under the mask of love and honesty, the anxious watchfulness, the cool earnestness, and if we may so say, the *passion* of hypocrisy, marked in every line, received their last finishing in that inconceivable burst of pretended indignation at Othello's doubts of his sincerity.

'O grace! O Heaven forgive me!

Are you a man? Have you a soul or sense?

God be wi' you; take mine office. O wretched fool,

That lov'st to make thine honesty a vice!

Oh monstrous world! Take note, take note, O world!

To be direct and honest, is not safe.

I thank you for this profit, and from hence

I'll have no friend, since love breeds such offence.'[38]

If Iago is detestable enough when he has business on his hands and all his engines at work, he is still worse when he has nothing to do, and we only see into the hollowness of his heart. His indifference when Othello falls into a swoon, is perfectly diabolical.

Iago.   How is it, General? Have you not hurt your head? .

Othello.   Do'st thou mock me?

Iago.   I mock you not, by Heaven,' etc.[39]

The part indeed would hardly be tolerated, even as a foil to the virtue and generosity of the other characters in the play, but for its indefatigable industry and inexhaustible resources, which divert the attention of the spectator (as well as his own) from the end he has in view to the means by which it must be accomplished. - Edmund the Bastard in *Lear* is something of the same character, placed in less prominent circumstances. Zanga is a vulgar caricature of it.[40]

18.   'TIMON OF ATHENS'

The opening to this essay has become a well-known starting-point for modern essays on the play. The play dwells on the subjects of social and economic injustice which were Hazlitt's preoccupations.

TIMON OF ATHENS always appeared to us to be written with as intense a feeling of his subject as any one play of Shakespear. It is one of the few in which he seems to be in earnest throughout, never to trifle nor go out of his way. He does not relax in his efforts, nor lose sight of the unity of his design. It is the only play of our author in which spleen is the predominant feeling of the mind. It is as much a satire as a play: and contains some of the finest pieces of invective possible to be conceived, both in the snarling, captious answers of the cynic Apemantus, and in the impassioned and more terrible imprecations of Timon. The latter remind the classical reader of the force and swelling impetuosity of the moral declamations in *Juvenal*,[1] while the former have all the keenness and caustic severity of the old Stoic philosophers.[2] The soul of Diogenes[3] appears to have been seated on the lips of Apemantus. The churlish profession of misanthropy in the cynic is contrasted with the profound feeling of it in Timon, and also with the soldier-like and determined resentment of Alcibiades against his countrymen, who have banished him, though this forms only an incidental episode in the tragedy.

The fable consists of a single event; - of the transition from the highest pomp and profusion of artificial refinement to the most abject state of savage life, and privation of all social intercourse. The change is as rapid as it is complete; nor is the description of the rich and generous Timon, banqueting in gilded palaces, pampered by every luxury, prodigal of his hospitality, courted by crowds of flatterers, poets, painters, lords, ladies, who -

> 'Follow his strides, his lobbies fill with tendance,
> Rain sacrificial whisperings in his ear;
> And through him drink the free air' [4]

more striking than that of the sudden falling off of his friends and fortune, and his naked exposure in a wild forest digging roots from the earth for his sustenance, with a lofty spirit of self-denial, and bitter scorn of the world, which raise him higher in our esteem than the dazzling gloss of prosperity could do. He grudges himself the means of life, and is only busy in preparing his grave. How forcibly is the difference between what he was, and what he is, described in Apemantus's taunting questions, when he comes to reproach him with the change in his way of life!

> - 'What, think'st thou,
>
> That the bleak air, thy boisterous chamberlain,
>
> Will put thy shirt on warm? will these moist trees
>
> That have outlived the eagle, page thy heels,
>
> And skip when thou point'st out? Will the cold brook,
>
> Candied with ice, caudle thy morning taste
>
> To cure thy o'er-night's surfeit? Call the creatures,
>
> Whose naked natures live in all the spight
>
> Of wreakful heav'n, whose bare unhoused trunks,
>
> To the conflicting elements expos'd,
>
> Answer mere nature, bid them flatter thee.'[5]

The manners are every where preserved with distinct truth. The poet and painter are very skilfully played off against one another, both affecting great attention to the other, and each taken up with his own vanity, and the superiority of his own art. Shakespear has put into the mouth of the former a very lively description of the genius of poetry and of his own in particular.

> - 'A thing slipt idly from me.
>
> Our poesy is as a gum, which issues
>
> From whence 'tis nourish'ed. The fire i' th' flint
>
> Shews not till it be struck: our gentle flame
>
> Provokes itself - and like the current flies
>
> Each bound it chafes.'[6]

The hollow friendship and shuffling evasions of the Athenian lords, their smooth professions and pitiful ingratitude, are very satisfactorily exposed, as well as the different disguises to which the meanness of self-love resorts in such cases to hide a want of generosity and good faith. The lurking selfishness of Apemantus does not pass undetected amidst the grossness of his sarcasms and his contempt for the pretensions of others. Even the two courtezans who accompany Alcibiades to the cave of Timon are very characteristically sketched; and the thieves who come to visit him are also 'true men' in their way. - An exception to this general picture of selfish depravity is found in the old and honest steward Flavius, to whom Timon pays a full tribute of tenderness. Shakespear was unwilling to draw a picture *'ugly all over with hypocrisy.'*[7] He owed this character to the good-natured solicitations of his Muse. His mind might well have been said to be the 'sphere of humanity.'

The moral sententiousness of this play equals that of Lord Bacon's Treatise on the Wisdom of the Ancients,[8] and is indeed seasoned with greater variety. Every topic of contempt or indignation is here exhausted; but while the sordid licentiousness of Apemantus, which turns every thing to gall and bitterness, shews only the natural virulence of his temper and antipathy to good or evil alike, Timon does not utter an imprecation without betraying the extravagant workings of disappointed passion, of love altered to hate. Apemantus sees nothing good in any object, and exaggerates whatever is disgusting: Timon is tormented with the perpetual contrast between things and appearances, between the fresh, tempting outside and the rottenness within, and invokes mischiefs on the heads of mankind proportioned to the sense of his wrongs and of their treacheries. He impatiently cries out, when he finds the gold,

> This yellow slave
> Will knit and break religions; bless the accurs'd;
> Make the hoar leprosy ador'd; place thieves,
> And give them title, knee, and approbation,
> With senators on the bench; this is it,
> That makes the wappen'd widow wed again;
> She, whom the spital-house
> Would cast the gorge at, *this embalms and spices*
> *To th' April day again.*[9]

One of his most dreadful imprecations is that which occurs immediately on his leaving Athens.

[Quotes IV.i.1-32]

Timon is here just as ideal in his passion for ill as he had been before in his belief of good. Apemantus was satisfied with the mischief existing in the world, and with his own ill-nature. One of the most decisive intimations of Timon's morbid jealousy of appearances is in his answer to Apemantus, who asks him,

> 'What things in the world can'st thou nearest compare with thy flatterers?
>
> *Timon.* Women nearest: but men, men are the things themselves.'[10]

Apemantus, it is said, 'loved few things better than to abhor himself.'[11] This is not the case with Timon, who neither loves to abhor himself nor others. All his vehement misanthropy is forced, up-hill work. From the slippery turns of fortune, from the turmoils of passion and adversity, he wishes to sink into the quiet of the grave. On that subject his thoughts are intent, on that he finds time and place to grow romantic. He digs his own grave by the sea-shore; contrives his funeral ceremonies amidst the pomp of desolation, and builds his mausoleum of the elements.

> 'Come not to me again; but say to Athens,
> Timon hath made his everlasting mansion
> Upon the beached verge of the salt flood;
> Which once a-day with his embossed froth
> The turbulent surge shall cover. - Thither come,
> And let my grave-stone be your oracle.'[1]

And again, Alcibiades, after reading his epitaph, says of him,

> 'These well express in thee thy latter spirits:
> Though thou abhorred'st in us our human griefs,
> Scorn'd'st our brain's flow, and those our droplets, which
> From niggard nature fall; yet rich conceit
> Taught thee to make vast Neptune weep for aye
> On thy low grave' [13]

thus making the winds his funeral dirge, his mourner the murmuring ocean; and seeking in the everlasting solemnities of nature oblivion of the transitory splendour of his life-time.

19. FROM 'CORIOLANUS'

This powerful and important essay, first printed in *The Examiner*, December 15, 1816, and subsequently reprinted in *A View of the English Stage*, occasioned controversy on its publication in the *Characters*. William Gifford, Hazlitt's most persistent critic in the Tory press, went on the attack in the *Quarterly Review*, January, 1818, against Hazlitt's political critique of poetry as the medium for aristocracy and power against democracy and liberty. Gifford was undoubtedly replying to the political thesis rather than, as he initially pretends, the fact that Hazlitt accuses Shakespeare of bias. Gifford's review provoked a stormy answer from Hazlitt (below, no. 48). The argument pursued by Hazlitt, that the poetic imagination by its exaggerating effect and its utility in the service of power can ambush the desire for justice and right, is an important statement indicating not only his beliefs but his doubts and worries about poetry and about Shakespeare. Although he gives himself the leeway of qualification, emphasised in his reply to Gifford, that the imagination may be consistent with the greatest good if it is braced with the 'republican faculty' of understanding (discriminating reason), the argument reveals a paradox in Hazlitt's thought. He is torn between admiration and suspicion in his attitude towards poetic imagination and its power. However, his scepticism about the poetic imagination takes its place beside many Puritan and nonconformist opinions voiced, for example, by Milton, Marvell and Bunyan. His other essays show that Hazlitt confines his strongest strictures to *Coriolanus* and does not extend them to other plays.

SHAKESPEAR has in this play shewn himself well versed in history and state-affairs. CORIOLANUS is a store-house of political common-places. Any one who studies it may save himself the trouble of reading Burke's *Reflections*,[1] or Paine's *Rights of Man*,[2] or the Debates in both Houses of Parliament since the French Revolution or our own. The arguments for and against aristocracy or democracy, on the privileges of the few and the claims of the many, on liberty and slavery, power and the abuse of it, peace and war, are here very ably handled, with the spirit of a poet and the acuteness of a philosopher. Shakespear himself seems to have had a leaning to the arbitrary side of the question, perhaps from some feeling of contempt for his own origin; and to have spared no occasion of baiting the rabble. What he says of them is very true: what he says of their betters is also very true, though he dwells less upon it. - The cause of the people is indeed but little calculated as a subject for poetry: it admits of rhetoric, which goes into argument and explanation, but it presents no immediate or distinct images to the mind, 'no jutting frieze, buttress, or coigne of vantage' for poetry 'to make its pendant bed and procreant cradle in.'[3] The language of poetry naturally falls in with the language of power. The imagination is an exaggerating and exclusive faculty: it takes from one thing to add to another: it accumulates circumstances together to give the greatest possible effect to a favourite object.[4] The understanding is a dividing and measuring faculty: it judges of things not according to their immediate impression on the mind, but according to their relations to one another. The one is a monopolising faculty, which seeks the greatest quantity of present excitement by inequality and disproportion; the other is a distributive faculty, which seeks the greatest quantity of ultimate good, by justice and proportion. The one is an aristocratical, the other a republican faculty. The principle of poetry is a very anti-levelling principle. It aims at effect, it exists by contrast. It admits of no medium. It is every thing by excess. It rises above the ordinary standard of sufferings and crimes. It presents a dazzling appearance. It shows its head turreted, crowned, and crested. Its front is gilt and blood-stained. Before it 'it carries noise, and behind it leaves tears.'[5] It has its altars and its victims, sacrifices, human sacrifices. Kings, priests, nobles, are its train-bearers, tyrants and slaves its executioners. - 'Carnage is its daughter.'[6] - Poetry is right-royal. It puts the individual for the species, the one above the infinite many, might before right. A lion hunting a flock of sheep or a herd of wild asses is a more poetical object than they; and we even take part with the lordly beast, because our vanity or some other feeling makes us disposed to place ourselves in the situation of the strongest party. So we feel some concern for the poor citizens of Rome when they meet together to compare their wants and grievances, till Coriolanus comes in and with blows and big words drives this set of 'poor rats,'[7] this rascal scum, to their homes and beggary before him. There is nothing heroical in a multitude of miserable rogues not wishing to be starved, or complaining that they are like to be so: but when a single man comes forward to brave their cries and to make them submit to the last indignities, from mere pride and self-will, our admiration of his prowess is immediately converted into contempt for their pusillanimity. The insolence of power is stronger than the plea of necessity. The tame submission to usurped authority or even the natural resistance to it has nothing to excite or flatter the imagination: it is the assumption of a right to insult or oppress others that carries an imposing air of superiority with it. We had rather be the oppressor than the oppressed. The love of power in ourselves and the admiration of it in others are both natural to man: the one makes him a tyrant, the other a slave. Wrong dressed out in pride, pomp, and circumstance, has more attraction than abstract right. - Coriolanus complains of the fickleness of the people: yet, the instant he cannot gratify his pride and obstinacy at their expense, he turns his arms against his country. If his country was not worth defending, why did he build his pride on its defence? He is a conquerer and a hero; he conquers other countries, and makes this a plea for enslaving his own; and when he is prevented from doing so, he leagues with its enemies to destroy his country. He rates the people 'as if he were a God to punish, and not a man of their infirmity.'[8] He scoffs at one of their tribunes for maintaining their rights and franchises: 'Mark you his absolute *shall*?'[9] not marking his own absolute *will* to take every thing from them, his impatience of the slightest opposition to his own pretensions being in proportion to their arrogance and absurdity. If the great and powerful had the beneficence and wisdom of Gods, then all this would have been well: if with a greater knowledge of what is good for the people, they had as great a care for their interest as they have themselves, if they were seated above the world, sympathising with the welfare, but not feeling the passions of men, receiving neither good nor hurt from them, but bestowing their benefits as free gifts on them, they might then rule over them like another Providence. But this is not the case. Coriolanus is unwilling that the senate should shew their 'cares'[10] for the people, lest their 'cares' should be construed into 'fears,' to the subversion of all due authority; and he is no sooner disappointed in his schemes to deprive the people not only of the cares of the state, but of all power to redress themselves, than Volumnia is made madly to exclaim,

> 'Now the red pestilence strike all trades in Rome,
> And occupations perish.'[11]

This is but natural: it is but natural for a mother to have more regard for her son than for a whole city; but then the city should be left to take some care of itself. The care of the state cannot, we here see, be safely entrusted to maternal affection, or to the domestic charities of high life. The great have private feelings of their own, to which the interests of humanity and justice must courtesy. Their interests are so far from being the same as those of the community, that they are in direct and necessary opposition to them; their power is at the expense of *our* weakness;

their riches of *our* poverty; their pride of *our* degradation; their splendour of *our* wretchedness; their tyranny of *our* servitude. If they had the superior knowledge ascribed to them (which they have not) it would only render them so much more formidable; and from Gods would convert them into Devils. The whole dramatic moral of CORIOLANUS is that those who have little shall have less, and that those who have much shall take all that others have left. The people are poor; therefore they ought to be starved. They are slaves; therefore they ought to be beaten. They work hard; therefore they ought to be treated like beasts of burden. They are ignorant; therefore they ought not to be allowed to feel that they want food, or clothing, or rest, that they are enslaved, oppressed, and miserable. This is the logic of the imagination and the passions; which seek to aggrandize what excites admiration and to heap contempt on misery, to raise power into tyranny, and to make tyranny absolute; to thrust down that which is low still lower, and to make wretches desperate: to exalt magistrates into kings, kings into gods; to degrade subjects to the rank of slaves, and slaves to the condition of brutes.[12] The history of mankind is a romance, a mask, a tragedy, constructed upon the principles of *poetical justice*; it is a noble or royal hunt, in which what is sport to the few is death to the many, and in which the spectators halloo and encourage the strong to set upon the weak, and cry havoc in the chase though they do not share in the spoil. We may depend upon it that what men delight to read in books, they will put in practice in reality.

.   .   .

Coriolanus himself is a complete character: his love of reputation, his contempt of popular opinion, his pride and modesty, are consequences of each other. His pride consists in the inflexible sternness of his will; his love of glory is a determined desire to bear down all opposition, and to extort the admiration both of friends and foes. His contempt for popular favour, his unwillingness to hear his own praises, spring from the same source. He cannot contradict the praises that are bestowed upon him; therefore he is impatient at hearing them. He would enforce the good opinion of others by his actions, but does not want their acknowledgments in words

> 'Pray now, no more: my mother,
> Who has a charter to extol her blood,

When she does praise me, grieves me.'13

His magnanimity is of the same kind. He admires in an enemy that courage which he honours in himself; he places himself on the hearth of Aufidius with the same confidence that he would have met him in the field, and feels that by putting himself in his power, he takes from him all temptation for using it against him.

.   .   .

[At this stage Hazlitt simply quotes from North's translation of Plutarch, to demonstrate how closely Shakespeare has adhered to his source.]

20.   FROM 'TROILUS AND CRESSIDA'

One or two comments betray the fact that Hazlitt is still wrestling with his doubts (expressed in 'Coriolanus') about Shakespeare's politics, and this time he concludes that the dramatist 'makes infinite excursions to the right and left'. Such flexibility marks Shakespeare's genius as 'dramatic' in contrast to Chaucer's 'historical' bent.

This is one of the most loose and desultory of our author's plays: it rambles on just as it happens, but it overtakes, together with some indifferent matter, a prodigious number of fine things in its way. Troilus himself is no character: he is merely a common lover: but Cressida and her uncle Pandarus are hit off with proverbial truth. By the speeches given to the leaders of the Grecian host, Nestor, Ulysses, Agamemnon, Achilles, Shakespear seems to have known them as well as if he had been a spy sent by the Trojans into the enemy's camp - to say nothing of their affording very lofty examples of didactic eloquence. The following is a very stately and spirited declamation:

[Quotes Ulysses' speech on 'order', I.iii.75-136, omitting 78-84]

It cannot be said of Shakespear, as was said of some one, that he was 'without o'erflowing full.'1 He was full, even to o'erflowing. He gave heaped measure, running over. This was his greatest fault. He was only in danger 'of losing distinction in his thoughts'2 (to borrow his own expression)

'As doth a battle when they charge on heaps
The enemy flying.'3

There is another passage, the speech of Ulysses to Achilles, shewing him the thankless nature of popularity, which has a still greater depth of moral observation and richness of illustration than the former. It is long, but worth the quoting. The sometimes giving an entire argument from the unacted plays of our author may with one class of readers have almost the use of restoring a lost passage; and may serve to convince another class of critics, that the poet's genius was not confined to the production of stage effect by preternatural means. -

[Quotes *in toto* III.iii.145-87, stopping mid-sentence]

The throng of images in the above lines is prodigious; and though they sometimes jostle against one another, they every where raise and carry on the feeling, which is intrinsically true and profound. The debates between Trojan chiefs on the restoring of Helen are full of knowledge of human motives and character. Troilus enters well into the philosophy of war, when he says in answer to something that falls from Hector,

> 'Why there you touch'd the life of our design:
> Were it not glory that we more affected,
> Than the performance of our heaving spleens,
> I would not wish a drop of Trojan blood
> Spent more in her defence. But, worthy Hector,
> She is a theme of honour and renown,
> A spur to valiant and magnanimous deeds.'[4]

The character of Hector, in a few slight indications which appear of it, is made very amiable. His death is sublime, and shews in a striking light the mixture of barbarity and heroism of the age. The threats of Achilles are fatal; they carry their own means of execution with them.

> 'Come here about me, you my myrmidons,
> Mark what I say. - Attend me where I wheel:
> Strike not a stroke, but keep yourselves in breath;
> And when I have the bloody Hector found,
> Empale him with your weapons round about,
> In fellest manner execute your arms.
> Follow me, sirs, and my proceeding eye.'[5]

He then finds Hector and slays him, as if he had been hunting down a wild beast. There is something revolting as well as terrific in the ferocious coolness with which he singles out his prey: nor does the splendour of the achievement reconcile us to the cruelty of the means.

The characters of Cressida and Pandarus are very amusing and instructive. The disinterested willingness of Pandarus to serve his friend in an affair which lies next his heart is immediately brought forward. 'Go thy way, Troilus, go thy way; had I a sister were a grace, or a daughter were a goddess, he should take his choice. O admirable man! Paris, Paris is dirt to him, and I warrant Helen, to change, would give money to boot.'[6] This is the language he addresses to his niece: nor is she much behindhand in coming into the plot. Her head is as light and fluttering as her heart. 'It is the prettiest villain, she fetches her breath so short as a new-ta'en sparrow.'[7] Both characters are originals, and quite different from what they are in Chaucer. In Chaucer, Cressida is represented a grave, sober, considerate personage (a widow - he cannot tell her age, nor whether she has children or no) who has an alternate eye to her character, her interest, and her pleasure: Shakespear's Cressida is a giddy girl, an unpractised jilt, who falls in love with Troilus, as she afterwards deserts him, from mere levity and thoughtlessness of temper. She may be wooed and won to any thing and from any thing, at a moment's warning; the other knows very well what she would be at, and sticks to it, and is more governed by substantial reasons than by caprice or vanity. Pandarus again, in Chaucer's story, is a friendly sort of go-between, tolerably busy, officious, and forward in bringing matters to bear: but in Shakespear he has 'a stamp exclusive and professional':[8] he wears the badge of his trade; he is a regular knight of the game. The difference of the manner in which the subject is treated arises perhaps less from intention, than from the different genius of the two poets. There is no *double entendre* in the characters of Chaucer: they are either quite serious or quite comic. In Shakespear the ludicrous and ironical are constantly blended with the stately and the impassioned. We see Chaucer's characters as they saw themselves, not as they appeared to others or might have appeared to the poet. He is as deeply implicated in the affairs of his personages as they could be themselves. He had to go a long journey with each of them, and became a kind of necessary confidant. There is little relief, or light and shade in his pictures. The conscious smile is not seen lurking under the brow of grief or impatience. Every thing with him is intense and continuous - a working out of what went before. - Shakespear never committed himself to his characters. He trifled, laughed, or wept with them as he chose. He has no prejudices for or against them; and it seems a matter of perfect indifference whether he shall be in jest or earnest. According to him 'the web of our lives is of a mingled yarn, good and ill together.'9 His genius was dramatic, as Chaucer's was historical. He saw both sides of a question, the different views taken of it according to the different interests of the parties concerned, and he was at once an actor and spectator in the scene. If any thing, he is too various and flexible: too full of transitions, of glancing lights, of salient points. If Chaucer followed up his subject too doggedly, perhaps Shakespear was too volatile and heedless. The Muse's wing too often lifted him from off his feet. He made infinite excursions to the right and the left.

> - 'He hath done
> Mad and fantastic execution,
> Engaging and redeeming of himself
> With such a careless force and forceless care,
> As if that luck in very spite of cunning
> Bad him win all.'10

Chaucer attended chiefly to the real and natural, that is, to the involuntary and inevitable impressions on the mind in given circumstance; Shakespear exhibited also the possible and the fantastical, - not only what things are in themselves, but whatever they might seem to be, their different reflections, their endless combinations. He lent his fancy, wit, invention, to others, and borrowed their feelings in return. Chaucer excelled in the force of habitual sentiment; Shakespear added to it every variety of passion, every suggestion of thought or accident. Chaucer described external objects with the eye of a painter, or he might be said to have embodied them with the hand of a sculptor, every part is so thoroughly made out, and tangible:- Shakespear's imagination threw over them a lustre

> - 'Prouder than when blue Iris bends.'11

Every thing in Chaucer has a downright reality. A simile or a sentiment is as if it were given in upon evidence. In Shakespear the commonest matter-of-fact has a romantic grace about it; or seems to float with the breath of imagination in a freer element. No one could have more depth of feeling or observation than Chaucer, but he wanted resources of invention to lay open the stores of nature or the human heart with the same radiant light that Shakespear has done. However fine or profound the thought, we know what is coming, whereas the effect of reading Shakespear is 'like the eye of vassalage at unawares encountering majesty.'[12] Chaucer's mind was consecutive, rather than discursive. He arrived at truth through a certain process; Shakespear saw every thing by intuition. Chaucer had a great variety of power, but he could do only one thing at once. He set himself to work on a particular subject. His ideas were kept separate, labelled, ticketed and parcelled out in a set form, in pews and compartments by themselves. They did not play into one another's hands. They did not re-act upon one another, as the blower's breath moulds the yielding glass. There is something hard and dry in them. What is the most wonderful thing in Shakespear's faculties is their excessive sociability, and how they gossiped and compared notes together.

21.   'ANTONY AND CLEOPATRA'

The essay is quoted in full, since Hazlitt writes with enthusiasm, although he does not place *Antony and Cleopatra* 'in the first class of Shakespear's productions'. Hazlitt's statement that Shakespeare '*becomes*' his characters, 'and speaks and acts for them' occurs with different wording in other essays and should be compared with Coleridge's repeated stance that 'Shakespeare becomes all things, yet for ever remaining himself' (Hawkes, 74; cf. 79-80 and elsewhere). But there is a difference of emphasis. Coleridge, as the philosopher of organic growth, is interested in the 'Protean' dramatist's capacity to reveal himself through his characters and yet remain 'aloof' as a man. (For a full account of Coleridge's ideas on this matter, see Jonathan Bate (1987, pp.14-16). He points out that Edward Capell first used the term 'this *Proteus*' of Shakespeare, in his 1768 edition of the plays.) Hazlitt, with his greater interest in stage-representation, does not enquire philosophically into the matter of the author's presence, but instead becomes interested in the principles upon which the characters themselves are created so as not to be 'stage-puppets or poetical machines'. Keats was influenced by Hazlitt's characterization of Cleopatra which is generally sympathetic while admitting 'great and unpardonable faults' in the woman (see White, pp.137-9). Once again, it is clear that Hazlitt's concept of characterization is not exclusive from the poetry, 'the splendour of the imagery, the semblance of reality...' but is instead intrinsically linked with the poetic representation of a world. In this he differs from the eighteenth century critics of character.

This is a very noble play. Though not in the first class of Shakespear's productions, it stands next to them, and is, we think, the finest of his historical plays, that is, of those in which he made poetry the organ of history, and assumed a certain tone of character and sentiment, in conformity to known facts, instead of trusting to his observations of general nature or to the unlimited indulgence of his own fancy. What he has added to the actual story, is upon a par with it. His genius was, as it were, a match for history as well as nature, and could grapple at will with either. The play is full of that pervading comprehensive power by which the poet could always make himself master of time and circumstances. It presents a fine picture of Roman pride and Eastern magnificence: and in the struggle between the two, the empire of the world seems suspended, 'like the swan's down-feather,'

> That stands upon the swell at full of tide,
> And neither way inclines.'[1]

The characters breathe, move, and live. Shakespear does not stand reasoning on what his characters would do or say, but at once *becomes* them, and speaks and acts for them. He does not present us with groups of stage-puppets or poetical machines making set speeches on human life, and acting from a calculation of problematical motives, but he brings living men and women on the scene, who speak and act from real feelings, according to the ebbs and flows of passion, without the least tincture of pedantry of logic or rhetoric. Nothing is made out by inference and analogy, by climax and antithesis, but every thing takes place just as it would have done in reality, according to the occasion. - The character of Cleopatra is a master-piece. What an extreme contrast it affords to Imogen! One would think it almost impossible for the same person to have drawn both. She is voluptuous, ostentatious, conscious, boastful of her charms, haughty, tyrannical, fickle. The luxurious pomp and gorgeous extravagance of the Egyptian queen are displayed in all their force and lustre, as well as the irregular grandeur of the soul of Mark Antony. Take only the first four lines that they speak as an example of the regal style of love-making.

> '*Cleopatra.*   If it be love indeed, tell me how much?
> *Antony.*   There's beggary in the love that can be reckon'd.

> *Cleopatra.* I'll set a bourn how far to be belov'd.
>
> *Antony.*   Then must thou needs find out new heav'n, new earth.'[2]

The rich and poetical description of her person beginning -

> 'The barge she sat in, like a burnish'd throne,
>
> Burnt on the water; the poop was beaten gold,
>
> Purple the sails, and so perfumed, that
>
> The winds were love-sick' [3]

seems to prepare the way for, and almost to justify the subsequent infatuation of Antony when in the sea-fight at Actium, he leaves the battle, and 'like a doating mallard'[4] follows her flying sails.

Few things in Shakespear (and we know of nothing in any other author like them) have more of that local truth of imagination and character than the passage in which Cleopatra is represented conjecturing what were the employments of Antony in his absence - 'He's speaking now, or murmuring - *Where's my serpent of old Nile?*'[5] Or again, when she says to Antony, after the defeat at Actium, and his summoning up resolution to risk another fight - 'It is my birthday; I had thought to have held it poor; but since my lord is Antony again, I will be Cleopatra.'[6] Perhaps the finest burst of all is Antony's rage after his final defeat when he comes in, and surprises the messenger of Cæsar kissing her hand -

> 'To let a fellow that will take rewards,
>
> And say God quit you, be familiar with,
>
> My play-fellow, your hand; this kingly seal,
>
> And plighter of high hearts.'[7]

It is no wonder that he orders him to be whipped; but his low condition is not the true reason: there is another feeling which lies deeper, though Antony's pride would not let him shew it, except by his rage; he suspects the fellow to be Cæsar's proxy.

Cleopatra's whole character is the triumph of the voluptuous, of the love of pleasure and the power of giving it, over every other consideration. Octavia is a dull foil to her, and Fulvia a shrew and shrill-tongued. What a picture do those lines give of her -

'Age cannot wither her, nor custom stale
Her infinite variety. Other women cloy
The appetites they feed, but she makes hungry
Where most she satisfies.'[8]

What a spirit and fire in her conversation with Antony's messenger who brings her the unwelcome news of his marriage with Octavia! How all the pride of beauty and of high rank breaks out in her promised reward to him -

- 'There's gold, and here
My bluest veins to kiss!' [9]

She had great and unpardonable faults, but the grandeur of her death almost redeems them. She learns from the depth of despair the strength of her affections. She keeps her queen-like state in the last disgrace, and her sense of the pleasurable in the last moments of her life. She tastes a luxury in death. After applying the asp, she says with fondness -

'Dost thou not see my baby at my breast,
That sucks the nurse asleep?
As sweet as balm, as soft as air, as gentle.
Oh Antony!'[10]

It is worth while to observe that Shakespear has contrasted the extreme magnificence of the descriptions in this play with pictures of extreme suffering and physical horror, not less striking - partly perhaps to place the effeminate character of Mark Antony in a more favourable light, and at the same time to preserve a certain balance of feeling in the mind. Cæsar says, hearing of his rival's conduct at the court of Cleopatra,

[Quotes I.iv.55-71]

The passage after Antony's defeat by Augustus, where he is made to say -

'Yes, yes; he at Philippi kept
His sword e'en like a dancer; while I struck
The lean and wrinkled Cassius, and 'twas I
That the mad Brutus ended' [11]

is one of those fine retrospections which show us the winding and eventful march of human life. The jealous attention which has been paid to the unities both of time and place has taken away the principle of perspective in the drama, and all the interest which objects derive from distance, from contrast, from privation, from change of fortune, from long-cherished passion; and contrasts our view of life from a strange and romantic dream, long, obscure, and infinite, into a smartly contested, three hours' inaugural disputation on its merits by the different candidates for theatrical applause.

The latter scenes of ANTONY AND CLEOPATRA are full of changes of accident and passion. Success and defeat follow one another with startling rapidity. Fortune sits upon her wheel more blind and giddy than usual. This precarious state and the approaching dissolution of his greatness are strikingly displayed in the dialogue of Antony with Eros.

> '*Antony.*   Eros, thou yet behold'st me?
>
> *Eros.*   Ay, noble lord.
>
> *Antony.*   Sometime we see a cloud that's dragonish,
>
>   A vapour sometime, like a bear or lion,
>
>   A towered citadel, a pendant rock,
>
>   A forked mountain, or blue promontory
>
>   With trees upon't, that nod unto the world
>
>   And mock our eyes with air. Thou hast seen these signs,
>
>   They are black vesper's pageants.
>
> *Eros.*   Ay, my lord.
>
> *Antony.*   That which is now a horse, even with a thought
>
>   The rack dislimns, and makes it indistinct
>
>   As water is in water.
>
> *Eros.*   It does, my lord.
>
> *Antony.*   My good knave, Eros, now thy captain is
>
>   Even such a body,' etc.[12]

This is, without doubt, one of the finest pieces of poetry in Shakespear. The splendour of the imagery, the semblance of reality, the lofty range of picturesque objects hanging over the world, their evanescent nature, the total uncertainty of what is left behind, are just like the mouldering schemes of human greatness. It is finer than Cleopatra's passionate lamentation over his fallen grandeur, because it is more dim, unstable, unsubstantial. Antony's headstrong presumption and infatuated determination to yield to Cleopatra's wishes to fight by sea instead of land, meet a merited punishment; and the extravagance of his resolutions, increasing with the desperateness of his circumstances, is well commented upon by Œnorbarbus.

> - 'I see men's judgments are
> A parcel of their fortunes, and things outward
> Do draw the inward quality after them
> To suffer all alike'[13]

The repentance of Œnorbarbus after his treachery to his master is the most affecting part of the play. He cannot recover from the blow which Antony's generosity gives him, and he dies broken-hearted, 'a master-leaver and a fugitive.'[14]

Shakespear's genius has spread over the whole play a richness like the overflowing of the Nile.

22. 'HAMLET'

Hazlitt's 'It is *we* who are Hamlet' is a typically Romantic approach, to be compared with Coleridge's 'I have a smack of Hamlet myself, if I may say so' and Keats's 'axioms in philosophy are not axioms until they are proved on the pulses ... you will know exactly my meaning when I say, that now I shall relish Hamlet more than I ever have done' (*Letters*, I, 279). Hazlitt once again refers to 'mixed motives'. He also memorably contrasts the acting styles of Kemble and Kean.

This is that Hamlet the Dane, whom we read of in our youth, and whom we may be said almost to remember in our after-years; he who made that famous soliloquy on life, who gave the advice to the players, who thought 'this goodly frame, the earth, a sterile promontory, and this brave o'er-hanging firmament, the air, this majestical roof fretted with golden fire, a foul and pestilent congregation of vapours';[1] whom 'man delighted not, nor woman neither';[2] he who talked with the grave-diggers, and moralised on Yorick's skull; the school-fellow of Rosencrans and Guildenstern at Wittenberg; the friend of Horatio; the lover of Ophelia; he that was mad and sent to England; the slow avenger of his father's death; who lived at the court of Horwendillus five hundred years before we were born, but all whose thoughts we seem to know as well as we do our own, because we have read them in Shakespear.

Hamlet is a name; his speeches and sayings but the idle coinage of the poet's brain. What then, are they not real? They are as real as our own thoughts. Their reality is in the reader's mind. It is *we* who are Hamlet. This play has a prophetic truth, which is above that of history. Whoever has become thoughtful and melancholy through his own mishaps or those of others; whoever has borne about with him the clouded brow of reflection, and thought himself 'too much i' th' sun';[3] whoever has seen the golden lamp of day dimmed by envious mists rising in his own breast, and could find in the world before him only a dull blank with nothing left remarkable in it; whoever has known 'the pangs of despised love, the insolence of office, or the spurns which patient merit of the unworthy takes';[4] he who has felt his mind sink within him, and sadness cling to his heart like a malady, who has had his hopes blighted and his youth staggered by the apparitions of strange things; who cannot be well at ease, while he sees evil hovering near him like a spectre; whose powers of action have been eaten up by thought, he to whom the universe seems infinite, and himself nothing; whose bitterness of soul makes him careless of consequences, and who goes to a play as his best resource to shove off, to a second remove, the evils of life by a mock representation of them - this is the true Hamlet.

We have been so used to this tragedy that we hardly know how to criticise it any more than we should know how to describe our own faces. But we must make such observations as we can. It is the one of Shakespear's plays that we think of the oftenest, because it abounds most in striking reflections on human life, and because the distresses of Hamlet are transferred, by the turn of his mind, to the general account of humanity. Whatever happens to him we apply to ourselves, because he applies it to himself as a means of general reasoning. He is a great moraliser; and what makes him worth attending to is, that he moralises on his own feelings and experience. He is not a common-placed pedant. If *Lear* is distinguished by the greatest dept of passion, HAMLET is the most remarkable for the ingenuity, originality, and unstudied development of character. Shakespear had more magnanimity than any other poet, and he has shewn more of it in this play than in any other. There is no attempt to force an interest: every thing is left for time and circumstances to unfold. The attention is excited without effort, the incidents succeed each other as matters of course, the characters think and speak and act just as they might do, if left entirely to themselves. There is no set purpose, no straining at a point. The observations are suggested by the passing scene - the gusts of passion come and go like sounds of music borne on the wind. The whole play is an exact transcript of what might be supposed to have taken place at the court of Denmark, at the remote period of time fixed upon, before the modern refinements in morals and manners were heard of. It would have been interesting enough to have been admitted as a by-stander in such a scene, at such a time, to have heard and witnessed something of what was going on. But here we are more than spectators. We have not only 'the outward pageants and the signs of grief';[5] but 'we have that within which passes shew.'[6] We read the thoughts of the heart, we catch the passions living as they rise. Other dramatic writers give us very fine versions and paraphrases of nature; but Shakespear, together with his own comments, gives us the original text, that we may judge for ourselves. This is a very great advantage.

The character of Hamlet stands quite by itself.[7] It is not a character marked by strength of will or even of passion, but by refinement of thought and sentiment. Hamlet is as little of the hero as a man can well be: but he is a young and princely novice, full of high enthusiasm and quick sensibility - the sport of circumstances, questioning with fortune and refining on his own feelings, and forced from the natural bias of his disposition by the strangeness of his situation. He seems incapable of deliberate action, and is only hurried into extremities on the spur of the occasion, when he has no time to reflect, as in the scene where he kills Polonius, and again, where he alters the letters which Rosencrans and Guildenstern are taking with them to England, purporting his death. At other times, when he is most bound to act, he remains puzzled, undecided, and sceptical, dallies with his purposes, till the occasion is lost, and finds out some pretence to relapse into indolence and thoughtfulness again. For this reason he refused to kill the King when he is at his prayers, and by a refinement in malice, which is in truth only an excuse for his own want of resolution, defers his revenge to a more fatal opportunity, when he shall be engaged in some act 'that has no relish of salvation in it.'[8]

'He kneels and prays,

And now I'll do 't, and so he goes to heaven,

And so am I reveng'd: *that would be scann'd*.

He kill'd my father, and for that,

I, his sole son, send him to heaven.

Why this is reward, not revenge.

Up sword and know thou a more horrid time,

When he is drunk, asleep, or in a rage.'9

He is the prince of philosophical speculators; and because he cannot have his revenge perfect, according to the most refined idea his wish can form, he declines it altogether. So he scruples to trust the suggestions of the ghost, contrives the scene of the play to have surer proof of his uncle's guilt, and then rests satisfied with this confirmation of his suspicions, and the success of his experiment, instead of acting upon it. Yet he is sensible of his own weakness, taxes himself with it, and tries to reason himself out of it.

[Quotes IV.iv.32-66]

Still he does nothing; and this very speculation on his own infirmity only affords him another occasion for indulging it. It is not from any want of attachment to his father or of abhorrence of his murder that Hamlet is thus dilatory, but it is more to his taste to indulge his imagination in reflecting upon the enormity of the crime and refining on his schemes of vengeance, than to put them into immediate practice. His ruling passion is to think, not to act: and any vague pretext that flatters this propensity instantly diverts him from his previous purposes.

The moral perfection of this character has been called in question, we think, by those who did not understand it. It is more interesting than according to rules; amiable, though not faultless. The ethical delineations of 'that noble and liberal casuist'10 (as Shakespear has been well called) do not exhibit the drab-coloured quakerism of morality. His plays are not copied either from The Whole Duty of Man,11 or from The Academy of Compliments!12 We confess we are a little shocked at the want of refinement in those who are shocked at the want of refinement in Hamlet. The neglect of punctilious exactness in his behaviour either partakes of the 'licence of the time,'13 or else belongs to the very excess of intellectual refinement in the character, which makes the common rules of life, as well as his own purposes, sit loose upon him. He may be said to be amenable only to the tribunal of his own thoughts, and is too much taken up with the airy world of contemplation to lay as much stress as he ought on the practical consequences of things. His habitual principles of action are unhinged and out of joint with the time. His conduct to Ophelia is quite natural in his circumstances. It is that of assumed severity only. It is the effect of disappointed hope, of bitter regrets, of affection suspended, not obliterated, by the distractions of the scene around him! Amidst the natural and preternatural horrors of his situation, he might be excused in delicacy from carrying on a regular courtship. When 'his father's spirit was in arms,'[14] it was not a time for the son to make love in. He could neither marry Ophelia, nor wound her mind by explaining the cause of his alienation, which he durst hardly trust himself to think of. It would have taken him years to have come to a direct explanation on the point. In the harassed state of his mind, he could not have done much otherwise than he did. His conduct does not contradict what he says when he sees her funeral,

> 'I loved Ophelia: forty thousand brothers
> Could not with all their quantity of love
> Make up my sum.'[15]

Nothing can be more affecting or beautiful than the Queen's apostrophe to Ophelia on throwing the flowers into the grave.

> - 'Sweets to the sweet, farewell.
> I hop'd thou should'st have been my Hamlet's wife:
> I thought thy bride-bed to have deck'd, sweet maid,
> And not have strew'd thy grave.'[16]

Shakespear was thoroughly a master of the mixed motives of human character, and he here shews us the Queen, who was so criminal in some respects, not without sensibility and affection in other relations of life. - Ophelia is a character almost too exquisitely touching to be dwelt upon. Oh rose of May,[17] oh flower too soon faded! Her love, her madness, her death, are described with the truest touches of tenderness and pathos. It is a character which nobody but Shakespear could have drawn in the way that he has done, and to the conception of which there is not even the smallest approach, except in some of the old romantic ballads.[18]

Her brother, Laertes, is a character we do not like so well: he is too hot and choleric, and somewhat rhodomontade. Polonius is a perfect character in its kind; nor is there any foundation for the objections which have been made to the consistency of this part. It is said that he acts very foolishly and talks very sensibly. There is no inconsistency in that. Again, that he talks wisely at one time and foolishly at another; that his advice to Laertes is very excellent, and his advice to the King and Queen on the subject of Hamlet's madness very ridiculous. But he gives the one as a father, and is sincere in it; he gives the other as a mere courtier, a busy-body, and is accordingly officious, garrulous, and impertinent. In short, Shakespear has been accused of inconsistency in this and other characters, only because he has kept up the distinction which there is in nature, between the understandings and the moral habits of men, between the absurdity of their ideas and the absurdity of their motives. Polonius is not a fool, but he makes himself so. His folly, whether in his actions or speeches, comes under the head of impropriety of intention.

We do not like to see our author's plays acted, and least of all, HAMLET. There is no play that suffers so much in being transferred on the stage.[19] Hamlet himself seems hardly capable of being acted. Mr Kemble unavoidably fails in this character from a want of ease and variety. The character of Hamlet is made up of undulating lines; it has the yielding flexibility of 'a wave o' th' sea.'[20] Mr Kemble plays it like a man in armour, with a determined inveteracy of purpose, in one undeviating straight line, which is as remote from the natural grace and refined susceptibility of the character, as the sharp angles and abrupt starts which Mr Kean introduces into the part. Mr Kean's Hamlet is as much too splenetic and rash[21] as Mr Kemble's is too deliberate and formal. His manner is too strong and pointed. He throws a severity, approaching to virulence, into the common observations and answers. There is nothing of this in Hamlet. He is, as it were, wrapped up in his reflections, and only *thinks aloud*. There should therefore be no attempt to impress what he says upon others by a studied exaggeration of emphasis or manner; no *talking at* his hearers. There should be as much of the gentleman and scholar as possible infused into the part, and as little of the actor. A pensive air of sadness should sit reluctantly upon his brow, but no appearance of fixed and sullen gloom. He is full of weakness and melancholy, but there is no harshness in his nature. He is the most amiable of misanthropes.

23. 'THE TEMPEST'

Hazlitt's essay on *The Tempest* is dominated by an interest in Caliban. Although (as he acknowledges) the germs for his account of the character may come from Schlegel's statement that Caliban 'is a poetical character', Hazlitt goes further than his contemporaries in weighing the bestial against the noble. Coleridge described Caliban as having 'the dawnings of understanding without reason or the moral sense' (Hawkes, 226), arguing that the deficiency cuts the character off from the 'truly human'. He emphasises 'the appearance of vice'. Hazlitt's account is more sympathetic, distinguishing between the 'vulgarity' of Trinculo and Stephano, in contrast to whom Caliban has 'a classical dignity' and a childlike simplicity, 'uncramped by any of the meannesses of custom'. It is Caliban's eloquent poetry and his lack of 'conventional coarseness, learnt from others' which draw Hazlitt's admiration, an attitude shared by Keats (*Letters*, 1, 214). Hazlitt also, characteristically, quotes Gonzalo's description of 'the commonwealth', a passage in which, it is said 'Shakespear has anticipated nearly all the arguments on the Utopian schemes of modern philosophy'.

There can be little doubt that Shakespear was the most universal genius that ever lived. 'Either for tragedy, comedy, history, pastoral, pastoral-comical, historical-pastoral, scene individable or poem unlimited, he is the only man. Seneca cannot be too heavy, nor Plautus too light for him.'[1] He has not only the same absolute command over our laughter and our tears, all the resources of passion, of wit, of thought, of observation, but he has the most unbounded range of fanciful invention, whether terrible or playful, the same insight into the world of imagination that he has into the world of reality; and over all there presides the same truth of character and nature, and the same spirit of humanity. His ideal beings are as true and natural as his real characters; that is, as consistent with themselves, or if we suppose such beings to exist at all, they could not act, speak, or feel otherwise than as he makes them. He has invented for them a language, manners, and sentiments of their own, from the tremendous imprecations of the Witches in *Macbeth*, when they do 'a deed without a name,'[2] to the sylph-like expressions of Ariel, who 'does his spiriting gently';[3] the mischievous tricks and gossipping of Robin Goodfellow, or the uncouth gabbling and emphatic gesticulations of Caliban in this play.

The TEMPEST is one of the most original and perfect of Shakespear's productions, and he has shewn in it all the variety of his powers. It is full of grace and grandeur. The human and imaginary characters, the dramatic and the grotesque, are blended together with the greatest art, and without any appearance of it. Though he has here given 'to airy nothing a local habitation and a name,'[4] yet that part which is only the fantastic creation of his mind, has the same palpable texture, and coheres 'semblably'[5] with the rest. As the preternatural part has the air of reality, and almost haunts the imagination with a sense of truth, the real characters and events partake of the wildness of a dream. The stately magician, Prospero, driven from his dukedom, but around whom (so potent is his art) airy spirits throng numberless to do his bidding; his daughter Miranda ('worthy of that name')[6] to whom all the power of his art points, and who seems the goddess of the isle; the princely Ferdinand, cast by fate upon the haven of his happiness in this idol of his love; the delicate Ariel; the savage Caliban, half brute, half demon; the drunken ship's crew - are all connected parts of the story, and can hardly be spared from the place they fill. Even the local scenery is of a piece and character with the subject. Prospero's enchanted island seems to have risen up out of the sea; the airy music, the tempest-tost vessel, the turbulent waves, all have the effect of the landscape background of some fine picture. Shakespear's pencil is (to use an allusion of his own) 'like the dyer's hand, subdued to what it works in.'[7] Every thing in him, though it partakes of 'the liberty of wit,' is also subjected to 'the law' of the understanding.[8] For instance, even the drunken sailors, who are made reeling-ripe, share in the disorder of their minds and bodies, in the tumult of the elements, and seem on shore to be as much at the mercy of chance as they were before at the mercy of the winds and waves. These fellows with their sea-wit are the least to our taste of any part of the play: but they are as like drunken sailors as they can be, and are an indirect foil to Caliban, whose figure acquires a classical dignity in the comparison.

The character of Caliban is generally thought (and justly so) to be one of the author's master-pieces. It is not indeed pleasant to see this character on the stage any more than it is to see the god Pan personated there. But in itself it is one of the wildest and most abstracted of all Shakespear's characters, whose deformity whether of body or mind is redeemed by the power and truth of the imagination displayed in it. It is the essence of grossness, but there is not a particle of vulgarity in it. Shakespear has described the brutal mind of Caliban in contact with the pure and original forms of nature; the character grows out of the soil where it is rooted, uncontrouled, uncouth and wild, uncramped by any of the meannesses of custom. It is 'of the earth, earthy,'9 It seems almost to have been dug out of the ground, with a soul instinctively superadded to it answering to its wants and origin. Vulgarity is not natural coarseness, but conventional coarseness, learnt from others, contrary to, or without an entire conformity of natural power and disposition; as fashion is the common-place affectation of what is elegant and refined without any feeling of the essence of it. Schlegel, the admirable German critic on Shakespear, observes that Caliban is a poetical character, and 'always speaks in blank verse.'10

[Quotes I.ii.321-44 and II.ii.160-72]

In conducting Stephano and Trinculo to Prospero's cell, Caliban shews the superiority of natural capacity over greater knowledge and greater folly; and in a former scene, when Ariel frightens them with his music, Caliban to encourage them accounts for it in the eloquent poetry of the senses.

> - 'Be not afraid, the isle is full of noises,
> Sounds, and sweet airs, that give delight and hurt not.
> Sometimes a thousand twanging instruments
> Will hum about mine ears, and sometimes voices,
> That if I then had waked after long sleep,
> Would make me sleep again; and then in dreaming,
> The clouds methought would open, and shew riches
> Ready to drop upon me: when I wak'd,
> I cried to dream again.'11

This is not more beautiful than it is true. The poet here shews us the savage with the simplicity of a child, and makes the strange monster amiable. Shakespear had to paint the human animal rude and without choice in its pleasures, but not without the sense of pleasure or some germ of the affections. Master Barnardine in *Measure for Measure*, the savage of civilized life, is an admirable philosophical counterpart to Caliban.

Shakespear has, as it were by design, drawn off from Caliban the elements of whatever is ethereal and refined, to compound them in the unearthly mould of

Ariel. Nothing was ever more finely conceived than this contrast between the material and the spiritual, the gross and delicate. Ariel is imaginary power, the swiftness of thought personified. When told to make good speed by Prospero, he says, 'I drink the air before me.'[12] This is something like Puck's boast on a similar occasion, 'I'll put a girdle round about the earth in forty minutes.'[13] But Ariel differs from Puck in having a fellow feeling in the interests of those he is employed about. How exquisite is the following dialogue between him and Prospero!

> '*Ariel.*   Your charm so strongly works 'em,
>
>   That if you now beheld them, your affections
>
>   Would become tender.
>
> *Prospero.* Dost thou think so, spirit?
>
> *Ariel.*   Mine would, sir, were I human.
>
> *Prospero.* And mine shall.
>
>   Hast thou, which art but air, a touch, a feeling
>
>   Of their afflictions, and shall not myself,
>
>   One of their kind, that relish all as sharply,
>
>   Passion'd as they, be kindlier moved than thou art?'[14]

It has been observed that there is a peculiar charm in the songs introduced in Shakespear, which, without conveying any distinct images, seem to recall all the feelings connected with them, like snatches of half-forgotten music heard indistinctly and at intervals. There is this effect produced by Ariel's songs, which (as we are told) seem to sound in the air, and as if the person playing them were invisible.

.   .   .

The courtship between Ferdinand and Miranda is one of the chief beauties of this play. It is the very purity of love. The pretended interference of Prospero with it heightens its interest, and is in character with the magician, whose sense of preternatural power makes him arbitrary, tetchy, and impatient of opposition.

The TEMPEST is a finer play than the *Midsummer Night's Dream*, which has sometimes been compared with it; but it is not so fine a poem. There are a greater number of beautiful passages in the latter. Two of the most striking in the

TEMPEST are spoken by Prospero. The one is that admirable one when the vision which he has conjured up disappears, beginning 'The cloud-capp'd towers, the gorgeous palaces,'[15] etc., which has been so often quoted, that every school-boy knows it by heart; the other is that which Prospero makes in abjuring his art.

[Quotes V.i.33-57]

We must not forget to mention among other things in this play, that Shakespear has anticipated nearly all the arguments on the Utopian schemes of modern philosophy.[16]

[Quotes II.i.144-69]

24. 'THE MIDSUMMER NIGHT'S DREAM'

This essay was first printed in *The Examiner*, November 26, 1815 as a review, reprinted in *The Round Table*, and the last paragraph comes from an article in *The Examiner*, January 21, 1816. It amplifies Hazlitt's comment in the preceding essay that *The Tempest* is a finer play than the *Dream* ' but it is not so fine a poem'. The idea that 'Poetry and the stage do not agree well together' (echoing Bottom's 'reason and love keep little company together now-a-days' at III.i.131) could be taken as an epigrammatic summation of a common romantic attitude shared by Coleridge and Lamb in particular. However, when it comes from such an experienced and enthusiastic theatre-goer as Hazlitt it perhaps carries a greater authority. Hazlitt's characteristic interests reveal themselves in his preference of a passage over a Titian painting from the effect of 'gusto', and his stress on 'the mixed impression' of the poetry.

BOTTOM the Weaver is a character that has not had justice done him. He is the most romantic of mechanics. And what a list of companions he has - Quince the Carpenter, Snug the Joiner, Flute the Bellows-mender, Snout the Tinker, Starveling the Tailor; and then again, what a group of fairy attendants, Puck, Peaseblossom, Cobweb, Moth, and Mustard-seed! It has been observed that Shakespear's characters are constructed upon deep physiological principles; and there is something in this play which looks very like it. Bottom the Weaver, who takes the lead of

> 'This crew of patches, rude mechanicals,
> That work for bread upon Athenian stalls,'[1]

follows a sedentary trade, and he is accordingly represented as conceited, serious, and fantastical. He is ready to undertake any thing and every thing, as if it was as much a matter of course as the motion of his loom and shuttle. He is for playing the tyrant, the lover, the lady, the lion. 'He will roar that it shall do any man's heart good to hear him';[2] and this being objected to as improper, he still has a resource in his good opinion of himself, and 'will roar you an 'twere any nightingale.'[3] Snug the Joiner is the moral man of the piece, who proceeds by measurement and discretion in all things. You see him with his rule and compasses in his hand 'Have you the lion's part written? Pray you, if it be, give it me, for I am slow of study.' - 'You may do it extempore,' says Quince, 'for it is nothing but roaring.'[4] Starveling the Tailor keeps the peace, and objects to the lion and the drawn sword. 'I believe we must leave the killing out when all's done.'[5] Starveling, however, does not start the objections himself, but seconds them when made by others, as if he had not spirit to express his fears without encouragement. It is too much to suppose all this intentional: but it very luckily falls out so. Nature includes all that is implied in the most subtle analytical distinctions; and the same distinctions will be found in Shakespear. Bottom, who is not only chief actor, but stage-manager for the occasion, has a device to obviate the danger of frightening the ladies: 'Write me a prologue, and let the prologue seem to say, we will do no harm with our swords, and that Pyramus is not killed indeed; and for better assurance, tell them that I, Pyramus, am not Pyramus, but Bottom the Weaver: this will put them out of fear.'[6] Bottom seems to have understood the subject of dramatic illusion at least as well as any modern essayist. If our holiday mechanic rules the roost among his fellows, he is no less at home in his new character of an ass, 'with amiable cheeks, and fair large ears.'[7] He instinctively acquires a most learned taste, and grows fastidious in the choice of dried peas and bottled hay. He is quite familiar with his new attendants, and assigns them their parts with all due gravity. 'Monsieur Cobweb, good Monsieur, get your weapon in your hand, and kill me a red-hipt humble bee on the top of a thistle, and, good Monsieur, bring me the honey-bag.'[8] What an exact knowledge is here shewn of natural history!

Puck, or Robin Goodfellow, is the leader of the fairy band. He is the Ariel of the MIDSUMMER NIGHT'S DREAM; and yet as unlike as can be to the Ariel in *The Tempest*. No other poet could have made two such different characters out of the same fanciful materials and situations. Ariel is a minister of retribution, who is touched with the sense of pity at the woes he inflicts. Puck is a mad-cap sprite, full of wantonness and mischief, who laughs at those whom he misleads - 'Lord, what fools these mortals be!' Ariel cleaves the air, and executes his mission with the zeal of a winged messenger; Puck is borne along on his fairy errand like the light and glittering gossamer before the breeze. He is, indeed, a most Epicurean little gentleman, dealing in quaint devices, and faring in dainty delights. Prospero and his world of spirits are a set of moralists: but with Oberon and his fairies we are launched at once into the empire of the butterflies. How beautifully is this race of beings contrasted with the men and women actors in the scene, by a single epithet which Titania gives to the latter, 'the human mortals!'9 It is astonishing that Shakespear should be considered, not only by foreigners, but by many of our own critics, as a gloomy and heavy writer, who painted nothing but 'gorgons and hydras, and chimeras dire.'10 His subtlety exceeds that of all other dramatic writers, insomuch that a celebrated person of the present day said that he regarded him rather as a metaphysician than a poet.11 His delicacy and sportive gaiety are infinite. In the MIDSUMMER NIGHT'S DREAM alone, we should imagine, there is more sweetness and beauty of description than in the whole range of French poetry put together. What we mean is this, that we will produce out of that single play ten passages, to which we do not think any ten passages in the works of the French poets can be opposed, displaying equal fancy and imagery. Shall we mention the remonstrance of Helena to Hermia, or Titania's description of her fairy train, or her disputes with Oberon about the Indian boy, or Puck's account of himself and his employments, or the Fairy Queen's exhortation to the elves to pay due attendance upon her favourite, Bottom; or Hippolita's description of a chase, or Theseus's answer? The two last are as heroical and spirited as the others are full of luscious tenderness. The reading of this play is like wandering in a grove by moonlight: the descriptions breathe a sweetness like odours thrown from beds of flower.

Titania's exhortation to the fairies to wait upon Bottom, which is remarkable for a certain cloying sweetness in the repetition of the rhymes, is as follows:-

'Be kind and courteous to this gentleman.

Hop in his walks, and gambol in his eyes,

Feed him with apricocks and dewberries,

With purple grapes, green figs and mulberries;

The honey-bags steal from the humble bees,

And for night tapers crop their waxen thighs,

And light them at the fiery glow-worm's eyes,

To have my love to bed, and to arise:

And pluck the wings from painted butterflies,

To fan the moon-beams from his sleeping eyes;

Nod to him, elves, and do him courtesies.'[12]

The sounds of the lute and of the trumpet are not more distinct than the poetry of the foregoing passage, and of the conversation between Theseus and Hippolita.

[Quotes IV.i.103-27]

Even Titian never made a hunting-piece of a *gusto* so fresh and lusty, and so near the first ages of the world as this.

It had been suggested to us, that the MIDSUMMER NIGHT'S DREAM would do admirably to get up as a Christmas after-piece; and our prompter proposed that Mr Kean should play the part of Bottom, as worthy of his great talents. He might, in the discharge of his duty, offer to play the lady like any of our actresses that he pleased, the lover or the tyrant like any of our actors that he pleased, and the lion like 'the most fearful wild-fowl living.'[13] The carpenter, the tailor, and joiner, it was thought, would hit the galleries. The young ladies in love would interest the side-boxes; and Robin Goodfellow and his companions excite a lively fellow-feeling in the children from school. There would be two courts, an empire within an empire, the Athenian and the Fairy King and Queen, with their attendants, and with all their finery. What an opportunity for processions, for the sound of trumpets and glittering of spears! What a fluttering of urchins' painted wings; what a delightful profusion of gauze clouds and airy spirits floating on them!

Alas the experiment has been tried, and has failed; not through the fault of Mr Kean, who did not play the part of Bottom, nor of Mr Liston, who did, and who played it well, but from the nature of things. The MIDSUMMER NIGHT'S DREAM, when acted, is converted from a delightful fiction into a dull pantomime.

All that is finest in the play is lost in the representation. The spectacle was grand: but the spirit was evaporated, the genius was fled. - Poetry and the stage do not agree well together. The attempt to reconcile them in this instance fails not only of effect, but of decorum. The *ideal* can have no place upon the stage, which is a picture without perspective; everything there is in the fore-ground. That which was merely an airy shape, a dream, a passing thought, immediately becomes an unmanageable reality. Where all is left to the imagination (as is the case in reading) every circumstance, near or remote, has an equal chance of being kept in mind, and tells according to the mixed impression of all that has been suggested. But the imagination cannot sufficiently qualify the actual impressions of the senses. Any offence given to the eye is not to be got rid of by explanation. Thus Bottom's head in the play is a fantastic illusion, produced by magic spells: on the stage it is an ass's head, and nothing more; certainly a very strange costume for a gentleman to appear in. Fancy cannot be embodied any more than a simile can be painted; and it is as idle to attempt it as to personate *Wall* or *Moonshine*. Fairies are not incredible, but fairies six feet high are so. Monsters are not shocking, if they are seen at a proper distance. When ghosts appear at mid-day, when apparitions stalk along Cheapside, then may the MIDSUMMER NIGHT'S DREAM be represented without injury at Covent Garden or at Drury Lane. The boards of a theatre and the regions of fancy are not the same thing.

25.   'ROMEO AND JULIET'

This essay is one of Hazlitt's most personal and well-rounded statements of the relation between literature and life. In attempting to capture the special impression of nostalgia which he finds in himself on reading the play, he ventures a general theory of the preciousness of youth as a function of its lack of knowledge of the future. In doing so he makes a sideswipe at 'the modern philosophy' (Hartley and Locke) and at Wordsworth's account of childhood. Hazlitt notes the effect of introducing characters representative of youth and age, admires Juliet as a character and remarks that 'Romeo is Hamlet in love', amplifying this provocative statement. His parenthesis '(actors are the best commentators on the poets)' can be compared with his assertion that Kean gives 'a new reading' of a passage in *Hamlet* (below, number 50). I have argued that the essay influenced Keats's 'Eve of St. Agnes' and perhaps the Odes (White, p.168). In an age when scholarly opinion on the chronology of Shakespeare's plays was largely undeveloped, it need not be held against Hazlitt that he does not question the supposition that *Romeo and Juliet* was the first play in the canon.

ROMEO AND JULIET is the only tragedy which Shakespear has written entirely on a love-story. It is supposed to have been his first play, and it deserves to stand in that proud rank. There is the buoyant spirit of youth in every line, in the rapturous intoxication of hope, and in the bitterness of despair. It has been said of ROMEO AND JULIET by a great critic, that 'whatever is most intoxicating in the odour of a southern spring, languishing in the song of the nightingale, or voluptuous in the first opening of the rose, is to be found in this poem.'[1] The description is true; and yet it does not answer to our idea of the play. For if it has the sweetness of the rose, it has its freshness too; if it has the languor of the nightingale's song, it has also its giddy transport; if it has the softness of a southern spring, it is as glowing and as bright. There is nothing of a sickly and sentimental cast. Romeo and Juliet are in love, but they are not love-sick. Every thing speaks the very soul of pleasure, the high and healthy pulse of the passions: the heart beats, the blood circulates and mantles throughout. Their courtship is not an insipid interchange of sentiments lip-deep, learnt at second-hand from poems and plays, - made up of beauties of the most shadowy kind, of 'fancies wan that hang the pensive head,'[2] of evanescent smiles, and sighs that breathe not, of delicacy that shrinks from the touch, and feebleness that scarce supports itself, an elaborate vacuity of thought, and an artificial dearth of sense, spirit, truth, and nature. It is the reverse of all this. It is Shakespear all over, and Shakespear when he was young.

We have heard it objected[3] to ROMEO AND JULIET, that it is founded on an idle passion between a boy and a girl, who have scarcely seen and can have but little sympathy or rational esteem for one another, who have had no experience of the good or ills of life, and whose raptures or despair must be therefore equally groundless and fantastical. Whoever objects to the youth of the parties in this play as 'too unripe and crude'[4] to pluck the sweets of love, and wishes to see a first-love carried on into a good old age, and the passions taken at the rebound, when their force is spent, may find all this done in the *Stranger*[5] and in other German plays, where they do things by contraries, and transpose nature to inspire sentiment and create philosophy. Shakespear proceeded in a more strait-forward, and, we think, effectual way. He did not endeavour to extract beauty from wrinkles, or the wild throb of passion from the last expiring sigh of indifference. He did not 'gather grapes of thorns nor figs of thistles.'6 It was not his way. But he has given a picture of human life, such as it is in the order of nature. He has founded the passion of the two lovers not on the pleasures they had experienced, but on all the pleasures they had *not* experienced. All that was to come of life was theirs. At that untried source of promised happiness they slaked their thirst, and the first eager draught made them drunk with love and joy. They were in full possession of their senses and their affections. Their hopes were of air, their desires of fire. Youth is the season of love, because the heart is then first melted in tenderness from the touch of novelty, and kindled to rapture, for it knows no end of its enjoyments or its wishes. Desire has no limit but itself. Passion, the love and expectation of pleasure, is infinite, extravagant, inexhaustible, till experience come to check and kill it. Juliet exclaims on her first interview with Romeo -

'My bounty is as boundless as the sea,
My love as deep.'7

And why should it not? What was to hinder the thrilling tide of pleasure, which had just gushed from her heart, from flowing on without stint or measure, but experience which she was yet without? What was to abate the transport of the first sweet sense of pleasure, which her heart and her senses had just tasted, but indifference which she was yet a stranger to? What was there to check the ardour of hope, of faith, of constancy, just rising in her breast, but disappointment which she had not yet felt! As there are the desires and the hopes of youthful passion, such as the keenness of its disappointments, and their baleful effect. Such is the transition in this play from the highest bliss to the lowest despair, from the nuptial couch to an untimely grave. The only evil that even in apprehension befalls the two lovers is the loss of the greatest possible felicity, yet this loss is fatal to both, for they had rather part with life than bear the thought of surviving all that had made life dear to them. In all this, Shakespear has but followed nature, which existed in his time, as well as now. The modern philosophy, which reduces the whole theory of the mind to habitual impressions, and leaves the natural impulses of passion and imagination out of the account, had not then been discovered; or if it had, would have been little calculated for the uses of poetry.

It is the inadequacy of the same false system of philosophy to account for the strength of our earliest attachments, which has led Mr Wordsworth to indulge in the mystical visions of Platonism in his Ode on the Progress of Life. He has very admirably described the vividness of our impressions in youth and childhood, and how 'they fade by degrees into the light of common day,'[8] and he ascribes the change to the supposition of a pre-existent state, as if our early thoughts were nearer heaven, reflections of former trails of glory, shadows of our past being. This is idle. It is not from the knowledge of the past that the first impressions of things derive their gloss and splendour, but from our ignorance of the future, which fills the void to come with the warmth of our desires, with our gayest hopes, and brightest fancies. It is the obscurity spread before it that colours the prospect of life with hope, as it is the cloud which reflects the rainbow. There is no occasion to resort to any mystical union and transmission of feeling through different states of being to account for the romantic enthusiasm of youth; nor to plant the root of hope in the grave, nor to derive it from the skies. Its root is in the heart of man: it lifts its head above the stars. Desire and imagination are inmates of the human breast. The heaven 'that lies about us in our infancy'[9] is only a new world, of which we know nothing but what we wish it to be, and believe all that we wish. In youth and boyhood, the world we live in is the world of desire, and of fancy: it is experience that brings us down to the world of reality. What is it that in youth sheds a dewy light round the evening star? That makes the daisy look so bright? That perfumes the hyacinth? That embalms the first kiss of love? It is the delight of novelty, and the seeing no end to the pleasure that we fondly believe is still in store for us. The heart revels in the luxury of its own thoughts, and is unable to sustain the weight of hope and love that presses upon it. - The effects of the passion of love alone might have dissipated Mr Wordsworth's theory, if he means any thing more by it than an ingenious and poetical allegory. *That* at least is not a link in the chain let down from other worlds; 'the purple light of love'[10] is not a dim reflection of the smiles of celestial bliss. It does not appear till the middle of life, and then seems like 'another morn risen on mid-day.'[11] In this respect the soul comes into the world 'in utter nakedness.'[12] Love waits for the ripening of the youthful blood. The sense of pleasure precedes the love of pleasure, but with the sense of pleasure, as soon as it is felt, come thronging infinite desires and hopes of pleasure, and love is mature as soon as born. It withers and it dies almost as soon!

This play presents a beautiful *coup-d'oeil* of the progress of human life. In thought it occupies years, and embraces the circle of the affections from childhood to old age. Juliet has become a great girl, a young woman since we first remember her a little thing in the idle prattle of the nurse. Lady Capulet was about her age when she became a mother, and old Capulet somewhat impatiently tells his younger visitors,

> - 'I've seen the day,
> That I have worn a visor, and could tell
> A whispering tale in a fair lady's ear,
> Such as would please: 'tis gone, 'tis gone, 'tis gone.'[13]

Thus one period of life makes way for the following, and one generation pushes another off the stage. One of the most striking passages to show the intense feeling of youth in this play is Capulet's invitation to Paris to visit his entertainment.

> 'At my poor house, look to behold this night
> Earth-treading stars that make dark heav'n light;
> Such comfort as do lusty young men feel
> When well-apparel'd April on the heel
> Of limping winter treads, even such delight
> Among fresh female-buds shall you this night
> Inherit at my house.'[14]

The feelings of youth and of the spring are here blended together like the breath of opening flowers. Images of vernal beauty appear to have floated before the author's mind, in writing this poem, in profusion. Here is another of exquisite beauty, brought in more by accident than by necessity. Montague declares of his son smit with a hopeless passion, which he will not reveal -

> 'But he, his own affection's counsellor
> Is to himself so secret and so close,
> So far from sounding and discovery,
> As is the bud bit with an envious worm,
> Ere he can spread his sweet leaves to the air,
> Or dedicate his beauty to the sun.'[15]

This casual description is as full of passionate beauty as when Romeo dwells in frantic fondness on 'the white wonder of his Juliet's hand.'[16] The reader may, if he pleases, contrast the exquisite pastoral simplicity of the above lines with the gorgeous description of Juliet when Romeo first sees her at her father's house, surrounded by company and artificial splendour.

> 'What lady's that which doth enrich the hand
> Of yonder knight?
> O she doth teach the torches to burn bright;
> Her beauty hangs upon the cheek of night,
> Like a rich jewel in an Æthiop's ear.'[17]

It would be hard to say which of the two garden scenes is the finest, that where he first converses with his love, or takes leave of her the morning after their marriage. Both are like a heaven upon earth; the blissful bowers of Paradise let down upon this lower world. We will give only one passage of these well known scenes to shew the perfect refinement and delicacy of Shakespear's conception of the female character. It is wonderful how Collins, who was a critic and a poet of great sensibility, should have encouraged the common error on this subject by saying - 'But stronger Shakespear felt for man alone.'[18]

The passage we mean is Juliet's apology for her maiden boldness.

[Quotes II.ii.85-106]

In this and all the rest, her heart, fluttering between pleasure, hope, and fear, seems to have dictated to her tongue, and 'calls true love spoken simple modesty.'[19] Of the same sort, but bolder in virgin innocence, is her soliloquy after her marriage with Romeo.

[Quotes III.ii.1-31]

We [would] the rather insert this passage here, inasmuch as we have no doubt it has been expunged from the Family Shakespear.[20] Such critics do not perceive that the feelings of the heart sanctify, without disguising, the impulses of nature. Without refinement themselves, they confound modesty with hypocrisy. Not so the German critic, Schlegel. Speaking of ROMEO AND JULIET, he says, 'It was reserved for Shakespear to unite purity of heart and the glow of imagination, sweetness and dignity of manners and passionate violence, in one ideal picture.'[21]

The character is indeed one of perfect truth and sweetness. It has nothing forward, nothing coy, nothing affected or coquettish about it; - it is a pure effusion of nature. It is as frank as it is modest, for it has no thought that it wishes to conceal. It reposes in conscious innocence on the strength of its affections. Its delicacy does not consist in coldness and reserve, but in combining warmth of imagination and tenderness of heart with the most voluptuous sensibility. Love is a gentle flame that rarifies and expands her whole being. What an idea of trembling haste and airy grace, borne upon the thoughts of love, does the Friar's exclamation give of her, as she approaches his cell to be married -

'Here comes the lady. Oh, so light of foot
Will ne'er wear out the everlasting flint;
A lover may bestride the gossamer,
That idles in the wanton summer air,
And yet not fall, so light is vanity.'[22]

The tragic part of this character is of a piece with the rest. It is the heroic founded on tenderness and delicacy. Of this kind are her resolution to follow the Friar's advice, and the conflict in her bosom between apprehension and love when she comes to take the sleeping poison. Shakespear is blamed for the mixture of low characters. If this is a deformity, it is the source of a thousand beauties. One instance is the contrast between the guileless simplicity of Juliet's attachment to her first love, and the convenient policy of the nurse in advising her to marry Paris, which excites such indignation in her mistress. 'Ancient damnation! oh most wicked fiend,'[23] etc.

Romeo is Hamlet in love. There is the same rich exuberance of passion and sentiment in the one, that there is of thought and sentiment in the other. Both are absent and self-involved, both live out of themselves in a world of imagination. Hamlet is abstracted from every thing; Romeo is abstracted from every thing but his love, and lost in it. His 'frail thoughts dally with faint surmise,'[24] and are fashioned out of the suggestions of hope, 'the flatteries of sleep.'[25] He is himself only in his Juliet; she is his only reality, his heart's true home and idol. The rest of the world is to him a passing dream. How finely is this character pourtrayed where he recollects himself on seeing Paris slain at the tomb of Juliet!-

'What said my man, when my betossed soul
Did not attend him as we rode? I think
He told me Paris should have married Juliet.'[26]

And again, just before he hears the sudden tidings of her death -

'If I may trust the flattery of sleep,
My dreams presage some joyful news at hand;
My bosom's lord sits lightly on his throne,
And all this day an unaccustom'd spirit
Lifts me above the ground with cheerful thoughts.
I dreamt my lady came and found me dead,
(Strange dream! that gives a dead man leave to think)
And breath'd such life with kisses on my lips,
That I reviv'd and was an emperour.
Ah me! how sweet is love itself possess'd,
When but love's shadows are so rich in joy!'[27]

Romeo's passion for Juliet is not a first love: it succeeds and drives out his passion for another mistress, Rosaline, as the sun hides the stars. This is perhaps an artifice (not absolutely necessary) to give us a higher opinion of the lady, while the first absolute surrender of her heart to him enhances the richness of the prize. The commencement, progress, and ending of his second passion are however complete in themselves, not injured if they are not bettered by the first. The outline of the play is taken from an Italian novel;[28] but the dramatic arrangement of the different scenes between the lovers, the more than dramatic interest in the progress of the story, the development of the characters with time and circumstances, just according to the degree and kind of interest excited, are not inferior to the expression of passion and nature. It has been ingeniously remarked among other proofs of skill in the contrivance of the fable, that the improbability of the main incident in the piece, the administering of the sleeping-potion, is softened and obviated from the beginning by the introduction of the Friar on his first appearance culling simples and descanting on their virtues. Of the passionate scenes in this tragedy, that between the Friar and Romeo when he is told of his sentence of banishment, that between Juliet and the Nurse when she hears of it, and of the death of her cousin Tybalt (which bear no proportion in her mind, when passion after the first shock of surprise throws its weight into the scale of her affections) and the last scene at the tomb, are among the most natural and overpowering. In all of these it is not merely the force of any one passion that is given, but the slightest and most unlooked-for transitions from one to another, the mingling currents of every different feeling rising up and prevailing in turn, swayed by the master-mind of the poet, as the waves undulate beneath the gliding storm. Thus when Juliet has by her complaints encouraged the Nurse to say, 'Shame come to Romeo,' she instantly repels the wish, which she had herself occasioned, by answering -

	'Blister'd be thy tongue
	For such a wish! He was not born to shame,
	Upon his brow shame is ashamed to sit,
	'For 'tis a throne where honour may be crown'd
	Sole monarch of the universal earth!
	O, what a beast was I to chide him so?
Nurse.	Will you speak well of him that kill'd your cousin?
Juliet.	Shall I speak ill of him that is my husband?
	Ah my poor lord, what tongue shall smooth thy name,
	When I, thy three-hours' wife, have mangled it?'[29]

And then follows on the neck of her remorse and returning fondness, that wish treading almost on the brink of impiety, but still held back by the strength of her devotion to her lord, that 'father, mother, nay, or both were dead,' rather than Romeo banished. If she requires any other excuse, it is in the manner in which Romeo echoes her frantic grief and disappointment in the next scene at being banished for her. Perhaps one of the finest pieces of acting that ever was witnessed on the stage, is Mr Kean's manner of doing this scene and his repetition of the word, *Banished.* He treads close indeed upon the genius of his author.[30]

.   .   .

We can more easily decide between Shakespear and any other author, than between him and himself. - Shall we quote any more passages to shew his genius or the beauty of ROMEO AND JULIET? At that rate, we might quote the whole. The late Mr Sheridan, on being shewn a volume of the Beauties of Shakespear,[31] very properly asked - 'But where are the other eleven?' The character of Mercutio in this play is one of the most mercurial and spirited of the productions of

Shakespear's comic muse.

26.   FROM 'LEAR'

King Lear has intimidated and inhibited many critics (Coleridge was apparently reluctant to lecture on it; Hawkes, p.18) and Hazlitt also confesses himself in awe of the play. He goes further, however, than any of his contemporaries or predecessors towards saying that it is Shakespeare's greatest play. Certainly, his concluding remarks indicate that *King Lear* represented for him an apex of tragic poetry, and something of a touchstone for judging all art. He concentrates on the emotional power of the play, placing its first three acts with the third act of *Othello* as 'Shakespear's great master-pieces in the logic of passion'. This 'logic' (involving contrast, controlled emotional expressiveness, rhythm and 'the sense of sympathy in the reader') is described with impressionistic force in the context of certain scenes. Perhaps as a consequence of his profound admiration for the poetry, in this essay Hazlitt quotes virtually entire scenes and sequences with minimal comment, and he quotes a long passage from Schlegel condemning the 'happy ending' devised by Nahum Tate ('approved of by Dr Johnson') which held the stage for 142 years. Schlegel's passage begins 'The LEAR of Shakespear cannot be acted'. Since the length of these various quotations is not justified in the present selection, they are omitted. The 'four things which have struck us in reading LEAR' listed at the end of the essay interested Keats enough for him to underline them in his copy of Hazlitt's *Characters*, and they indeed express beliefs that Keats either shared with or learned from Hazlitt. In annotating his copy, Keats finds a 'contradiction' in Hazlitt's comments on the Fool's role, and he himself stresses the pathos of this character rather than his humour.

It should be stressed that *King Lear* was a controversial play in Hazlitt's time for political reasons. From 1810 to 1820 the play was banned in any form from the stage because of the madness of George III, and even before this Tate's rewriting had held the stage from 1681 (to 1823). Lamb said it could not be staged in the original for artistic reasons.

We wish that we could pass this play over, and say nothing about it. All that we can say must fall far short of the subject; or even of what we ourselves conceive of it. To attempt to give a description of the play itself or of its effect upon the mind, is mere impertinence: yet we must say something. - It is then the best of all Shakespear's plays, for it is the one in which he was the most in earnest.[1] He was here fairly caught in the web of his own imagination. The passion which he has taken as his subject is that which strikes its root deepest into the human heart; of which the bond is the hardest to be unloosed; and the cancelling and tearing to pieces of which gives the greatest revulsion to the frame. This depth of nature, this force of passion, this tug and war of the elements of our being, this firm faith in filial piety, and the giddy anarchy and whirling tumult of the thoughts at finding this prop failing it, the contrast between the fixed, immoveable basis of natural affection, and the rapid, irregular starts of imagination, suddenly wrenched from all its accustomed holds and resting-places in the soul, this is what Shakespear has given, and what nobody else but he could give. So we believe. - The mind of Lear, staggering between the weight of attachment and the hurried movements of passion, is like a tall ship driven about by the winds, buffeted by the furious waves, but that still rides above the storm, having its anchor fixed in the bottom of the sea; or it is like the sharp rock circled by the eddying whirlpool that foams and beats against it, or like the solid promontory pushed from its basis by the force of an earthquake.

The character of Lear itself is very finely conceived for the purpose. It is the only ground on which such a story could be built with the greatest truth and effect. It is his rash haste, his violent impetuosity, his blindness to every thing but the dictates of his passions or affections, that produces all his misfortunes, that aggravates his impatience of them, that enforces our pity for him. That part which Cordelia bears in the scene is extremely beautiful: the story is almost told in the first words she utters. We see at once the precipice on which the poor old king stands from his own extravagant and credulous importunity, the indiscreet simplicity of her love (which, to be sure, has a little of her father's obstinacy in it) and the hollowness of her sisters' pretensions. Almost the first burst of that noble tide of passion, which runs through the play, is in the remonstrance of Kent to his royal master on the injustice of his sentence against his youngest daughter - 'Be Kent unmannerly, when Lear is mad!'[2] This manly plainness, which draws down on him the displeasure of the unadvised king, is worthy of the fidelity with which he adheres to his fallen fortunes. The true character of the two eldest daughters, Regan and Gonerill (they are so thoroughly hateful that we do not even like to repeat their names) breaks out in their answer to Cordelia who desires them to treat their father well - 'Prescribe not us our duties'[3] - their hatred of advice being in proportion to their determination to do wrong, and to their hypocritical pretensions to do right. Their deliberate hypocrisy adds the last finishing to the odiousness of their characters. It is the absence of this detestable quality that is the only relief in the character of Edmund the Bastard, and that at times reconciles us to him. We are not tempted to exaggerate the guilt of his conduct, when he himself gives it up as a bad business, and writes himself down 'plain villain.' Nothing more can be said about it. His religious honesty in this respect is admirable. One speech of his is worth a million. His father, Gloster, whom he has just deluded with a forged story of his brother Edgar's designs against his life, accounts for his unnatural behaviour and the strange depravity of the times from the late eclipses in the sun and moon. Edmund, who is in the secret, says when he is gone - 'This is the excellent foppery of the world, that when we are sick in fortune (often the surfeits of our own behaviour) we make guilty of our disasters the sun, the moon, and stars: as if we were villains on necessity; fools by heavenly compulsion; knaves, thieves, and treacherous by spherical predominance; drunkards, liars, and adulterers by an enforced obedience of planetary influence; and all that we are evil in, by a divine thrusting on. An admirable evasion of whore-master man, to lay his goatish disposition on the charge of a star! My father compounded with my mother under the Dragon's tail, and my nativity was under Ursa Major: so that it follows, I am rough and lecherous. Tut! I should have been what I am, had the maidenliest star in the firmament twinkled on my bastardising.'[4] - The whole character, its careless, light-hearted villainy, contrasted with the sullen, rancorous malignity of Regan and Gonerill, its connection with the conduct of the under-plot, in which Gloster's persecution of one of his sons and the ingratitude of another, form a counterpart to the mistakes and misfortunes of Lear, - his double amour with the two sisters, and the share which he has in bringing about the fatal catastrophe, are all managed with an uncommon degree of skill and power.

It has been said, and we think justly, that the third act of *Othello* and the three first acts of LEAR, are Shakespear's great master-pieces in the logic of passion: that they contain the highest examples not only of the force of individual passion, but of its dramatic vicissitudes and striking effects arising from the different circumstances and characters of the persons speaking. We see the ebb and flow of the feeling, its pauses and feverish starts, its impatience of opposition, its accumulating force when it has time to recollect itself, the manner in which it avails itself of every passing word or gesture, its haste to repel insinuation, the alternate contraction and dilatation of the soul, and all 'the dazzling fence of controversy'[5] in this mortal combat with poisoned weapons, aimed at the heart, where each wound is fatal. We have seen in *Othello*, how the unsuspecting frankness and impetuous passions of the Moor are played upon and exasperated by the artful dexterity of Iago. In the present play, that which aggravates the sense of sympathy in the reader, and of uncontroulable anguish in the swoln heart of Lear, is the petrifying indifference, the cold calculating, obdurate selfishness of his daughters. His keen passions seem whetted on their stony hearts. The contrast would be too painful, the shock too great, but for the intervention of the Fool, whose well-timed levity comes in to break the continuity of feeling when it can no longer be borne, and to bring into play again the fibres of the heart just as they are growing rigid from over-strained excitement. The imagination is glad to take refuge in the half-comic, half-serious comments of the Fool, just as the mind under the extreme anguish of a surgical operation vents itself in sallies of wit. The character was also a grotesque ornament of the barbarous times, in which alone the tragic ground-work of the story could be laid. In another point of view it is indispensable, inasmuch as while it is a diversion to the too great intensity of our disgust, it carries the pathos to the highest pitch of which it is capable, by shewing the pitiable weakness of the old king's conduct and its irretrievable consequences in the most familiar point of view. Lear may well 'beat at the gate which let his folly in,'[6] after, as the Fool says, 'he has made his daughters his mothers.'[7] The character is dropped in the third act to make room for the entrance of Edgar as Mad Tom, which well accords with the increasing bustle and wildness of the incidents; and nothing can be more complete than the distinction between Lear's real and Edgar's assumed madness, while the resemblance in the cause of their distresses, from the severing of the nearest ties of natural affection, keeps up a unity of interest. Shakespear's mastery over his subject, if it was not art, was owing to a knowledge of the connecting links of the passions, and their effect upon the mind, still more wonderful than any systematic adherence to rules, and that anticipated and outdid all the efforts of the most refined art, not inspired and rendered instinctive by genious.

One of the most perfect displays of dramatic power is the first interview between Lear and his daughter, after the designed affronts upon him, which till one of his knights reminds him of them, his sanguine temperament had led him to overlook. He returns with his train from hunting, and his usual impatience breaks out in his first words, 'Let me not stay a jot for dinner; go, get it ready.' He then encounters the faithful Kent in disguise, and retains him in his service; and the first trial of his honest duty is to trip up the heels of the officious Steward who makes so prominent and despicable a figure through the piece. On the entrance of Gonerill the following dialogue takes place:-

[Quotes I.iv.187-310 entirely]

This is certainly fine: no wonder that Lear says after it, 'O let me not be mad, not mad, sweet heavens,'[8] feeling its affects by anticipation; but fine as is this burst of rage and indignation at the first blow aimed at his hopes and expectations, it is nothing near so fine as what follows from his double disappointment, and his lingering efforts to see which of them he shall lean upon for support and find comfort in, when both his daughters turn against his age and weakness. It is with some difficulty that Lear gets to speak with his daughter Regan, and her husband, at Gloster's castle. In concert with Gonerill they have left their own home on purpose to avoid him. His apprehensions are first alarmed by this circumstance, and when Gloster, whose guests they are, urges the fiery temper of the Duke of Cornwall as an excuse for not importuning him a second time, Lear breaks out -

'Vengeance! Plague! Death! Confusion! -
Fiery? What quality? Why, Gloster, Gloster,
I'd speak with the Duke of Cornwall, and his wife.'[9]

Afterwards, feeling perhaps not well himself, he is inclined to admit their excuse from illness, but then recollecting that they have set his messenger (Kent) in the stocks, all his suspicions are roused again and he insists on seeing them.

[Quotes II.iv.127-286 in entirety, the scene where Lear confronts Regan and then both daughters with Cornwall.]

If there is any thing in any author like this yearning of the heart, these throes of tenderness, this profound expression of all that can be thought and felt in the most heart-rending situations, we are glad of it; but it is in some author that we have not read.

The scene in the storm, where he is exposed to all the fury of the elements, though grand and terrible, is not so fine, but the moralising scenes with Mad Tom, Kent, and Gloster, are upon a par with the former. His exclamation in the supposed trial-scene of his daughters, 'See the little dogs and all, Tray, Blanch, and Sweetheart, see they bark at me,'[10] his issuing his orders, 'Let them anatomize Regan, see what breeds about her heart,'[11] and his reflection when he sees the misery of Edgar, 'Nothing but his unkind daughters could have brought him to this,'[12] are in a style of pathos, where the extremest resources of the imagination are called in to lay open the deepest movements of the heart, which was peculiar to Shakespear. In the same style and spirit is his interrupting the Fool who asks 'whether a madman be a gentleman or a yeoman,' by answering 'A king, a king.'[13] -

The indirect part that Gloster takes in these scenes where his generosity leads him to relieve Lear and resent the cruelty of his daughters, at the very time that he is himself instigated to seek the life of his son, and suffering under the sting of his supposed ingratitude, is a striking accompaniment to the situation of Lear. Indeed, the manner in which the threads of the story are woven together is almost as wonderful in the way of art as the carrying on the tide of passion, still varying and unimpaired, is on the score of nature. Among the remarkable instances of this kind are Edgar's meeting with his old blind father; the deception he practises upon him when he pretends to lead him to the top of Dover-cliff - 'Come on, sir, here's the place,'[14] to prevent his ending his life and miseries together; his encounter with the perfidious Steward whom he kills, and his finding the letter from Gonerill to his brother upon him which leads to the final catastrophe, and brings the wheel of Justice 'full circle home'[15] to the guilty parties. The bustle and rapid succession of events in the last scenes is surprising. But the meeting between Lear and Cordelia is by far the most affecting part of them. It has all the wildness of poetry, and all the heart-felt truth of nature. The previous account of her reception of the news of his unkind treatment, her involuntary reproaches to her sisters, 'Shame, ladies, shame,'[16] Lear's backwardness to see his daughter, the picture of the desolate state to which he is reduced, 'Alack, 'tis he; why he was met even now, as mad as the vex'd sea, singing aloud,'[17] only prepare the way for and heighten our expectation of what follows, and assuredly this expectation is not disappointed when through the tender care of Cordelia he revives and recollects her.

[Quotes IV.vii.43-9]

Almost equal to this in awful beauty is their consolation of each other when, after the triumph of their enemies, they are led to prison.

[Quotes V.iii.3-21]

The concluding events are sad, painfully sad; but their pathos is extreme. The oppression of the feelings is relieved by the very interest we take in the misfortunes of others, and by the reflections to which they give birth. Cordelia is hanged in prison by the orders of the bastard Edmund, which are known too late to be countermanded, and Lear dies broken-hearted, lamenting over her.

> '*Lear.*   And my poor fool is hang'd! No, no, no life:
> Why should a dog, a horse, a rat, have life,
> And thou no breath at all? O, thou wilt come no more,
> Never, never, never, never, never! -
> Pray you, undo this button: thank you, sir.'[18]

He dies, and indeed we feel the truth of what Kent says on the occasion -

> 'Vex not his ghost: O, let him pass! he hates him,
> That would upon the rack of this rough world
> Stretch him out longer.'[19]

.   .   .

Four things have struck us in reading LEAR:

1. That poetry is an interesting study, for this reason, that it relates to whatever is most interesting in human life. Whoever therefore has a contempt for poetry, has a contempt for himself and humanity.

2. That the language of poetry is superior to the language of painting; because the strongest of our recollections relate to feelings, not to faces.

3. That the greatest strength of genius is shewn in describing the strongest passion: for the power of the imagination, in works of invention, must be in proportion to the force of the natural impressions, which are the subject of them.

4. That the circumstance which balances the pleasure against the pain in tragedy is, that in proportion to the greatness of the evil, is our sense and desire of the opposite good excited; and that our sympathy with actual suffering is lost in the strong impulse given to our natural affections, and carried away with the swelling tide of passion, that gushes from and relieves the heart.

tide of passion, that gushes from and relieves the heart.

27.   FROM 'RICHARD II'

Hazlitt takes this opportunity to attack the arbitrariness of monarchy and the expediency of contemporary politicians, subjects dear to his heart.

RICHARD II. is a play little known compared with *Richard III.* which last is a play that every unfledged candidate for theatrical fame chuses to strut and fret his hour upon the stage in; yet we confess that we prefer the nature and feeling of the one to the noise and bustle of the other; at least, as we are so often forced to see it acted. In RICHARD II. the weakness of the king leaves us leisure to take a greater interest in the misfortunes of the man. After the first act, in which the arbitrariness of his behaviour only proves his want of resolution, we see him staggering under the unlooked-for blows of fortune, bewailing his loss of kingly power, not preventing it, sinking under the aspiring genius of Bolingbroke, his authority trampled on, his hopes failing him, and his pride crushed and broken down under insults and injuries, which his own misconduct had provoked, but which he has not courage or manliness to resent. The change of tone and behaviour in the two competitors for the throne according to their change of fortune, from the capricious sentence of banishment passed by Richard upon Bolingbroke, the suppliant offers and modest pretensions of the latter on his return to the high and haughty tone with which he accepts Reichard's resignation of the crown after the loss of all his power, the use which he makes of the deposed king to grace his triumphal progress through the streets of London, and the final intimation of his wish for his death, which immediately finds a servile executioner, is marked throughout with complete effect and without the slightest appearance of effort. The steps by which Bolingbroke mounts the throne are those by which Richard sinks into the grave. We feel neither respect nor love for the deposed monarch; for he is as wanting in energy as in principle: but we pity him, for he pities himself. His heart is by no means hardened against himself, but bleeds afresh at every new stroke of mischance, and his sensibility, absorbed in his own person, and unused to misfortune, is not only tenderly alive to its own sufferings, but without the fortitude to bear them. He is, however, human in his distresses; for to feel pain, and sorrow, weakness, disappointment, remorse and anguish, is the lot of make us forget that he ever was a king. .

The right assumed by sovereign power to trifle at its will with the happiness of others as a matter of course, or to remit its exercise as a matter of favour, is strikingly shewn in the sentence of banishment so unjustly pronounced on Bolingbroke and Mowbray, and in what Bolingbroke says when four years of his banishment are taken off, with as little reason.

> 'How long a time lies in one little word!
> Four lagging winters and four wanton springs
> End in a word: such is the breath of kings.'[1]

.   .   .

The truth is, that there is neither truth nor honour in all these noble persons: they answer words with words, as they do blows with blows, in mere self defence: nor have they any principle whatever but that of courage in maintaining any wrong they dare commit, or any falsehood which they find it useful to assert. How different were these noble knights and 'barons bold'[2] from their more refined descendants in the present day, who, instead of deciding questions of right by brute force, refer everything to convenience, fashion, and good breeding! In point of any abstract love of truth or justice, they are just the same now that they were then.

The characters of old John of Gaunt and of his brother York, uncles to the King, the one stern and foreboding, the other honest, good-natured, doing all for the best, and therefore doing nothing, are well kept up. The speech of the former, in praise of England, is one of the most eloquent that ever was penned. We should perhaps hardly be disposed to feed the pampered egotism of our countrymen by quoting this description, were it not that the conclusion of it (which looks prophetic) may qualify any improper degree of exultation.

[Quotes II.i.40-66]

The character of Bolingbroke, afterwards Henry IV, is drawn with a masterly hand: - patient for occasion, and then steadily availing himself of it, seeing his advantage afar off, but only seizing on it when he has it within his reach, humble, crafty, bold, and aspiring, encroaching by regular but slow degrees, building power on opinion, and cementing opinion by power.

His bold assertion of his own rights, his pretended submission to the king, and the ascendancy which he tacitly assumes over him without openly claiming it, as soon as he has him in his power, are characteristic traits of this ambitious and politic usurper. But the part of Richard himself gives the chief interest to the play. His folly, his vices, his misfortunes, his reluctance to part with the crown, his fear to keep it, his weak and womanish regrets, his starting tears, his fits of hectic passion, his smothered majesty, pass in succession before us, and make a picture as natural as it is affecting. Among the most striking touches of pathos are his wish 'O that I were a mockery king of snow to melt away before the sun of Bolingbroke,'[3] and the incident of the poor groom who comes to visit him in prison, and tells him how 'it yearned his heart that Bolingbroke upon his coronation-day rode on Roan Barbary.'[4]

28.   FROM 'HENRY IV IN TWO PARTS'

The 'heroic and serious part of these two plays' does not detain Hazlitt long in what is really an essay in praise of Falstaff, 'an actor in himself almost as upon the stage'. Hazlitt's account of Falstaff is still worth close study.

If Shakespear's fondness for the ludicrous sometimes led to faults in his tragedies (which was not often the case) he has made us amends by the character of Falstaff. This is perhaps the most substantial comic character that ever was invented. Sir John carries a most portly presence in the mind's eye; and in him, not to speak it profanely, 'we behold the fulness of the spirit of wit and humour bodily.'[1] We are as well acquainted with his person as his mind, and his jokes come upon us with double force and relish from the quantity of flesh through which they make their way, as he shakes his fat sides with laughter, or 'lards the lean earth as he walks along.'[2] Other comic characters seem, if we approach and handle them, to resolve themselves into air, 'into thin air':[3] but this is embodied and palpable to the grossest apprehension: it lies 'three fingers deep upon the ribs,'[4] it plays about the lungs and the diaphragm with all the force of animal enjoyment. His body is like a good estate to his mind, from which he receives rents and revenues of profit and pleasure in kind, according to its extent, and the richness of the soil. Wit is often a meagre substitute for pleasurable sensation; an effusion of spleen and petty spite at the comforts of others, from feeling none in itself. Falstaff's wit is an emanation of a fine constitution; an exuberance of good-humour and good-nature; an overflowing of his love of laughter and good-fellowship; a giving vent to his heart's ease, and over-contentment with himself and others. He would not be in character, if he were not so fat as he is; for there is the greatest keeping in the boundless luxury of his imagination and the pampered self-indulgence of his physical appetites. He manures and nourishes his mind with jests, as he does his body with sack and sugar. He carves out his jokes, as he would a capon or a haunch of venison, where there is *cut and come again*; and pours out upon them the oil of gladness. His tongue drops fatness, and in the chambers of his brain 'it snows of meat and drink.'[5] He keeps up perpetual holiday and open house, and we live with him in a round of invitations to a rump and dozen. - Yet we are not to suppose that he was a mere sensualist. All this is as much in imagination as in reality. His sensuality does not engross and stupify his other faculties, but 'ascends me into the brain, clears away all the dull, crude vapours that environ it, and makes it full of nimble, fiery, and delectable shapes.'[6] His imagination keeps up the ball after his senses have done with it. He seems to have even a greater enjoyment of the freedom from restraint, of good cheer, of his ease, of his vanity, in the ideal exaggerated description which he gives of them, than in fact. He never fails to enrich his discourse with allusions to eating and drinking, but we never see him at table. He carries his own larder about with him, and he is himself 'a tun of man.'[7] His pulling out the bottle in the field of battle is a joke to shew his contempt for glory accompanied with danger, his systematic adherence to his Epicurean philosophy in the most trying circumstances. Again, such is his deliberate exaggeration of his own vices, that it does not seem quite certain whether the account of his hostess's bill, found in his pocket, with such an out-of-the-way charge for capons and sack with only one halfpenny-worth of bread, was not put there by himself as a trick to humour the jest upon his favourite propensities, and as a conscious caricature of himself. He is represented as a liar, a braggart, a coward, a glutton, etc. and yet we are not offended but delighted with him; for he is all these as much to amuse others as to gratify himself. He openly assumes all these characters to shew the humourous part of them. The unrestrained indulgence of his own ease, appetites, and convenience, has neither malice nor hypocrisy in it. In a word, he is an actor in himself almost as much as upon the stage, and we no more object to the character of Falstaff in a moral point of view than we should think of bringing an excellent comedian, who should represent him to the life, before one of the police offices. We only consider the number of pleasant lights in which he puts certain foibles (the more pleasant as they are opposed to the received rules and necessary restraints of society) and do not trouble ourselves about the consequences resulting from them, for no mischievous consequences do result. Sir John is old as well as fat, which gives a melancholy retrospective tinge to the character; and by the disparity between his inclinations and his capacity for enjoyment, makes it still more ludicrous and fantastical.

The secret of Falstaff's wit is for the most part a masterly presence of mind, an absolute self-possession, which nothing can disturb. His repartees are involuntary suggestions of his self-love; instinctive evasions of every thing that threatens to interrupt the career of his triumphant jollity and self-complacency. His very size floats him out of all his difficulties in a sea of rich conceits; and he turns round on the pivot of his convenience, with every occasion and at a moment's warning. His natural repugnance to every unpleasant thought or circumstance, of itself makes light of objections, and provokes the most extravagant and licentious answers in his own justification. His indifference to truth puts no check upon his invention, and the more improbable and unexpected his contrivances are, the more happily does he seem to be delivered of them, the anticipation of their effect acting as a stimulus to the gaiety of his fancy. The success of one adventurous sally gives him spirits to undertake another: he deals always in round numbers, and his exaggerations and excuses are 'open, palpable, monstrous as the father that begets them.'[8]

. . .

One of the topics of exulting superiority over others most common in Sir John's mouth is his corpulence and the exterior marks of good living which he carries about him, thus 'turning his vices into commodity.'[9] He accounts for the friendship between the Prince and Poins, from 'their legs being both of a bigness';[10] and compares Justice Shallow to 'a man made after supper of a cheese-paring.'[11] There cannot be a more striking gradation of character than that between Falstaff and Shallow, and Shallow and Silence. It seems difficult at first to fall lower than the squire; but this fool, great as he is, finds an admirer and humble foil in his cousin Silence. Vain of his acquaintance with Sir John, who makes a butt of him, he exclaims, 'Would, cousin Silence, that thou had'st seen that which this knight and I have seen!' - 'Aye, Master Shallow, we have heard the chimes at midnight,'[12] says Sir John. To Falstaff's observation 'I did not think Master Silence had been a man of this mettle,' Silence answers, 'Who, I? I have been merry twice and once ere now.[13] What an idea is here conveyed of a prodigality of living? What good husbandry and economical self-denial in his pleasures? What a stock of lively recollections? It is curious that Shakespear has ridiculed in Justice Shallow, who was 'in some authority under the king,'[14] that disposition to unmeaning tautology which is the regal infirmity of later times,[15] and which, it may be supposed, he acquired from talking to his cousin Silence, and receiving no answers.

> '*Falstaff.*   You have here a goodly dwelling, and a rich.
>
> *Shallow.*   Barren, barren, barren; beggars all, beggars all, Sir John:
> marry, good air. Spread Davy, spread Davy. Well said, Davy.
>
> *Falstaff.*   This Davy serves you for good uses.
>
> *Shallow.*   A good varlet, a good varlet, a very good varlet. By
> the mass, I have drank too much sack at supper. A good varlet.
> Now sit down, now sit down. Come, cousin.'[16]

The true spirit of humanity, the thorough knowledge of the stuff we are made of, the practical wisdom with the seeming fooleries in the whole of the garden-scene at Shallow's country-seat, and just before in the exquisite dialogue between him and Silence on the death of old Double, have no parallel any where else. In one point of view, they are laughable in the extreme; in another they are equally affecting, if it is affecting to shew *what a little thing is human life*, what a poor forked creature man is![17]

The heroic and serious part of these two plays founded on the story of Henry IV is not inferior to the comic and farcical. The characters of Hotspur and Prince Henry are two of the most beautiful and dramatic, both in themselves and from contrast, that ever were drawn. They are the essence of chivalry. We like Hotspur the best upon the whole, perhaps because he was unfortunate. - The characters of their fathers, Henry IV and old Northumberland, are kept up equally well. Henry naturally succeeds by his prudence and caution in keeping what he has got; Northumberland fails in his enterprise from an excess of the same quality, and is caught in the web of his own cold, dilatory policy. Owen Glendower is a masterly character. It is as bold and original as it is intelligible and thoroughly natural. The disputes between him and Hotspur are managed with infinite address and insight into nature. We cannot help pointing out here some very beautiful lines, where Hotspur describes the fight between Glendower and Mortimer.

[Quotes *1 Henry IV*, I.iii.98-107]

The peculiarity and the excellence of Shakespear's poetry is, that it seems as if he made his imagination the hand-maid of nature, and nature the plaything of his imagination. He appears to have been all the characters, and in all the situations he describes. It is as if either he had had all their feelings, or had lent them all his genius to express themselves. There cannot be stronger instances of this than Hotspur's rage when Henry IV forbids him to speak of Mortimer, his insensibility to all that his father and uncle urge to calm him, and his fine abstracted apostrophe to honour, 'By heaven methinks it were an easy leap to pluck bright honour from the moon,'[18] etc. After all, notwithstanding the gallantry, generosity, good temper, and idle freaks of the mad-cap Prince of Wales, we should not have been sorry, if Northumberland's force had come up in time to decide the fate of the battle at Shrewsbury; at least, we always heartily sympathise with Lady Percy's grief, when she exclaims,

> 'Had my sweet Harry had but half their numbers,
> To-day might I (hanging on Hotspur's neck)
> Have talked of Monmouth's grave.'[19]

The truth is, that we never could forgive the Prince's treatment of Falstaff; though perhaps Shakespear knew what was best, according to the history, the nature of the times, and of the man. We speak only as dramatic critics. Whatever terror the French in those days might have of Henry V yet, to the readers of poetry at present, Falstaff is the better man of the two. We think of him and quote him oftener.

29. FROM 'HENRY V'

Hazlitt's splendidly iconoclastic essay on this patriotic play was calculated to be as provocative as possible, not only because of his anti-monarchical beliefs but because he was bitterly disappointed by the fall of Napoleon and what that event represented - the defeat of the French Revolution. The personal emotion accounts for Hazlitt's fiery prose. The latter part of the essay (largely omitted here) consists of quotation of 'the well-known *Beauties* of Shakespear'.

HENRY V is a very favourite monarch with the English nation, and he appears to have been also a favourite with Shakespear, who labours hard to apologise for the actions of the king, by shewing us the character of the man, as 'the king of good fellows.' He scarcely deserves this honour. He was fond of war and low company: - we know little else of him. He was careless, dissolute, and ambitious: - idle, or doing mischief. In private, he seemed to have no idea of the common decencies of life, which he subjected to a kind of regal licence; in public affairs, he seemed to have no idea of any rule of right or wrong, but brute force, glossed over with a little religious hypocrisy and archiepiscopal advice. His principles did not change with his situation and professions. His adventure on Gadshill was a prelude to the affair of Agincourt, only a bloodless one; Falstaff was a puny prompter of violence and outrage, compared with the pious and politic Archbishop of Canterbury, who gave the king *carte blanche*, in a genealogical tree of his family, to rob and murder in circles of latitude and longitude abroad - to save the possessions of the church at home. This appears in the speeches in Shakespear, where the hidden motives that actuate princes and their advisers in war and policy are better laid open than in speeches from the throne or woolsack. Henry, because he did not know how to govern his own kingdom, determined to make war upon his neighbours. Because his own title to the crown was doubtful, he laid claim to that of France. Because he did not know how to exercise the enormous power, which had just dropped into his hands, to any one good purpose, he immediately undertook (a cheap and obvious resource of sovereignty) to do all the mischief he could. Even if absolute monarchs had the wit to find out objects of laudable ambition, they could only 'plume up their wills'[1] in adhering to the more sacred formula of the royal prerogative, 'the right divine of kings to govern wrong,'[2] because will is only then triumphant when it is opposed to the will of others, because the pride of power is only then shewn, not when it consults the rights and interest of others, but when it insults and tramples on all justice and all humanity. Henry declares his resolution 'when France is his, to bend it to his awe, or break it all to pieces'[3] - a resolution worthy of a conqueror, to destroy all that he cannot enslave; and what adds to the joke, he lays all the blame of the consequences of his ambition on those who will not submit tamely to his tyranny. Such is the history of kingly power, from the beginning to the end of the world; - with this difference, that the object of war formerly, when the people adhered to their allegiance, was to depose kings; the object latterly, since the people swerved from their allegiance, has been to restore kings, and to make common cause against mankind. The object of our late invasion and conquest of France was to restore the legitimate monarch, the descendant of Hugh Capet, to the throne: Henry V in his time made war on and deposed the descendant of this very Hugh Capet, on the plea that he was a usurper and illegitimate. What would the great modern catspaw of legitimacy and restorer of divine right have said to the claim of Henry and the title of the descendants of Hugh Capet? Henry V it is true, was a hero, a King of England, and the conqueror of the king of France. Yet we feel little love or admiration for him. He was a hero, that is, he was ready to sacrifice his own life for the pleasure of destroying thousands of other lives: he was a king of England, but not a constitutional one, and we only like kings according to the law; lastly, he was a conqueror of the French king, and for this we dislike him less than if he had conquered the French people. How then do we like him? We like him in the play. There he is a very amiable monster, a very splendid pageant. As we like to gaze at a panther or a young lion in their cages in the Tower, and catch a pleasing horror from their glistening eyes, their velvet paws, and dreadless roar, so we take a very romantic, heroic, patriotic, and poetical delight in the boasts and feats of our younger Harry, as they appear on the stage and are confined to lines of ten syllables; where no blood follows the stroke that wounds our ears, where no harvest bends beneath horses' hoofs, no city flames, no little child is butchered, no dead men's bodies are found piled on heaps and festering the next morning - in the orchestra!

So much for the politics of this play; now for the poetry. Perhaps one of the most striking images in all Shakespear is that given of war in the first lines of the Prologue.

> 'O for a muse of fire, that would ascend
> The brightest heaven of invention,

> A kingdom for a stage, princes to act,
> And monarchs to behold the swelling scene!
> Then should the warlike Harry, like himself,
> Assume the port of Mars, and *at his heels*
> *Leash'd in like hounds, should famine, sword, and fire*
> *Crouch for employment.*[4]

Rubens, if he had painted it, would not have improved upon this simile.

. . .

Another characteristic instance of the blindness of human nature to every thing but its own interests, is the complaint made by the king of 'the ill neighbourhood' of the Scot in attacking England when she was attacking France.

> 'For once the eagle England being in prey,
> To her unguarded nest the weazel Scot
> Comes sneaking, and so sucks her princely eggs.'[5]

It is worth observing that in all these plays, which give an admirable picture of the spirit of the *good old times*, the moral inference does not at all depend upon the nature of the actions, but on the dignity or meanness of the persons committing them. 'The eagle England' has a right 'to be in prey,' but 'the weazel Scot' has none 'to come sneaking to her nest,' which she has left to pounce upon others. Might was right, without equivocation or disguise, in that heroic and chivalrous age. The substitution of right for might, even in theory, is among the refinements and abuses of modern philosophy.

. . .

HENRY V is but one of Shakespear's second-rate plays. Yet by quoting passages, like this, from his second-rate plays alone, we might make a volume 'rich with his praise,'

> 'As is the oozy bottom of the sea
> With sunken wrack and sumless treasuries.'[6]

. . .

The comic parts of HENRY V are very inferior to those of *Henry IV*. Falstaff is dead, and without him, Pistol, Nym, and Bardolph, are satellites without a sun. Fluellen the Welshman is the most entertaining character in the piece. He is good-natured, brave, choleric, and pedantic. His parallel between Alexander and Harry of Monmouth, and his desire to have 'some disputations' with Captain Macmorris on the discipline of the Roman wars, in the heat of the battle, are never to be forgotten. His treatment of Pistol is as good as Pistol's treatment of his French prisoner. There are two other remarkable prose passages in this play: the conversation of Henry in disguise with the three centinels on the duties of a soldier, and his courtship of Katherine in broken French. We like them both exceedingly, though the first savours perhaps too much of the king, and the last too little of the lover.

30. FROM 'HENRY VI IN THREE PARTS'

The essay largely consists of quotations contrasting Richard II ('the splenetic effusion of disappointed ambition') and Henry VI ('a naturally quiet and contented disposition'). Here we reproduce a more general reflection on contrasts among characters, reprinted from 'Shakespear's Exact Discrimination of Nearly Similar Characters' in *The Examiner*, May 12, 1816.

During the time of the civil wars of York and Lancaster, England was a perfect bear-garden, and Shakespear has given us a very lively picture of the scene. The three parts of HENRY VI convey a picture of very little else; and are inferior to the other historical plays. They have brilliant passages; but the general ground-work is comparatively poor and meagre, the style 'flat and unraised.'

. . .

We have already observed that Shakespear was scarcely more remarkable for the force and marked contrasts of his characters than for the truth and subtlety with which he has distinguished those who approached the nearest to each other. For instance, the soul of Othello is hardly more distinct from that of Iago than that of Desdemona is shewn to be from Æmilia's; the ambition of Macbeth is as distinct from the ambition of Richard III as it is from the meekness of Duncan; the real madness of Lear is as different from the feigned madness of Edgar[1] as from the babbling of the fool; the contrast between wit and folly in Falstaff and Shallow is not more characteristic though more obvious than the gradations of folly, loquacious or reserved, in Shallow and Silence; and again, the gallantry of Prince Henry is as little confounded with that of Hotspur as with the cowardice of Falstaff, or as the sensual and philosophic cowardice of the Knight is with the pitiful and cringing cowardice of Parolles. All these several personages were as different in Shakespear as they would have been in themselves: his imagination borrowed from the life, and every circumstance, object, motive, passion, operated there as it would in reality, and produced a world of men and women as distinct, as true and as various as those that exist in nature. The peculiar property of Shakespear's imagination was this truth, accompanied with the unconsciousness of nature: indeed, imagination to be perfect must be unconscious, at least in production; for nature is so. - We shall attempt one example more in the characters of Richard II and Henry VI.

The characters and situations of both these persons were so nearly alike, that they would have been completely confounded by a commonplace poet. Yet they are kept quite distinct in Shakespear. Both were kings, and both unfortunate. Both lost their crowns owing to their mismanagement and imbecility; the one from a thoughtless, wilful abuse of power, the other from an indifference to it. The manner in which they bear their misfortunes corresponds exactly to the causes which led to them. The one is always lamenting the loss of his power which he has not the spirit to regain; the other seems only to regret that he had ever been king, and is glad to be rid of the power, with the trouble; the effeminacy of the one is that of a voluptuary, proud, revengeful, impatient of contradiction, and inconsolable in his misfortunes; the effeminacy of the other is that of an indolent, good-natured mind, naturally averse to the turmoils of ambition and the cares of greatness, and who wishes to pass this time in monkish indolence and contemplation. - Richard bewails the loss of the kingly power only as it was the means of gratifying his pride and luxury; Henry regards it only as a means of doing right, and is less desirous of the advantages to be derived from possessing it than afraid of exercising it wrong.

31. 'RICHARD III'

The opening sentence sets the tone for several of Hazlitt's stage reviews, in which he comments on the theatrical potential of *Richard III* when played by Kean. No other writer of his time wrote so much or so perceptively on this character, whom Hazlitt often compares and contrasts with Iago as studies in evil. He shows sensitivity to gesture and expression of an actor in conveying an impression. Hazlitt also indicates the way in which the text had been hacked about in Colley Cibber's acting version which held the stage until 1821.

RICHARD III may be considered as properly a stage-play: it belongs to the theatre, rather than to the closet. We shall therefore criticise it chiefly with a reference to the manner in which we have seen it performed. It is the character in which Garrick came out:[1] it was the second character in which Mr Kean appeared, and in which he acquired his fame.[2] Shakespear we have always with us: actors we have only for a few seasons; and therefore some account of them may be acceptable, if not to our contemporaries, to those who come after us, if 'the rich and idle personage, Posterity,'[3] should deign to look into our writings.

It is possible to form a higher conception of the character of Richard than that given by Mr Kean: but we cannot imagine any character represented with greater distinctness and precision, more perfectly *articulated* in every part. Perhaps indeed there is too much of what is technically called execution. When we first saw this celebrated actor in the part, we thought he sometimes failed from an exuberance of manner, and dissipated the impression of the general character by the variety of his resources. To be complete, his delineation of it should have more solidity, depth, sustained and impassioned feeling, with somewhat less brilliancy, with fewer glancing lights, pointed transitions, and pantomimic evolutions.

The Richard of Shakespear is towering and lofty; equally impetuous and commanding; haughty, violent, and subtle; bold and treacherous; confident in his strength as well as in his cunning; raised high by his birth, and higher by his talents and his crimes; a royal usurper, a princely hypocrite, a tyrant, and a murderer of the house of Platagenet.

> 'But I was born so high:
> Our aery buildeth in the cedar's top,
> And dallies with the wind, and scorns the sun.'[4]

The idea conveyed in these lines (which are indeed omitted in the miserable medley acted for RICHARD III) is never lost sight of by Shakespear, and should not be out of the actor's mind for a moment. The restless and sanguinary Richard is not a man striving to be great, but to be greater than he is; conscious of his strength of will, his power of intellect, his daring courage, his elevated station; and making use of these advantages to commit unheard-of crimes, and to shield himself from remorse and infamy.

If Mr Kean does not entirely succeed in concentrating all the lines of the character, as drawn by Shakespear, he gives an animation, vigour, and relief to the part which we have not seen equalled. He is more refined than Cooke; more bold, varied, and original than Kemble in the same character. In some parts he is deficient in dignity, and particularly in the scenes of state business, he has by no means an air of artificial authority. There is at times an aspiring elevation, an enthusiastic rapture in his expectations of attaining the crown, and at others a gloating expression of sullen delight, as if he already clenched the bauble, and held it in his grasp. The courtship scene with Lady Anne is an admirable exhibition of smooth and smiling villainy. The progress of wily adulation, of encroaching humility, is finely marked by his action, voice and eye. He seems, like the first Tempter, to approach his prey, secure of the event, and as if success had smoothed his way before him. The late Mr Cooke's manner of representing this scene was more vehement, hurried, and full of anxious uncertainty. This, though more natural in general, was less in character in this particular instance. Richard should woo less as a lover than as an actor - to shew his mental superiority, and power of making others the playthings of his purposes. Mr Kean's attitude in leaning against the side of the stage before he comes forward to address Lady Anne, is one of the most graceful and striking ever witnessed on the stage. It would do for Titian to paint. The frequent and rapid transition of his voice from the expression of the fiercest passion to the most familiar tones of conversation was that which gave a peculiar grace of novelty to his acting on his first appearance. This has been since imitated and caricatured by others, and he himself uses the artifice more sparingly than he did. His bye-play is excellent.[5] His manner of bidding his friends 'Good night,' after pausing with the point of his sword, drawn slowly backward and forward on the ground, as if considering the plan of the battle next day, is a particularly happy and natural thought. He gives to the two last acts of the play the greatest animation and effect. He fills every part of the stage; and makes up for the deficiency of his person by what has been sometimes objected to as an excess of action. The concluding scene in which he is killed by Richmond is the most brilliant of the whole. He fights at last like one drunk with wounds; and the attitude in which he stands with his hands stretched out, after his sword is wrested from him, has a preternatural and terrific grandeur, as if his will could not be disarmed, and the very phantoms of his despair had power to kill. - Mr Kean has since in a great measure effaced the impression of his Richard III by the superior efforts of his genius in Othello (his master-piece), in the murder-scene in Macbeth, in Richard II, in Sir Giles Overreach,[6] and lastly in Oroonoko;[7] but we still like to look back to his first performance of this part, both because it first assured his admirers of his future success, and because we bore our feeble but, at that time, not useless testimony to the merits of this very original actor, on which the town was considerably divided for no other reason than because they *were* original.

The manner in which Shakespear's plays have been generally altered or rather mangled by modern mechanists, is a disgrace to the English stage. The patch-work RICHARD III which acted under the sanction of his name, and which was manufactured by Cibber,[8] is a striking example of this remark.

The play itself is undoubtedly a very powerful effusion of Shakespear's genius. The ground-work of the character of Richard, that mixture of intellectual vigour with moral depravity, in which Shakespear delighted to shew his strength - gave full scope as well as temptation to the exercise of his imagination. The character of his hero is almost every where predominant, and marks its lurid track throughout. The original play is however too long for representation, and there are some few scenes which might be better spared than preserved, and by omitting which it would remain a complete whole. The only rule, indeed, for altering Shakespear is to retrench certain passages which may be considered either as superfluous or obsolete, but not to add or transpose any thing. The arrangement and development of the story, and the mutual contrast and combination of the *dramatis persona*, are in general as finely managed as the development of the characters or the expression of the passions.

. . .

To make room for these worse than needless additions, many of the most striking passages in the real play have been omitted by the foppery and ignorance of the prompt-book critics. We do not mean to insist merely on passages which are fine as poetry and to the reader, such as Clarence's dream,[9] etc. but on those which are important to the understanding of the character, and peculiarly adapted for stage-effect. We will give the following as instances among several others. The first is the scene where Richard enters abruptly to the queen and her friends to defend himself:-

[Quotes I.iii.42-58]

Nothing can be more characteristic than the turbulent pretensions to meekness and simplicity in this address. Again, the versatility and adroitness of Richard is admirably described in the following ironical conversation with Brakenbury:-

[Quotes I.i.84-102]

The feigned reconciliation of Gloucester with the queen's kinsmen is also a master-piece. One of the finest strokes in the play, and which serves to shew as much as any thing the deep, plausible manners of Richard, is the unsuspecting security of Hastings, at the very time when the former is plotting his death, and when that very appearance of cordiality and good-humour on which Hastings builds his confidence arises from Richard's consciousness of having betrayed him to his ruin. This, with the whole character of Hastings, is omitted.

Perhaps the two most beautiful passages in the original play are the farewell apostrophe of the queen to the Tower, where the children are shut up from her, and Tyrrel's description of their death. We will finish our quotations with them.

> 'Queen. Stay, yet look back with me unto the Tower;
> Pity, you ancient stones, those tender babes,
> Whom envy hath immured within your walls;
> Rough cradle for such little pretty ones,
> Rude, rugged nurse, old sullen play-fellow,
> For tender princes!'[10]

The other passage is the account of their death by Tyrrel:-

[Quotes IV.iii.4-19]

These are some of those wonderful bursts of feeling, done to the life, to the very height of fancy and nature, which our Shakespear alone could give. We do not insist on the repetition of these last passages as proper for the stage: we should indeed be loth to trust them in the mouth of almost any actor: but we should wish them to be retained in preference at least to the fantoccini[11] exhibition of the young princes, Edward and York, bandying childish wit with their uncle.

32. FROM 'HENRY VIII'

As in other accounts of History Plays, one detects Hazlitt's blistering, anti-monarchical bias.

This play contains little action or violence of passion, yet it has considerable interests of a more mild and thoughtful cast, and some of the most striking passages in the author's works. The character of Queen Katherine is the most perfect delination of matronly dignity, sweetness, and resignation, that can be conceived.

.   .   .

The character of Henry VIII is drawn with great truth and spirit. It is like a very disagreeable portrait, sketched by the hand of a master. His gross appearance, his blustering demeanour, his vulgarity, his arrogance, his sensuality, his cruelty, his hypocrisy, his want of common decency and common humanity, are marked in strong lines. His traditional peculiarities of expression complete the reality of the picture. The authoritative expletive, 'Ha!' with which he intimates his indignation or surprise, has an effect like the first startling sound that breaks from a thunder-cloud. He is of all the monarchs in our history the most disgusting: for he unites in himself all the vices of barbarism and refinement, without their virtues. Other kings before him (such as Richard III) were tyrants and murderers out of ambition or necessity: they gained or established unjust power by violent means: they destroyed their enemies, or those who barred their access to the throne or made its tenure insecure. But Henry VIII's power is most fatal to those whom he loves: he is cruel and remorseless to pamper his luxurious appetites: bloody and voluptuous; an amorous murderer; an uxorious debauchee. His hardened insensibility to the feelings of others is strengthened by the most profligate self-indulgence. The religious hypocrisy, under which he masks his cruelty and his lust, is admirably displayed in the speech in which he describes the first misgivings of his conscience and its increasing throes and terrors, which have induced him to divorce his queen. The only thing in his favour in this play is his treatment of Cranmer: there is also another circumstance in his favour, which is his patronage of Hans Holbein. - It has been said of Shakespear - 'No maid could live near such a man.'[1] It might with as good reason be said - 'No king could live near such a man.' His eye would have penetrated through the pomp of circumstance and the veil of opinion. As it is, he has represented such persons to the life - his plays are in this respect the glass of history - he has done them the same justice as if he had been a privy counsellor all his life, and in each successive reign. Kings ought never to be seen upon the stage. In the abstract, they are very disagreeable characters: it is only while living that they are 'the best of kings.'[2] It is their power, their splendour, it is the apprehension of the personal consequences of their favour or their hatred that dazzles the imagination and suspends the judgment of their favourites or their vassals; but death cancels the bond of allegiance and of interest; and seen *as they were*, their power and their pretensions look monstrous and ridiculous. The charge brought against modern philosophy as inimical to loyalty is unjust, because it might as well be brought against other things. No reader of history can be a lover of kings. We have often wondered that Henry VIII as he is drawn by Shakespear, and as we have seen him represented in all the bloated deformity of mind and person, is not hooted from the English stage.

33.   FROM 'KING JOHN'

KING JOHN is the last of the historical plays we shall have to speak of; and we are not sorry that it is. If we are to indulge our imaginations, we had rather do it upon an imaginary theme; if we are to find subjects for the exercise of our pity and terror, we prefer seeking them in fictitious danger and fictitious distress. It gives a *soreness* to our feelings of indignation or sympathy, when we know that in tracing the progress of sufferings and crimes, we are treading upon real ground, and recollect that the poet's dream 'denoted a foregone conclusion' - irrevocable ills, not conjured up by fancy, but placed beyond the reach of poetical justice. That the treachery of King John, the death of Arthur, the grief of Constance, had a real truth in history, sharpens the sense of pain, while it hangs a leaden weight on the heart and the imagination. Something whispers us that we have no right to make a mock of calamities like these, or to turn the truth of things into the puppet and plaything of our fancies. 'To consider thus' may be 'to consider too curiously';[2] but still we think that the actual truth of the particular events, in proportion as we are conscious of it, is a drawback on the pleasure as well as the dignity of tragedy.

KING JOHN has all the beauties of language and all the richness of the imagination to relieve the painfulness of the subject. The character of King John himself is kept pretty much in the background; it is only marked in by comparatively slight indications. The crimes he is tempted to commit are such as are thrust upon him rather by circumstances and opportunity than of his own seeking: he is here represented as more cowardly than cruel, and as more contemptible than odious. The play embraces only a part of his history. There are however few characters on the stage that excite more disgust and loathing. He has no intellectual grandeur or strength of character to shield him from the indignation which his immediate conduct provokes: he stands naked and defenceless, in that respect, to the worst we can think of him: and besides, we are impelled to put the very worst construction on his meanness and cruelty by the tender picture of the beauty and helplessness of the object of it, as well as by the frantic and heart-rending pleadings of maternal despair. We do not forgive him the death of Arthur, because he had too late revoked his doom and tried to prevent it; and perhaps because he has himself repented of his black design, our *moral sense* gains courage to hate him the more for it. We take him at his word, and think his purposes must be odious indeed, when he himself shrinks back from them. The scene in which King John suggests to Hubert the design of murdering his nephew is a master-piece of dramatic skill, but it is still inferior, very inferior to the scene between Hubert and Arthur, when the latter learns the orders to put out his eyes. If any thing ever was penned, heart-piercing, mixing the extremes of terror and pity, of that which shocks and that which soothes the mind, it is this scene.

.   .   .

The contrast between the mild resignation of Queen Katherine to her own wrongs, and the wild, uncontroulable affliction of Constance for the wrongs which she sustains as a mother, is no less naturally conceived than it is ably sustained throughout these two wonderful characters.

The accompaniment of the comic character of the Bastard was well chosen to relieve the poignant agony of suffering, and the cold cowardly policy of behaviour in the principal characters of this play. Its spirit, invention, volubility of tongue and forwardness in action, are unbounded. *Aliquando sufflaminandus erat*, says Ben Jonson of Shakespear.[3] But we should be sorry if Ben Jonson had been his licenser. We prefer the heedless magnanimity of his wit infinitely to all Jonson's laborious caution. The character of the Bastard's comic humour is the same in essence as that of other comic characters in Shakespear; they always run on with good things and are never exhausted; they are always daring and successful. They have words at will, and a flow of wit like a flow of animal spirits. The difference between Falconbridge and the others is that he is a soldier, and brings his wit to bear upon action, is courageous with his sword as well as tongue, and stimulates his gallantry by his jokes, his enemies feeling the sharpness of his blows and the sting of his sarcasms at the same time. Among his happiest sallies are his descanting on the composition of his own person, his invective against 'commodity, tickling commodity,'[4] and his expression of contempt for the Archduke of Austria, who had killed his father, which begins in jest but ends in serious earnest. His conduct at the siege of Angiers shews that his resources were not confined to verbal retorts. - The same exposure of the policy of courts and camps, of kings, nobles, priests, and cardinals, takes place here as in the other plays we have gone through, and we shall not go into a disgusting repetition.

This, like the other plays taken from English history, is written in a remarkably smooth and flowing style, very different from some of the tragedies, *Macbeth*, for instance. The passages consist of a series of single lines, not running into one another. This peculiarity in the versification, which is most common in the three parts of *Henry VI* has been assigned as a reason why those plays were not written by Shakespear. But the same structure of verse occurs in his other undoubted plays, as in *Richard II* and in KING JOHN.

34.   FROM 'TWELFTH NIGHT; OR, WHAT YOU WILL'

This essay reveals the analytical interest in comedy which informs the *Lectures on the English Comic Writers*, in which Hazlitt develops his distinction between 'natural' and 'artificial' comedy which almost certainly influenced Meredith. (Although the theory is not unique to Hazlitt, he develops it in a relatively original way.) The essay illustrates as well as any other in this volume Hazlitt's willingness to mingle general theory with specific comment on quotations. It illustrates also Hazlitt's preference for tragedy, and the graver effects in Shakespeare's comedies, as a reaction against Johnson, whom Hazlitt in fact misrepresents. Johnson did not say the comedies were 'better' than the tragedies but that comedy seemed more congenial to Shakespeare than tragedy: 'His tragedy seems to be skill, his comedy to be instinct' (Wimsatt, p.64).

This is justly considered as one of the most delightful of Shakespear's comedies. It is full of sweetness and pleasantry. It is perhaps too good-natured for comedy. It has little satire, and no spleen. It aims at the ludicrous rather than the ridiculous. It makes us laugh at the follies of mankind, not despise them, and still less bear any ill-will towards them. Shakespear's comic genius resembles the bee rather in its power of extracting sweets from weeds or poisons, than in leaving a sting behind it. He gives the most amusing exaggeration of the prevailing foibles of his characters, but in a way that they themselves, instead of being offended at, would almost join in to humour; he rather contrives opportunities for them to shew themselves off in the happiest lights, than renders them contemptible in the perverse construction of the wit or malice of others. - There is a certain stage of society in which people become conscious of their peculiarities and absurdities, affect to disguise what they are, and set up pretensions to what they are not. This gives rise to a corresponding style of comedy, the object of which is to detect the disguises of self-love, and to make reprisals on these preposterous assumptions of vanity, by marking the contrast between the real and the affected character as severely as possible, and denying to those, who would impose on us for what they are not, even the merit which they have. This is the comedy of artificial life, of wit and satire, such as we see it in Congreve, Wycherley, Vanbrugh, etc. To this succeeds a state of society from which the same sort of affectation and pretence are banished by a greater knowledge of the world or by their successful exposure on the stage; and which by neutralising the materials of comic character, both natural and artificial, leaves no comedy at all - but *the sentimental.* Such is our modern comedy. There is a period in the progress of manners anterior to both these, in which the foibles and follies of individuals are of nature's planting, not the growth of art or study; in which they are therefore unconscious of them themselves, or care not who knows them, if they can but have their whim out; and in which, as there is no attempt at imposition, the spectators rather receive pleasure from humouring the inclinations of the persons they laugh at, than wish to give them pain by exposing their absurdity. This may be called the comedy of nature, and it is the comedy which we generally find in Shakespear. - Whether the analysis here given be just or not, the spirit of his comedies is evidently quite distinct from that of the authors above mentioned, as it is in its essence the same with that of Cervantes, and also very frequently of Moliére, though he was more systematic in his extravagance than Shakespear. Shakespear's comedy is of a pastoral and poetical cast. Folly is indigenous to the soil, and shoots out with native, happy, unchecked luxuriance. Absurdity has every encouragement afforded it; and nonsense has room to flourish in. Nothing is stunted by the churlish, icy hand of indifference or severity. The poet runs riot in a conceit, and idolises a quibble.[1] His whole object is to turn the meanest or rudest objects to a pleasurable account. The relish which he has of a pun, or of the quaint humour of a low character, does not interfere with the delight with which he describes a beautiful image, or the most refined love. The clown's forced jests do not spoil the sweetness of the character of Viola; the same house is big enough to hold Malvolio, the Countess, Maria, Sir Toby, and Sir Andrew Ague-cheek. For instance, nothing can fall much lower than this last character in intellect or morals: yet how are his weaknesses nursed and dandled by Sir Toby into something 'high fantastical,'[2] when on Sir Andrew's commendation of himself for dancing and fencing, Sir Toby answers - 'Wherefore are these things hid? Wherefore have these gifts a curtain before them? Are they like to take dust like mistress Moll's picture? Why dost thou not go to church in a galliard, and come home in a coranto? My very walk should be a jig! I would not so much as make water but in a cinque-pace. What doest thou mean? Is this a world to hide virtues in? I did think by the excellent constitution of thy leg, it was framed under the star of a galliard!'[3] - How Sir Toby, Sir Andrew, and the Clown afterwards *chirp over their cups*, how they 'rouse the night-owl in a catch, able to draw three souls out of one weaver!'[4] What can be better than Sir Toby's unanswerable answer to Malvolio, 'Dost thou think, because thou art virtuous, there shall be no more cakes and ale?'[5] - In a word, the best turn is given to every thing, instead of the worst. There is a constant infusion of the romantic and enthusiastic, in proportion as the characters are natural and sincere: whereas, in the more artificial style of comedy, every thing gives way to ridicule and indifference, there being nothing left but affectation on one side, and incredulity on the other. - Much as we like Shakespear's comedies, we cannot agree with Dr Johnson that they are better than his tragedies;[6] nor do we like them half so well. If his inclination to comedy sometimes led him to trifle with the seriousness of tragedy, the poetical and impassioned passages are the best parts of his comedies. The great and secret charm of TWELFTH NIGHT is the character of Viola. Much as we like catches and cakes and ale, there is something that we like better. We have a friendship for Sir Toby; we patronise Sir Andrew; we have an understanding with the Clown, a sneaking kindness for Maria and her rogueries; we feel a regard for Malvolio, and sympathise with his gravity, his smiles, his cross garters, his yellow stockings, and imprisonment in the stocks. But there is something that excites in us a stronger feeling than all this - it is Viola's confession of her love.

.   .   .

We have already said something of Shakespear's songs. One of the most beautiful of them occurs in this play, with a preface of his own to it.

[Quotes II.iv.42-66 *passim*]

Who after this will say that Shakespear's genius was only fitted for comedy? Yet after reading other parts of this play, and particularly the garden-scene where Malvolio picks up the letter, if we were to say that his genius for comedy was less than his genius for tragedy, it would perhaps only prove that our own taste in such matters is more saturnine than mercurial.

35.   FROM 'THE TWO GENTLEMEN OF VERONA'

This is little more than the first outlines of a comedy loosely sketched in. It is the story of a novel dramatised with very little labour or pretension; yet there are passages of high poetical spirit, and of inimitable quaintness of humour, which are undoubtedly Shakespear's, and there is throughout the conduct of the fable and careless grace and felicity which marks it for his.

.   .   .

The tender scenes in this play, though not so highly wrought as in some others, have often much sweetness of sentiment and expression. There is something pretty and playful in the conversation of Julia with her maid, when she shews such a disposition to coquetry about receiving the letter from Proteus; and her behaviour afterwards and her disappointment, when she finds him faithless to his vows, remind us at a distance of Imogen's tender constancy. Her answer to Lucetta, who advises her against following her lover in disguise, is a beautiful piece of poetry.

> 'Lucetta.   I do not seek to quench your love's hot fire,
>
>   But qualify the fire's extremest rage,
>
>   Lest it should burn above the bounds of reason.
>
> Julia.   The more thou damm'st it up, the more it burns,
>
>   The current that with gentle murmur glides,
>
>   Thou know'st, being stopp'd, impatiently doth rage;
>
>   But when his fair course is not hindered,
>
>   He makes sweet music with th' enamell'd stones,
>
>   Giving a gentle kiss to every sedge
>
>   He overtaketh in his pilgrimage:
>
>   And so by many winding nooks he strays,
>
>   With willing sport, to the wild ocean.[1]

>   Then let me go, and hinder not my course;
>
>   I'll be as patient as a gentle stream,
>
>   And make a pastime of each weary step,
>
>   Till the last step have brought me to my love,
>
>   And there I'll rest, as after much turmoil,
>
>   A blesed soul doth in Elysium.'[2]

If Shakespear indeed had written only this and other passages in the TWO GENTLEMEN OF VERONA, he would *almost* have deserved Milton's praise of him-

> 'And sweetest Shakespear, Fancy's child,
>
> Warbles his native wood-notes wild.'[3]

But as it is, he deserves rather more praise than this.

36.   FROM 'THE MERCHANT OF VENICE'

Hazlitt deserves a place in the history of criticism of Shylock, a character in whom Charles Lamb was also very interested. The phrase 'Shylock is a good hater' is memorable and calculatedly ambivalent, glossed by the sentence 'There is a strong, quick, and deep sense of justice mixed up with the gall and bitterness of his resentment'. Some biographers have been tempted to see this as a fair comment on Hazlitt himself. We reproduce only the analysis of Shylock, since the rest of the essay is relatively perfunctory, and Hazlitt admits that Portia is 'no great favourite' of his.

This is a play that in spite of the change of manners and prejudices still holds undisputed possession of the stage. Shakespear's malignant has outlived Mr. Cumberland's benevolent Jew.[1] In the proportion as Shylock has ceased to be a popular bugbear, 'baited with the rabble's curse,'[2] he becomes a half-favourite with the philosophical part of the audience, who are disposed to think that Jewish revenge is at least as good as Christian injuries. Shylock is a *good hater;* 'a man no less sinned against than sinning.'[3] If he carried his revenge too far, yet he has strong grounds for 'the lodged hate he bears Anthonio,' [4] which he explains with equal force of eloquence and reason. He seems the depositary of the vengeance of his race; and though the long habit of brooding over daily insults and injuries has crusted over his temper with inveterate misanthropy, and hardened him against the contempt of mankind, this adds but little to the triumphant pretensions of his enemies. There is a strong, quick, and deep sense of justice mixed up with the gall and bitterness of his resentment. The constant apprehension of being burnt alive, plundered, banished, reviled, and trampled on, might be supposed to sour the most forbearing nature, and to take something from that 'milk of human kindness,'[5] with which his persecutors contemplated his indignities. The desire of revenge is almost inseparable from the sense of wrong; and we can hardly help sympathising with the proud spirit, hid beneath his 'Jewish gaberdine,'[6] stung to madness by repeated undeserved provocations, and labouring to throw off the load of obloquy and oppression heaped upon him and all his tribe by one desperate act of 'lawful' revenge, till the ferociousness of the means by which he is to execute his purpose, and the pertinacity with which he adheres to it, turns us against him; but even at last, when disappointed of the sanguinary revenge with which he had glutted his hopes, and exposed to beggary and contempt by the letter of the law on which he had insisted with so little remorse, we pity him, and think him hardly dealt with by his judges. In all his answers and retorts upon his adversaries, he has the best not only of the argument but of the question, reasoning on their own principles and practice. They are so far from allowing of any measure of equal dealing, of common justice or humanity between themselves and the Jew, that even when they come to ask a favour of him, and Shylock reminds them that 'on such a day they spit upon him, another spurned him, another called him dog,· and for these curtesies request he'll lend them so much monies'7- Anthonio, his old enemy, instead of any acknowledgment of the shrewdness and justice of his remonstrance, which would have been preposterous in a respectable Catholic merchant in those times, threatens him with a repetition of the same treatment-

'I am as like to call thee so again,
To spit on thee again, to spurn thee too.'8

After this, the appeal to the Jew's mercy, as if there were any common principle of right and wrong between them, is the rankest hypocrisy, or the blindest prejudice; and the Jew's answer to one of Anthonio's friends, who asks him what his pound of forfeit flesh is good for, is irresistible-

[Quotes III.i.53-73]

The whole of the trial-scene, both before and after the entrance of Portia, is a master-piece of dramatic skill. The legal acuteness, the passionate declamations, the sound maxims of jurisprudence, the wit and irony interspersed in it, the fluctuations of hope and fear in the different persons, and the completeness and suddenness of the catastrophe, cannot be surpassed, Shylock, who is his own counsel, defends himself well, and is triumphant on all the general topics that are urged against him, and only fails through a legal flaw.

. . .

The keenness of his revenge awakes all his faculties; and he beats back all opposition to his purpose, whether grave or gay, whether of wit or argument, with an equal degree of earnestness and self-possession. His character is displayed as distinctly in other less prominent parts of the play, and we may collect from a few sentences the history of his life - his descent and origin, his thrift and domestic economy, his affection for his daughter, whom he loves next to his wealth, his courtship and his first present to Leah, his wife! 'I would not have parted with it' (the ring which he first gave her) 'for a wilderness of monkies!'[9] What a fine Hebraism is implied in this expression![10]

.   .   .

When we first went to see Mr. Kean in Shylock, we expected to see, what we had been used to see, a decrepid old man, bent with age and ugly with mental deformity, grinning with deadly malice, with the venom of his heart congealed in the expression of his countenance, sullen, morose, gloomy, inflexible, brooding over one idea, that of his hatred, and fixed on one unalterable purpose, that of his revenge.[11] We were disappointed, because we had taken our idea from other actors, not from the play. There is no proof there that Shylock is old, but a single line, 'Bassanio and *old* Shylock, both stand forth,'[12] - which does not imply that he is infirm with age - and the circumstance that he has a daughter marriageable, which does not imply that he is old at all. It would be too much to say that his body should be made crooked and deformed to answer to his mind, which is bowed down and warped with prejudices and passion. That he has but one idea, is not true; he has more ideas than any other person in the piece; and if he is intense and inveterate in the pursuit of his purpose, he shows the utmost elasticity, vigour, and presence of mind, in the means of attaining it. But so rooted was our habitual impression of the part from seeing it caricatured in the representation, that it was only from a careful perusal of the play itself that we saw our error. The stage is not in general the best place to study our author's characters in. It is too often filled with traditional common-place conceptions of the part, handed down from sire to son, and suited to the taste of *the great vulgar and the small.*-' 'Tis an unweeded garden; things rank and gross do merely gender in it!'[13] If a man of genius comes once in an age to clear away the rubbish, to make it fruitful and wholesome, they cry, 'Tis a bad school: it may be like nature, it may be like Shakespear, but it is not like us.' Admirable critics!

37.   FROM 'THE WINTER'S TALE'

An otherwise rather inconsequential essay is distinguished by a passage on the style of Leontes' early speeches which shows that Hazlitt's metaphorical technique can be effective as 'close criticism'.

We wonder that Mr. Pope should have entertained doubts of the genuineness of this play. He was, we suppose, shocked (as a certain critic suggests)[1] at the Chorus, Time, leaping over sixteen years with his crutch between the third and fourth act, and at Antigonus's landing with the infant Perdita on the sea-coast of Bohemia. These slips or blemishes however do not prove it not to be Shake-spear's; for his was as likely to fall into them as any body; but we do not know any body but himself who could produce the beauties. The *stuff* of which the tragic passion is composed, the romantic sweetness, the comic humour, are evidently his. Even the crabbed and tortuous style of the speeches of Leontes, reasoning of his own jealousy, beset with doubts and fears, and entangled more and more in the thorny labyrinth, bears every mark of Shakespear's peculiar manner of conveying the painful struggle of different thoughts and feelings, labouring for utterance, and almost strangled in the birth. For instance:-

> 'Ha' not you seen, Camillo?
> (But that's past doubt; you have, or your eye-glass
> Is thicker than a cuckold's horn) or heard,
> (For to a vision so apparent, rumour
> Cannot be mute) or thought (for cogitation
> Resides not within man that does not think)
> My wife is slippery? If thou wilt, confess,
> Or else be impudently negative,
> To have nor eyes, nor ears, nor thought.'[2]

Here Leontes is confounded with his passion, and does not know which way to turn himself, to give words to the anguish, rage, and apprehension, which tug at his breast. It is only as he is worked up into a clearer conviction of his wrongs by insisting on the grounds of his unjust suspicions to Camillo, who irritates him by his opposition, that he bursts out into the following vehement strain of bitter indignation: yet even here his passion staggers, and is as it were oppressed with its own intensity.

> 'Is whispering nothing?
> Is leaning cheek to cheek? is meeting noses?
> Kissing with inside lip? stopping the career
> Of laughter with a sigh? (a note infallible

Of breaking honesty!) horsing foot on foot?
Skulking in corners? wishing clocks more swift?
Hours, minutes? the noon, midnight? and all eyes
Blind with the pin and web, but theirs; theirs only,
That would, unseen, be wicked? is this nothing?
Why then the world, and all that's in't, is nothing,
The covering sky is nothing, Bohemia's nothing,
My wife is nothing!'[3]

38.   FROM 'ALL'S WELL THAT ENDS WELL'

Hazlitt's admiration for *All's Well*, proclaimed in the first sentence, stems from his taste for
'serious' comedy (*Twelfth Night*), and from his fondness for the kind of Shakespearean heroine
represented by Helena, the strong but demure woman who shares some attributes with Imogen.
However, he does little to justify his judgment of the play, since the second half of the essay is
taken up with praise for the source-story in Boccaccio.

All's Well That Ends Well is one of the most pleasing of our author's comedies.
The interest is however more of a serious than of a comic nature. The character of
Helen is one of great sweetness and delicacy. She is placed in circumstances of the
most critical kind, and has to court her husband both as a virgin and a wife: yet the
most scrupulous nicety of female modesty is not once violated. There is not one
thought or action that ought to bring a blush into her cheeks, or that for a moment
lessens her in our esteem. Perhaps the romantic attachment of a beautiful and
virtuous girl to one placed above her hopes by the circumstances of birth and
fortune, was never so exquisitely expressed as in the reflections which she utters
when young Roussillon leaves his mother's house, under whose protection she has
been brought up with him, to repair to the French king's court.

[Quotes I.i.79-98]

The interest excited by this beautiful picture of a fond and innocent heart is kept
up afterwards by her resolution to follow him to France, the success of her
experiment in restoring the king's health, her demanding Bertram in marriage as a
recompense, his leaving her in disdain, her interview with him afterwards
disguised as Diana, a young lady whom he importunes with his secret addresses,

and their final reconciliation when the consequences of her stratagem and the proofs of her love are fully made known. The persevering gratitude of the French king to his benefactress, who cures him of a languishing distemper by a prescription hereditary in her family, the indulgent kindness of the Countess, whose pride of birth yields, almost without a struggle, to her affection for Helen, the honesty and uprightness of the good old lord Lafeu, make very interesting parts of the picture. The wilful stubbornness and youthful petulance of Bertram are also very admirably described. The comic part of the play turns on the folly, boasting and cowardice of Parolles, a parasite and hanger-on of Bertram's, the detection of whose false pretensions to bravery and honour forms a very amusing episode. He is first found out by the old lord Lafeu, who says, 'The soul of this man is in his clothes'[1]; and it is proved afterwards that his heart is in his tongue, and that both are false and hollow. The adventure of 'the bringing off of his drum'[2] has become proverbial as a satire on all ridiculous and blustering undertakings which the person never means to perform: nor can any thing by more severe than what one of the bye-standers remarks upon what Parolles says of himself, 'Is it possible he should know what he is, and be that he is?'[3] Yet Parolles himself gives the best solution of the difficulty afterwards when he is thankful to escape with his life and the loss of character; for, so that he can live on, he is by no means squeamish about the loss of pretensions, to which he had assumed only as a means to live.

[Quotes IV.iii.330-40]

The story of All's Well That Ends Well, and of several others of Shakespear's plays, is taken from Boccacio. The poet has dramatised the original novel with great skill and comic spirit, and has preserved all the beauty of character and sentiment without *improving upon* it, which was impossible. There is indeed in Boccacio's serious pieces a truth, a pathos, and an exquisite refinement of sentiment, which is hardly to be met with in any other prose writer whatever. Justice has not been done him by the world.

39.   FROM 'LOVE'S LABOUR'S LOST'

If we were to part with any of the author's comedies, it should be this. Yet we should be loth to part with Don Adriano de Armado, that mighty potentate of nonsense, or his page, that handful of wit; with Nathaniel the curate, or Holofernes the school-master, and their dispute after dinner on 'the golden cadences of poesy'; with Costard the clown, or Dull the constable. Biron is too accomplished a character to be lost to the world, and yet he could not appear without his fellow courtiers and the king: and if we were to leave out the ladies, the gentlemen would have no mistresses. So that we believe we may let the whole play stand as it is, and we shall hardly venture to 'set a mark of reprobation on it.'[1] Still we have some objections to the style, which we think savours more of the pedantic spirit of Shakespear's time than of his own genius; more of the controversial divinity, and the logic of Peter Lombard,[2] than of the inspiration of the Muse. It transports us quite as much to the manners of the court, and the quirks of courts of law, as to the scenes of nature or the fairy-land of his imagination. Shakespear has set himself to imitate the tone of polite conversation then prevailing among the fair, the witty, and the learned, and he has imitated it but too faithfully. It is as if the hand of Titian had been employed to give grace to the curls of a full-bottomed periwig, or Raphael had attempted to give expression to the tapestry figures in the House of Lords. Shakespear has put an excellent description of this fashionable jargon into the mouth of the critical Holofernes 'as too picked, too spruce, too affected, too odd, as it were, too peregrinate, as I may call it'[3]; and nothing can be more marked than the difference when he breaks loose from the trammels he had imposed on himself, 'as light as bird from brake,'[4] and speaks in his own person. We think, for instance, that in the following soliloquy the poet has fairly got the start of Queen Elizabeth and her maids of honour:-

[Quotes III.i.174-205]

40 FROM 'MUCH ADO ABOUT NOTHING'

The essay ends with a lighthearted but scathing jibe at authority in Hazlitt's own time.

This admirable comedy used to be frequently acted till of late years. Mr Garrick's Benedick was one of his most celebrated characters; and Mrs Jordan, we have understood, played Beatrice very delightfully. The serious part is still the most prominent here, as in other instances that we have noticed. Hero is the principal figure in the piece, and leaves an indelible impression on the mind by her beauty, her tenderness, and the hard trial of her love.

.   .   .

The principal comic characters in Much Ado About Nothing, Benedick and Beatrice, are both essences in their kind. His character as a woman-hater is admirably supported, and his conversion to matrimony is no less happily effected by the pretended story of Beatrice's love for him. It is hard to say which of the two scenes is the best, that of the trick which is thus practised on Benedick, or that in which Beatrice is prevailed on to take pity on him by overhearing her cousin and her maid declare (which they do on purpose) that he is dying of love for her.

.   .   .

These were happy materials for Shakespear to work on, and he has made a happy use of them. Perhaps that middle point of comedy was never more nicely hit in which the ludicrous blends with the tender, and our follies, turning around against themselves in support of our affections, retain nothing but their humanity.

Dogberry and Verges in this play are inimitable specimens of quaint blundering and misprisions of meaning; and are a standing record of that formal gravity of pretension and total want of common understanding, which Shakespear no doubt copied from real life, and which in the course of two hundred years appear to have ascended from the lowest to the highest offices in the state.

41.   FROM 'AS YOU LIKE IT'

Hazlitt's comments on Jaques are consistent with his repeated preference for the serious side of Shakespearean comedy. His statement 'It is not what is done, but what is said, that claims our attention' has been tacitly accepted by most modern critics of the play.

Shakespear has here converted the forest of Arden into another Arcadia, where they 'fleet the time carelessly, as they did in the golden world.'[1] It is the most ideal of any of this author's plays. It is a pastoral drama, in which the interest arises more out of the sentiments and characters than out of the actions or situations. It is not what is done, but what is said, that claims our attention. Nursed in solitude, 'under the shade of melancholy boughs,'[2] the imagination grows soft and delicate, and the wit runs riot in idleness, like a spoiled child, that is never sent to school. Caprice and fancy reign and revel here, and stern necessity is banished to the court. The mild sentiments of humanity are strengthened with thought and leisure; the echo of the cares and noise of the world strikes upon the ear of those 'who have felt them knowingly,'[3] softened by time and distance. 'They hear the tumult, and are still.'[4] The very air of the place seems to breathe a spirit of philosophical poetry: to stir the thoughts, to touch the heart with pity, as the drowsy forest rustles to the sighing gale. Never was there such beautiful moralising, equally free from pedantry or petulance.

> 'And this their life, exempt from public haunts,
> Finds tongues in trees, books in the running brooks,
> Sermons in stones, and good in every thing.'[5]

Jaques is the only purely contemplative character in Shakespear. He thinks, and does nothing. His whole occupation is to amuse his mind, and he is totally regardless of his body and his fortunes. He is the prince of philosophical idlers; his only passion is thought; he sets no value upon any thing but as it serves as food for reflection. He can 'suck melancholy out of a song, as a weasel sucks eggs';[6] the motley fool, 'who morals on the time,'[7] is the greatest prize he meets with in the forest. He resents Orlando's passion for Rosalind as some disparagement of his own passion for abstract truth; and leaves the Duke, as soon as he is restored to his sovereignty, to seek his brother out who has quitted it, and turned hermit.

> -'Out of these convertites
> There is much matter to be heard and learnt.'[8]

Within the sequestered and romantic glades of the forest of Arden, they find leisure to be good and wise, or to play the fool and fall in love. Rosalind's character is made up of sportive gaiety and natural tenderness: her tongue runs the faster to conceal the pressure at her heart. She talks herself out of breath, only to get deeper in love. The coquetry with which she plays with her lover in the double character which she has to support is managed with the nicest address. How full of voluble, laughing grace is all her conversation with Orlando-

> -'In heedless mazes running
> With wanton haste and giddy cunning.'[9]

How full of real fondness and pretended cruelty is her answer to him when he promises to love her 'For ever and a day!'[10]

[Quotes IV.i.146-58]

The silent and retired character of Celia is a necessary relief to the provoking loquacity of Rosalind, nor can anything be better conceived or more beautifully described than the mutual affection between the two cousins:-

> -'We still have slept together,
>
> Rose at an instant, learn'd, play'd, eat together,
>
> And wheresoe'r we went, like Juno's swans,
>
> Still we went coupled and inseparable.'[11]

The unrequited love of Silvius for Phebe shews the perversity of this passion in the commonest scenes of life, and the rubs and stops which nature throws in its way, where fortune has placed none. Touchstone is not in love, but he will have a mistress as a subject for the exercise of his grotesque humour, and to shew his contempt for the passion, by his indifference about the person. He is a rare fellow. He is a mixture of the ancient cynic philosopher with the modern buffoon, and turns folly into wit, and wit into folly, just as the fit takes him. His courtship of Audrey not only throws a degree of ridicule on the state of wedlock itself, but he is equally an enemy to the prejudices of opinion in other respects. The lofty tone of enthusiasm, which the Duke and his companions in exile spread over the stillness and solitude of the country life, receives a pleasant shock from Touchstone's sceptical determination of the question.

> 'Corin. And how like you this shepherd's life, Mr Touchstone?
>
> Clown. Truly, shepherd, in respect of itself, it is a good life; but in respect that it is a shepherd's life, it is naught. In respect that it is solitary, I like it very well; but in respect that it is private, it is a very vile life. Now in respect it is in the fields, it pleaseth me well; but in respect it is not in the court, it is tedious. As it is a spare life, look you, it fits my humour; but as there is no more plenty in it, it goes much against my stomach.'[12]

42. FROM 'THE TAMING OF THE SHREW'

The Taming Of The Shrew is almost the only one of Shakespear's comedies that has a regular plot, and downright moral. It is full of bustle, animation, and rapidity of action. It shews admirably how self-will is only to be got the better of by stronger will, and how one degree of ridiculous perversity is only to be driven out by another still greater. Petruchio is a madman in his senses; a very honest fellow, who hardly speaks a word of truth, and succeeds in all his tricks and impostures. He acts his assumed character to the life with the most fantastical extravagance, with complete presence of mind, with untired animal spirits, and without a particle of ill humour from beginning to end. - The situation of poor Katherine, worn out by his incessant persecutions, becomes at last almost as pitiable as it is ludicrous, and it is difficult to say which to admire most, the unaccountableness of his actions, or the unalterableness of his resolutions.

.   .   .

The most striking and at the same time laughable feature in the character of Petruchio throughout, is the studied approximation to the intractable character of real madness, his apparent insensibility to all external considerations, and utter indifference to every thing but the wild extravagant freaks of his own self-will. There is no contending with a person on whom nothing makes any impression but his own purposes, and who is bent on his own whims just in proportion as they seem to want common sense. With him a thing's being plain and reasonable is a reason against it. The airs he gives himself are infinite, and his caprices as sudden as they are groundless. The whole of his treatment of his wife at home is in the same spirit of ironical attention and inverted gallantry. Every thing flies before his will, like a conjurer's wand, and he only metamorphoses his wife's temper by metamorphosing her senses and all the objects she sees, at a word's speaking. Such are his insisting that it is the moon and not the sun which they see, etc. This extravagance reaches its most pleasant and poetical height in the scene where, on their return to her father's, they meet old Vincentio, whom Petruchio immediately addresses as a young lady:-

[Quotes IV.v.27-48]

The whole is carried off with equal spirit, as if the poet's comic Muse had wings of fire. It is strange how one man could be so many things; but so it is.

The Taming Of The Shrew is a play within a play. It is supposed to be a play acted for the benefit of Sly the tinker, who is made to believe himself a lord, when he wakes after a drunken brawl. The character of Sly and the remarks with which he accompanies the play are as good as the play itself. His answer when he is asked how he likes it, 'Indifferent well; 'tis a good piece of work, would 'twere done,'[1] is in good keeping, as if he were thinking of his Saturday night's job. Sly does not change his tastes with his new situation, but in the midst of splendour and luxury still calls out lustily and repeatedly 'for a pot o' the smallest ale.'[2] He is very slow in giving up his personal identity in his sudden advancement. 'I am Christopher Sly, call not me honour nor lordship. I ne'er drank sack in my life: and if you give me any conserves, give me conserves of beef: ne'er ask me what raiment I'll wear, for I have no more doublets than backs, no more stockings than legs, nor no more shoes than feet, nay, sometimes more feet than shoes, or such shoes as my toes look through the over-leather. - What, would you make me mad? Am not I Christophero Sly, old Sly's son of Burton-heath, by birth a pedlar, by education a card-maker, by transmutation a bear-herd, and now by present profession a tinker? Ask Marian Hacket, the fat alewife of Wincot, if she know me not; if she say I am not fourteen-pence on the score of sheer ale, score me up for the lying'st knave in Christendom.[3] This is honest. 'The Slies are no rogues,'[4] as he says of himself. We have a great predilection for this representative of the family; and what makes us like him the better is, that we take him to be of kin (not many degrees removed) to Sancho Panza.[5]

43.   FROM 'MEASURE FOR MEASURE'

Long before the term 'problem comedy' had been coined by F.S. Boas in 1896, Hazlitt clarified the problematic nature of *Measure for Measure* when he said 'there may be said to be a general system of cross-purposes between the feelings of the different characters and the sympathy of the reader or the audience'. Hazlitt's resolution of the problem lies in his perception of Shakespeare's apparently endless tolerance of idiosyncrasies, and his understanding of the sources for human behaviour. The assessment of the ethical status of each character (e.g. the Duke) made by Hazlitt is extremely balanced, and shines with sanity when set beside many modern critiques.

This is a play as full of genius as it is of wisdom. Yet there is an original sin in the nature of the subject, which prevents us from taking a cordial interest in it. 'The height of moral argument,'[1] which the author has maintained in the intervals of passion or blended with the more powerful impulses of nature, is hardly surpassed in any of his plays. But there is in general a want of passion; the affections are at a stand; our sympathies are repulsed and defeated in all directions. The only passion which influences the story is that of Angelo; and yet he seems to have a much greater passion for hypocrisy than for his mistress. Neither are we greatly enamoured of Isabella's rigid chastity, though she could not act otherwise than she did. We do not feel the same confidence in the virtue that is 'sublimely good'[2] at another's expense, as if it had been put to some less disinterested trial. As to the Duke, who makes a very imposing and mysterious stage-character, he is more absorbed in his own plots and gravity than anxious for the welfare of the state; more tenacious of his own character than attentive to the feelings and apprehensions of others. Claudio is the only person who feels naturally; and yet he is placed in circumstances of distress which almost preclude the wish for his deliverance. Mariana is also in love with Angelo, whom we hate. In this respect, there may be said to be a general system of cross-purposes between the feelings of the different characters and the sympathy of the reader or the audience. This principle of repugnance seems to have reached its height in the character of Master Barnardine, who not only sets at defiance the opinions of others, but has even thrown off all self regard, -' one that apprehends death no more dreadfully but as a drunken sleep; careless, reckless, and fearless of what's past, present, and to come.'[3] He is a fine antithesis to the morality and the hypocrisy of the other characters of the play. Barnardine is Caliban transported from Prospero's wizard island to the forests of Bohemia or the prisons of Vienna. He is the creature of bad habits as Caliban is of gross instincts. He has however a strong notion of the natural fitness of things, according to his own sensations - 'He has been drinking hard all night, and he will not be hanged that day'[4] - and Shakespear has let him off at last. We do not understand why the philosophical German critic, Schlegel, should be so severe on those pleasant persons, Lucio, Pompey, and Master Froth, as to call them 'wretches.' They appear all mighty comfortable in their occupations, and determined to pursue them, 'as the flesh and fortune should serve.'[5] A very good exposure of the want of self-knowledge and contempt for others, which is so common in the world, is put into the mouth of Abhorson, the jailer, when the Provost purposes to associate Pompey with him in his office - 'A bawd, sir? Fie upon him, he will discredit our mystery.' And the same answer will serve in nine instances out of ten to the same kind of remark, 'Go to, sir, you weigh equally; a feather will turn the scale.'[6] Shakespear was in one sense the least moral of all writers; for morality (commonly so called) is made up of antipathies; and his talent consisted in sympathy with human nature, in all its shapes, degrees, depressions, and elevations. The object of the pedantic moralist is to find out the bad in everything: his was to shew that 'there is some soul of goodness in things evil.'[7] Even Master Barnardine is not left to the mercy of what others think of him; but when he comes in, speaks for himself, and pleads his own cause, as well as if counsel had been assigned him. In one sense, Shakespear was no moralist at all: in another, he was the greatest of all moralists. He was a moralist in the same sense in which nature is one. He taught what he had learnt from her. He shewed the greatest knowledge of humanity with the greatest fellow-feeling for it.

One of the most dramatic passages in the present play is the interview between Claudio and his sister, when she comes to inform him of the conditions on which Angelo will spare his life.

44.   FROM 'THE MERRY WIVES OF WINDSOR'

The extract chosen for selection focuses on Falstaff, but it is worth adding the comment on Slender ('a very potent piece of imbecility'): 'Shakespear is the only writer who was as great in describing weakness as strength.'

THE MERRY WIVES OF WINDSOR is no doubt a very amusing play, with a great deal of humour, character, and nature in it: but we should have liked it much better, if any one else had been the hero of it, instead of Falstaff. We could have been contented if Shakespear had not been 'commanded to shew the knight in love.'[1] Wits and philosophers, for the most part, do not shine in that character; and Sir John himself, by no means, comes off with flying colours. Many people complain of the degradation and insults to which Don Quixote is so frequently exposed in his various adventures. But what are the unconscious indignities which he suffers, compared with the sensible mortifications which Falstaff is made to bring upon himself? What are the blows and buffetings which the Don receives from the staves of the Yanguesian carriers or from Sancho Panza's more hard-

hearted hands,[2] compared with the contamination of the buck-basket, the disguise
of the fat woman of Brentford, and the horns of Herne the hunter, which are
discovered on Sir John's head? In reading the play, we indeed wish him well
through all these discomfitures, but it would have been as well if he had not got
into them. Falstaff in *THE MERRY WIVES OF WINDSOR* is not the man he was
in the two parts of *Henry IV*. His wit and eloquence have left him. Instead of
making a butt of others, he is made a butt of by them. Neither is there a single
particle of love in him to excuse his follies: he is merely a designing, bare-faced
knave, and an unsuccessful one. The scene with Ford as Master Brook, and that
with Simple, Slender's man, who comes to ask after the Wise Woman, are almost
the only ones in which his old intellectual ascendancy appears. He is like a person
recalled to the stage to perform an unaccustomed and ungracious part; and in which
we perceive only 'some faint sparks of those flashes of merriment, that were wont
to set the hearers in a roar.'[3] But the single scene with Doll Tearsheet, or Mrs
Quickly's account of his desiring 'to eat some of housewife Keach's prawns,' and
telling her 'to be no more so familiarity with such people,'[4] is worth the whole of
THE MERRY WIVES OF WINDSOR put together.

45.   'THE COMEDY OF ERRORS'

Noting that Shakespear has faithfully followed his source, the *Menaechmi* of Plautus, Hazlitt
observes regretfully that the dramatist 'soared longest and best on unborrowed plumes'. He
comments that 'The only passage of a very Shakespearian cast in this comedy is the one in which
the Abbess, with admirable characteristic artifice, makes Adriana confess her own misconduct in
driving her husband mad' (quotes V.i.44-90).

46.   'DOUBTFUL PLAYS OF SHAKESPEAR'

It is true that Shakespear's best works are very superior to those of Marlow, or
Heywood, but it is not true that the best of the doubtful plays above enumerated are
superior or even equal to the best of theirs. *The Yorkshire Tragedy*, which
Schlegel speaks of as an undoubted production of our author's, is much more in
the manner of Heywood than of Shakespear. The effect is indeed overpowering,

but the mode of producing it is by no means poetical. The praise which Schlegel gives to *Thomas, Lord Cromwell*, and to *Sir John Oldcastle*, is altogether exaggerated. They are very indifferent compositions, which have not the slightest pretensions to rank with *Henry V.* or *Henry VIII.* We suspect that the German critic was not very well acquainted with the dramatic contemporaries of Shakespear, or aware of their general merits; and that he accordingly mistakes a resemblance in style and manner for an equal degree of excellence. Shakespear differed from the other writers of his age not in the mode of treating his subjects, but in the grace and power which he displayed in them. The reason assigned by a literary friend of Schlegel's for supposing *The Puritan; or, the Widow of Watling Street*, to be Shakespear's, viz. that it is in the style of Ben Jonson, that is to say, in a style just the reverse of his own, is not very satisfactory to a plain English understanding. *Locrine*, and *The London Prodigal,* if they were Shakespear's at all, must have been among the sins of his youth. *Arden of Feversham* contains several striking passages, but the passion which they express is rather that of a sanguine temperament than of a lofty imagination; and in this respect they approximate more nearly to the style of other writers of the time than of Shakespear's. *Titus Andronicus* is certainly as unlike Shakespear's usual style as it is possible. It is an accumulation of vulgar physical horrors, in which the power exercised by the poet bears no proportion to the repugnance excited by the subject. The character of Aaron the Moor is the only thing which shews any originality of conception; and the scene in which he expresses his joy 'at the blackness and ugliness of his child begot in adultery,'[1] the only one worthy of Shakespear. Even this is worthy of him only in the display of power, for it gives no pleasure. Shakespear managed these things differently. Nor do we think it a sufficient answer to say that this was an embryo or crude production of the author. In its kind it is full grown, and its features decided and overcharged. It is not like a first imperfect essay, but shews a confirmed habit, a systematic preference of violent effect to everything else. There are occasional detached images of great beauty and delicacy, but these were not beyond the powers of other writers then living. The circumstance which inclines us to reject the external evidence in favour of this play being Shakespear's is, that the grammatical construction is constantly false and mixed up with vulgar abbreviations, a fault that never occurs in any of his genuine plays. A similar defect, and the halting measure of the verse are the chief objections to *Pericles of Tyre*, if we except the far-fetched and complicated absurdity of the story. The movement of the thoughts and passions has something in it not unlike Shakespear, and several of the descriptions are either the original hints of passages which Shakespear has ingrafted on his other plays. The most memorable idea in it is in Marina's speech, where she compares the world to 'a lasting storm, hurrying her from her friends.'[2]

47.   FROM 'POEMS AND SONNETS'

Although Hazlitt was out of sympathy with Shakespeare's non-dramatic verse, the reasons are interesting since he believes the writer's real talent lay in inhabiting dramatic characters rather than expressing his own personal feelings and ideas.

Our idolatry of Shakespear (not to say our admiration) ceases with his plays. In his other productions, he was a mere author, though not a common author. It was only by representing others, that he became himself. He could go out of himself, and express the soul of Cleopatra; but in his own person, he appeared to be always waiting for the prompter's cue. In expressing the thoughts of others, he seems inspired; in expressing his own, he was a mechanic. The licence of an assumed character was necessary to restore his genius to the privileges of fashion, the trammels of custom. In his plays, he was 'as broad and casing as the general air'[1]: in his poems, on the contrary, he appears to be 'cooped, and cabined in'[2] by all the technicalities of art, by all the petty intricacies of thought and language, which poetry had learned from the controversial jargon of the schools, where words had been made a substitute for things. There was, if we mistake not, something of modesty, and a painful sense of personal propriety at the bottom of this. Shakespear's imagination, by identifying itself with the strongest characters in the most trying circumstances, grapples at once with nature, and trampled the littleness of art under his feet: the rapid changes of situation, the wide range of the universe, gave him life and spirit, and afforded full scope to his genius; but returned into his closet again, and having assumed the badge of his profession, he could only labour in his vocation, and conform himself to existing models. The thoughts, the passions, the words which the poet's pen, 'glancing from heaven to earth, from earth to heaven,'[3] lent to others, shook off the fetters of pedantry and affectation; while his own thoughts and feelings, standing by themselves, were seized upon as lawful prey, and tortured to death according to the established rules and practice of the day. In a word, we do not like Shakespear's poems, because we like his plays: the one, in all their excellencies, are just the reverse to the other. It has been the fashion of late to cry up our author's poems, as equal to his plays: this is the desperate cant of modern criticism.[4] We would ask, was there the slightest comparison between Shakespear, and either Chaucer or Spenser, as mere poets? Not any. - The two poems of Venus and Adonis and of Tarquin and Lucrece appear to us like a couple of ice-houses. They are about as hard, as glittering, and as cold. The author seems all the time to be thinking of his verses, and not of his subject, - not of what his characters would feel, but of what he shall say; and as it must happen in all such cases, he always puts into their mouths those things which they would be the last to think of, and which it shews the greatest ingenuity in him to find out. The whole is laboured, up-hill work. The poet is perpetually singling out the difficulties of the art to make an exhibition of his strength and skill in wrestling with them. He is making perpetual trials of them as if his mastery over them were doubted. The images, which are often striking, are generally applied to things which they are the least like: so that they do not blend with the poem, but seem stuck upon it, like splendid patch-work, or remain quite distinct from it, like detached substances, painted and varnished over. A beautiful thought is sure to be lost in an endless commentary upon it. The speakers are like persons who have both leisure and inclination to make riddles on their own situation, and to twist and turn every object or incident into acrostics and anagrams. Everything is spun out into allegory; and a digression is always preferred to the main story. Sentiment is built up upon plays of words; the hero or heroine feels, not from the impulse of passion, but from the force of dialectics. There is besides a strange attempt to substitute the language of painting for that of poetry, to make us *see* their feelings in the faces of the persons; and again, consistently with this, in the description of the picture in Tarquin and Lucrece, those circumstances are chiefly insisted on, which it would be impossible to convey except by words.

.   .   .

Of the Sonnets we do not well know what to say. The subject of them seems to be somewhat equivocal; but many of them are highly beautiful in themselves, and interesting as they relate to the state of the personal feelings of the author.

[Quotes Sonnets 25, 29, 102, 73]

In all these, as well as in many others, there is a mild tone of sentiment, deep, mellow, and sustained, very different from the crudeness of his earlier poems.

48. ADDENDUM TO *CHARACTERS*: FROM 'A LETTER TO WILLIAM GIFFORD ESQUIRE'

William Gifford, editor of the *Quarterly Review* which was sympathetic to the Tories, ferociously attacked Hazlitt, ostensibly for his books on literature but basically for his political attitudes. Hazlitt responded with equal or greater ferocity, carefully unpicking Gifford's arguments, exposing his prejudices and accusing him of being a 'cat's paw', 'the *Government Critic*, a character nicely differing from that of a government spy - the invisible link, that connects literature with the police' (Howe, ix, 13). Gifford was clearly responding to the political content in Hazlitt's writings on literature, and Hazlitt picks up the gauntlet by reasserting his attitudes. His comments on Coriolanus which should be compared with the essay in the *Characters* (above, number 19) were greatly admired by John Keats. Keats, in quoting the whole section on this play calls it a 'fine passage' and goes on:

> The manner in which this is managed: the force and innate power with which it yeasts and works up itself - the feeling for the costume of society; is in a style of genius - He (Hazlitt) hath a demon as he himself says of Lord Byron ...
> (Letter to the George Keatses, 13 March, 1819, *Letters*, ii, 76)

Gifford's attack, even though it is intemperate, cannot be said to be irrelevant, since the charges Hazlitt answers are very central to his own discipline of writing on Shakespeare: his readiness to draw political lessons from literature, his habit of quoting Shakespeare, his claims that 'sympathy' has an anatomical and moral significance, and that 'impressionism' is a rational and justifiable methodology when dealing with works of the imagination. The letter was written in February 1819 after the appearance (late in January) of *The Quarterly Review* dated the previous July. Hazlitt replies to this and to other reviews by Gifford in the *Quarterly*.

．　　　．　　　．

You do well to confine yourself to the hypocrite; for you have too little talent for the sophist. Yet in two instances you have attempted an answer to an opinion I had expressed; and in both you have shewn how little you can understand the commonest question. The first is as follows:- 'In his remarks upon Coriolanus, which contain the concentrated venom of his malignity, he has libelled our great poet as a friend of arbitrary power, in order that he may introduce an invective against human nature. "Shakespeare himself seems to have had a leaning to the arbitrary side of the question, perhaps from some feeling of contempt for his own origin; and to have spared no occasion of baiting the rabble."'

How do you prove that he did not? By shewing with a little delicate insinuation how he would have done just what I say he did. - 'Shall we not be dishonouring the gentle Shakespeare by answering such calumny, when every page of his works supplies its refutation?'[1] - 'Who has painted with more cordial feelings the tranquil innocence of humble life?' [True.] 'Who has furnished more instructive lessons to the great upon "the insolence of office" - "the oppressor's wrong"[2] - or the abuses of brief authority'[3] - [which you would hallow through all time] - 'or who has more severely stigmatised those "who crook the pregnant hinges of the knee where thrift may follow fawning?"[4]' [Granted, none better.] 'It is true he was not actuated by an envious hatred of greatness' - [so that to stigmatise servility and corruption does not always proceed from envy and a love of mischief] - 'he was not at all likely, had he lived in our time, to be an orator in Spa-fields or the editor of a seditious Sunday newspaper' - [To have delivered Mr Coleridge's *Conciones ad Populum*, or to have written Mr Southey's Wat Tyler[5]] -'he knew what discord would follow if degree were taken away'[6] - [As it did in France from the taking away the degree between the tyrant and the slave, and those little convenient steps and props of it, the Bastile, Lettres de Cachet, and Louis xv.'s *Palais aux cerfs*[7]] - 'And *therefore*, with the wise and good of every age, he pointed out the injuries that must arise to society from a turbulent rabble instigated to mischief by men not much more enlightened, and infinitely more worthless than themselves.'

So that it would appear by your own account that Shakspeare had a discreet leaning to the arbitrary side of the question, and, had he lived in our time, would probably have been a writer in the Courier, or a contributor to the Quarterly Review! It is difficult to know which to admire most in this, the weakness or the cunning. I have said that Shakspeare has described both sides of the question, and you ask me very wisely, 'Did he confine himself to one?' No, I say that he did not: but I suspect that he had a leaning to one side, and has given it more quarter than it deserved. My words are: '*Coriolanus* is a storehouse of political common-places. The arguments for and against aristocracy and democracy, on the privileges of the few and the claims of the many, on liberty and slavery, power and the abuse of it, peace and war, are here very ably handled, with the spirit of a poet and the acuteness of a philosopher. Shakspeare himself seems to have had a leaning to the arbitrary side of the question, perhaps from some feeling of contempt for his own origin, and to have spared no occasion of baiting the rabble. *What he says of them is very true: what he says of their betters is also very true, though he dwells less upon it.*'

I then proceed to account for this by shewing how it is that 'the cause of the people is but little calculated for a subject for poetry; or that the language of poetry naturally falls in with the language of power.' I affirm, Sir, that poetry, that the imagination, generally speaking, delights in power, in strong excitement, as well as in truth, in good, in right, whereas pure reason and the moral sense approve only of the true and good. I proceed to shew that this general love or tendency to immediate excitement or theatrical effect, no matter how produced, gives a bias to the imagination often inconsistent with the greatest good, that in poetry it triumphs over principle, and bribes the passions to make a sacrifice of common humanity. You say that it does not, that there is no such original sin in poetry, that it makes no such sacrifice or unworthy compromise between poetical effect and the still small voice of reason. And how do you prove that there is no such principle giving a bias to the imagination, and a false colouring to poetry? Why by asking in reply to the instances where this principle operates, and where no other can, with much modesty and simplicity - 'But are these the only topics that afford delight in poetry, &c.' No; but these objects do afford delight in poetry, and they afford it in proportion to their strong and often tragical effect, and not in proportion to the good produced, or their desirableness in a moral point of view. 'Do we read with more pleasure of the ravages of a beast of prey, than of the shepherd's pipe upon the mountain?' No; but we do read with pleasure of the ravages of a beast of prey, and we do so on the principle I have stated, namely, from the sense of power abstracted from the sense of good; and it is the same principle that makes us read with admiration and reconciles us in fact to the triumphant progress of the conquerors and mighty hunters of mankind, who come to stop the shepherd's pipe upon the mountains, and sweep away his listening flock. Do you mean to deny that there is anything imposing to the imagination in power, in grandeur, in outward shew, in the accumulation of individual wealth and luxury, at the expense of equal justice and the common weal? Do you deny that there is anything in 'the pride, pomp, and circumstance of glorious war, that makes ambition virtue,'[8] in the eyes of admiring multitudes? Is this a new theory of the Pleasures of the Imagination, which says that the pleasures of the imagination do not take rise solely in the calculations of the understanding? Is it a paradox of my making, that 'one murder makes a villain, millions a hero!'[9] Or is it not true that here, as in other cases, the enormity of the evil overpowers and makes a convert of the imagination by its very magnitude? You contradict my reasoning, because you know nothing of the question, and you think that no one has a right to understand what you do not. My offence against purity in the passage alluded to, 'which contains the concentrated venom of my malignity,' is, that I have admitted that there are tyrants and slaves abroad in the world; and you would hush the matter up, and pretend that there is no such thing, in order that there may be nothing else. Farther, I have explained the cause, the subtle sophistry of the human mind, that tolerates and pampers the evil, in order to guard against its approaches; you would conceal the cause in order to prevent the cure, and to leave the proud flesh about the heart to harden and ossify into one impenetrable mass of selfishness and hypocrisy, that we may not 'sympathise in the distresses of suffering virtue' in any case, in which they come in competition with the factitious wants and 'imputed weaknesses of the great.' You ask 'are we gratified by the cruelties of Domitian or Nero?' No, not we - they were too petty and cowardly to strike the imagination at a distance; but the Roman Senate tolerated them, addressed their perpetrators, exalted them into Gods, the Fathers of their people; they had pimps and scribblers of all sorts in their pay, their Senecas, &c. till a turbulent rabble thinking that there were no injuries to society greater than the endurance of unlimited and wanton oppression, put an end to the farce, and abated the nuisance as well as they could. Had you and I lived in those times, we should have been what we are now, I 'a sour mal-content,' and you 'a sweet courtier.'[10] Your reasoning is ill put together; it wants sincerity, it wants ingenuity. To prove that I am wrong in saying that the love of power and heartless submission to it extend beyond the tragic stage to real life, to prove that there has been nothing heard but the shepherd's pipe upon the mountain, and that the still sad music of humanity[11] has never filled up the pauses to the thoughtful ear, you bring in illustration the cruelties of Domitian and Nero, whom you suppose to have been without flatterers, train-bearers, or executioners, and 'the crime of revolutionary France of a still blacker die,' (a sentence which alone would have entitled you to a post of honour and secrecy under Sejanus,) which you suppose to have been without aiders and abettors. You speak of the horrors of Robespierre's reign; (there you tread on velvet;) do you mean that these atrocities excited nothing but horror in revolutionary France, in undelivered France, in Paris, the centre and focus of anarchy and crime; or that the enthusiasm and madness with which they were acted and applauded, was owing to nothing but a long-deferred desire for truth and justice, and the collected vengeance of the human race? You do not mean this, for you never mean anything that has even an approximation to unfashionable truth in it. You add, 'We cannot recollect, however, that these crimes were heard of with much satisfaction in this country.' Then you have forgotten the years 1793 and 94, you have forgotten the addresses against republicans and levellers, you have forgotten Mr Burke and his 80,000 incorrigible Jacobins.[12] - 'Nor had we the misfortune to know any individual, (though we will not take upon us to deny that Mr Hazlitt may have been of that description,)' (I will take upon me to deny that) 'who cried havoc, and enjoyed the atrocities of Robespierre and Carnot.' Then at that time, Sir, you had not the good fortune to know Mr Southey.[13]

To return, you find fault with my toleration of those pleasant persons, Lucio, Pompey, and Master Froth, in Measure for Measure, and with my use of the word 'natural morality.' And yet, 'the word is a good word, being whereby a man may be accommodated.'[14] If Pompey was a common bawd, you, Sir, are a court pimp. That is artificial morality. 'Go to, a feather turns the scale of your avoir-du-pois.'[15] I have also, it seems, erred in using the term *moral* in a way not familiar to you, as opposed to *physical*; and in that sense have applied it to the description of the mole on Imogen's neck, 'cinque-spotted, like the crimson drops i' th' bottom of a cowslip.'[16] I have stated that there is more than a physical - there is a moral beauty in this image, and I think so still, though you may not comprehend how.

.   .   .

I have commenced my observations on Lear, you say, with 'an acknowledgment remarkable for its *naiveté* and its truth'; the import of which remarkable acknowlegment is, that I find myself incompetent to do justice to this tragedy, by any criticism upon it. This you construe into a 'determination on my part to write nonsense'; you seem, Sir, to have sat down with a determination to write something worse than nonsense. As a proof of my having fulfilled the promise, (which I had *not* made,) you cite these words, 'It is then the best of all Shakespear's plays, for it is the one in which he was *most in earnest*'; and add significantly, 'Macbeth and Othello were mere *jeux d'esprit*, we presume.' You may presume so, but not from what I have said. You only aim at being a wordcatcher, and fail even in that. In like manner, you say, 'If this means that we sympathise so much with the feelings and sentiments of Hamlet, that we identify ourselves with the character, we have to accuse Mr Hazlitt of strangely misleading us a few pages back. "The moral of *Othello* comes directly home to the business and bosoms of men; the interest in *Hamlet* is more *remote* and reflex." And yet it is we who are Hamlet.' - Yes, because we sympathise with Hamlet, in the way I have explained, and which you ought to have endeavoured at least to understand, as reflecting and moralising on the general distresses of human life, and not as particularly affected by those which come home to himself, as we see in Othello. You accuse me of stringing words together without meaning, and it is you who cannot connect two ideas together.

You call me 'a poor cankered creature,' 'a trader in sedition,' 'a wicked sophist,' and yet you would have it believed that I am principally distinguished by an *indestructible* love of flowers and odours, and dews and clear waters, and soft airs and sounds and bright skies, and woodland solitudes and moonlight bowers.'[17] I do not understand how you reconcile such 'welcome and unwelcome things,'[18] but anything will do to feed your spleen at another's expence, when it is the person and not the thing you dislike. Thus you complain of my style, that it is at times figurative, at times poetical, at times familiar, not always the same flat dull thing that you would have it.

.   .   .

You know nothing of Shakespear, nor of what is thought about him: you mind only the text of the commentators. With respect to Mr Wordsworth's Ode,[19] which I have dragged into my account of Romeo and Juliet, I did not quarrel with the poetical conceit, but with the metaphysical doctrine founded upon it by his school. There is a difference between 'ends of verse and sayings of philosophers.' If Shakespear had been a great German transcendental philosopher (either at the first or second hand) his talking of the music of the spheres might have rendered him suspected. You compare my account of Hamlet to the dashing style of a showman: I think the showman's speech is proper to a show, and mine to Hamlet. You, Sir, have no sympathy in common with Hamlet; nothing to make him seem ever 'present to your mind's eye'; no feeling to produce such an hallucination in your mind, nor to make you tolerate it in others. You are an Ultra-Crepidarian critic.[20]

PART THREE

KEAN AS A SHAKESPEAREAN ACTOR

KEAN AS A SHAKESPEAREAN ACTOR

Hazlitt wrote a large number of theatre reviews between 1814 and 1820, for *The Morning Chronicle*, *The Examiner*, *The Champion* (for which Keats reviewed on at least one occasion), *The Times* and *The London Magazine*. Many of these were collected in *A View of the English Stage or A Series of Dramatic Criticisms* in 1818, and there are enough left out to furnish another substantial volume (Howe, vol. 18, *Dramatic Criticism*). This bulk of work gives a fascinating, certainly opinionated but always informed and detailed picture of the stage during these years. He had some of the most powerful Shakespearean actors to report - Edmund Kean, Mrs Siddons, Kemble and Booth. Of these, his undoubted favourite was Kean, whose career Hazlitt was able to trace from its beginning in January, 1814:

> I went to see him the first night of his appearing in Shylock. I remember it well...Mr Kean's appearance was the first gleam of genius breaking athwart the gloom of the Stage, and the public have since gladly basked in its ray, in spite of actors, managers, and critics. (Preface to *A View of the English Stage*)

So fulsome was his praise that Hazlitt was at one time suspected of being in the pay of the theatre in which the actor was playing. He could, however, be judiciously critical when he felt that Kean was either not playing up to his own standards or (as in the case of Coriolanus) not suited to the role. He could be ferocious and sarcastic by turns about bad performances from other actors, and he sadly lamented the falling-off of Mrs Siddons's performances late in her career. It is impossible in most cases to distinguish beween what is criticism of the play and what of the specific performance, so often does Hazlitt judge an actor against his own imaginative conception of the character in the totality of the text. Often he asserts (as Lamb did) the superiority of the text over the play in performance, but he is quick to accept 'new readings' of passages by inspired actors, an implicit acknowledgment of the plurality of possibilities in the text. The selection aims to represent the tight fit between Hazlitt's literary and theatrical ideas.

We are inclined to think of theatre reviewing as ephemeral in its nature. Quite often it is so in Hazlitt's practice, since many of the plays and players he comments upon have long since disappeared from critical notice. However, by collecting many reviews into a volume, Hazlitt signals that he believes reviewing has a permanent validity and interest, and he clearly also used reviews as a testing-ground for ideas which later appear in the *Characters*. In that volume, the essays on *A Midsummer Night's Dream*, *Henry VI* and *Coriolanus*, for example, first appeared as reviews. Hazlitt never believed in wasting a good phrase by publishing it only once:

> In fact, I have come to this determination in my own mind, that a work is as good as a *manuscript*, and is invested with all the same privileges, till it appears in a second edition - a rule which leaves me at liberty to make what use I please of what I have hitherto written, with the single exception of THE CHARACTERS OF SHAKESPEAR'S PLAYS. (Howe, v, 178)

This *credo*, expressed in the Preface to *A View of the English Stage*, means first that Hazlitt's work is littered with repetition (avoided as far as possible in this selection), and secondly - more pertinently - that he appears to have regarded his theatre criticism as an adjunct, in content and quality, to the *Characters*. Certainly, we find similar qualities in the two bodies of material. As we noticed in introducing the *Characters*, although Hazlitt is often regarded lazily as simply continuing the eighteenth-century tradition of 'character criticism', in fact character is invariably analysed as part of a larger dramatic context, and in particular as the product of a sharply observed, poetically felt 'impression' or atmosphere built up in the play through a tissue of imagery and rhythms and moral concerns. In these pieces we find the hallmarks of Hazlitt observed in his essays - the combination of trenchancy in expressing an opinion and subtlety in capturing the tone of a dramatic moment, the blend of the patrician attitude with radical and demotic beliefs. As elsewhere, he is more discursive, sustained and frankly entertaining than other reviewers, having a strong attachment to the theatre alongside a judicious wariness about abuses of its resources. What he lacks in comparison with Coleridge - deep shafts of insight and an architectonic grasp of dramatic structure - he makes up for in incisiveness, wit and good sense. At least he did not turn his back on the notion of Shakespeare's plays in performance, and instead embraced wholeheartedly the resources afforded the critic by the existence of the theatre. The selection here is only a fraction of Hazlitt's theatre criticism, and another whole volume would be an apt companion to this book.

49.   FROM 'MR KEAN'S SHYLOCK'

First published *The Morning Chronicle*, January 27, 1814. This passage is repeated in a later review in *The Examiner*, April 7, 1816.

Notwithstanding the complete success of Mr Kean in the part of Shylock, we question whether he will not become a greater favourite in other parts. There was a lightness and vigour in his tread, a buoyancy and elasticity of spirit, a fire and animation, which would accord better with almost any other character than with the morose, sullen, inward, inveterate, inflexible malignity of Shylock. The character of Shylock is that of a man brooding over one idea, that of its wrongs, and bent on one unalterable purpose, that of revenge. In conveying a profound impression of this feeling, or in embodying the general conception of rigid and uncontroulable self-will, equally proof against every sentiment of humanity or prejudice of opinion, we have seen actors more successful than Mr Kean; but in giving effect to the conflict of passions arising out of the contrasts of situation, in varied vehemence of declamation, in keenness of sarcasm, in the rapidity of his transitions from one tone and feeling to another, in propriety and novelty of action, presenting a succession of striking pictures, and giving perpetually fresh shocks of delight and surprise, it would be difficult to single out a competitor.

50.   FROM 'MR KEAN'S HAMLET'

First published in *The Morning Chronicle* on March 14, 1814, subsequently republished in *A View of the English Stage* (1818), and furnished some lines in the chapter on Hamlet in *Characters*. In praising Kean for introducing '*a new reading*', Hazlitt demonstrates his own fluid sense that the play in performance can help the critic in his own developing interpretation. In generalising about Shakespeare as 'ventriloquist', it is arguable whether Hazlitt is distancing himself consciously, or simply repeating without fully understanding, a distinction often made by Coleridge: 'Shakespeare seems characterless, because characteristic. The poet lost in his portraits contrasted with the poet as a mere ventriloquist' (Raysor, I, 73; see Raysor's footnote for other references). One would expect some difference of perspective between a poet/metaphysician and a person interested in the stage, on this complex matter. Keats adds his contribution when he calls

Shakespeare 'the camelion Poet' who has 'no self' but 'lives in gusto, be it foul or fair, high or low, rich or poor, mean or elevated. - It has as much delight in conceiving an Iago as an Imogen' in the exercise of 'Negative Capability' (Keats, *Letters*, I, 387). Whether protean or ventriloquial, Shakespeare provides his own paradoxical explanation, and a source for his Romantic interpreters:

> Then comes it that my name receives a brand,
>
> And almost thence my nature is sudu'd
>
> To what it works in, like the dyer's hand.
>
> (Sonnet 111)

The version of the text selected here is from *A View of the English Stage*.

This character is probably of all others the most difficult to personate on the stage. It is like the attempt to embody a shadow.

> 'Come then, the colours and the ground prepare,
>
> Dip in the rainbow, trick her off in air,
>
> Chuse a firm cloud, before it falls, and in it
>
> Catch, 'ere she change, the Cynthia of a minute.'[1]

Such nearly is the task which the actor imposes on himself in the part of Hamlet. It is quite remote from hardness and dry precision. The character is spun to the finest thread, yet never loses its continuity. It has the yielding flexibility of 'a wave of the sea.'[2] It is made up of undulating lines, without a single sharp angle. There is no set purpose, no straining at a point. The observations are suggested by the passing scene - the gusts of passion come and go, like the sounds of music borne on the wind. The interest depends not on the action, but on the thoughts - on 'that within which passeth shew.'[3] Yet, in spite of these difficulties, Mr Kean's representation of the character had the most brilliant success. It did not indeed come home to our feelings, as Hamlet (that very Hamlet whom we read of in our youth, and seem almost to remember in our after years), but it was a most striking and animated rehearsal of the part.

.   .   .

To point out the defects of Mr Kean's performance of the part, is a less grateful but a much shorter task, than to enumerate the many striking beauties which he gave to it, both by the power of his action and by the true feeling of nature. His surprise when he first sees the Ghost, his eagerness and filial confidence in following it, the impressive pathos of his action and voice in addressing it, 'I'll call thee Hamlet, *Father*, Royal Dane,'4 were admirable.

Mr Kean has introduced in this part a *new reading*, as it is called, which we think perfectly correct. In the scene where he breaks from his friends to obey the command of his father, he keeps his sword pointed behind him, to prevent them from following him, instead of holding it before him to protect him from the Ghost. The manner of his taking Guildenstern and Rosencrantz under each arm, under pretence of communicating his secret to them, when he only means to trifle with them, had the finest effect, and was, we conceive, exactly in the spirit of the character. So was the suppressed tone of irony in which he ridicules those who gave ducats for his uncle's picture, though they would 'make mouths at him,'5 while his father lived. Whether the way in which Mr Kean hesitates in repeating the first line of the speech in the interview with the player, and then, after several ineffectual attempts to recollect it, suddenly hurries on with it, 'The rugged Pyrrhus,' &c.6 is in perfect keeping, we have some doubts: but there was great ingenuity in the thought; and the spirit and life of the execution was beyond every thing. Hamlet's speech in describing his own melancholy, his instructions to the players, and the soliloquy on death, were all delivered by Mr Kean in a tone of fine, clear, and natural recitation. His pronunciation of the word 'contumely' in the last of these, we apprehend, not authorized by custom, or by the metre.

Both the closet scene with his mother, and his remonstrances to Ophelia, were highly impressive. If there had been less vehemence of effort in the latter, it would not have lost any of its effect. But whatever nice faults might be found in this scene, they were amply redeemed by the manner of his coming back after he has gone to the extremity of the stage, from a pang of parting tenderness to press his lips to Ophelia's hand. It had an electrical effect on the house. It was the finest commentary that was ever made on Shakespear. It explained the character at once (as he meant it), as one of disappointed hope, of bitter regret, of affection suspended, not obliterated, by the distractions of the scene around him! The manner in which Mr Kean acted in the scene of the Play before the King and Queen was most daring of any, and the force and animation which he gave to it, cannot be too highly applauded. Its extreme boldness 'bordered on the verge of all we hate,'[7] and the effect it produced, with a test of the extraordinary powers of this extraordinary actor.

.   .   .

51.   FROM 'MR KEAN'S IAGO' (i)

Although ostensibly an essay on Kean, the following piece belongs to Hazlitt's Shakespearean criticism, since he draws the character of Iago as he sees it in comparison with that of Richard. Hazlitt's picture of Iago as one of a class of characters in Shakespeare - 'that of great intellectual activity, accompanied with a total want of moral principle' - influenced Bradley. Behind the account, as Hazlitt makes clear, lies his repeated analysis of the dangers of 'curiosity and imagination' when these faculties are not 'under the restraint of humanity, or the sense of moral obligation'. He emphasises the 'amusement' and 'gaiety' of the 'dreadful sport' practised by Iago. The essay was first published in *The Examiner*, July 24, 1814 and concluded August 7, then in *The Round Table* (1817) and Hazlitt draws upon it in his essay on *Othello* in *Characters*. The text reproduced here is that which appears in *A View of the English Stage*.

There is no one within our remembrance, who has so completely foiled the critics as this celebrated actor: one sagacious person imagines that he must perform a part in a certain manner; another virtuoso chalks out a different path for him; and when the time comes, he does the whole off in a way, that neither of them had the least conception of, and which both of them are therefore very ready to condemn as entirely wrong. It was ever the trick of genius to be thus. We confess that Mr Kean has thrown us out more than once. For instance, we are very much inclined to persist in the objection we before made, that his Richard is not gay enough, and that his Iago is not grave enough. This he may perhaps conceive to be the mere caprice of captious criticism; but we will try to give our reasons, and shall leave them to Mr Kean's better judgment.

It is to be remembered, then, that Richard was a princely villain, borne along in a sort of triumphal car of royal state, buoyed up with the hopes and privileges of his birth, reposing even on the sanctity of religion, trampling on his devoted victims without remorse, and who looked out and laughed from the high watch-tower of his confidence and his expectations, on the desolation and misery he had caused around him. He held on his way, unquestioned, 'hedged in with the divinity of kings,'[1] amenable to no tribunal, and abusing his power *in contempt of mankind.* But as for Iago, we conceive differently of him. He had not the same natural advantages. He was a mere adventurer in mischief, a pains-taking, plodding knave, without patent or pedigree, who was obliged to work his uphill way by wit, not by will, and to be the founder of his own fortune. He was, if we may be allowed a vulgar allusion, a true prototype of modern Jacobinism, who thought that talents ought to decide the place; a man of 'morbid sensibility' (in the fashionable phrase), full of distrust, of hatred, of anxious and corroding thoughts, and who, though he might assume a temporary superiority over others by superior adroitness, and pride himself in his skill, could not be supposed to assume it as a matter of course, as if he had been entitled to it from his birth. We do not here mean to enter into the characters of the two men, but something must be allowed to the difference of their situations. There might be the same indifference in both as to the end in view, but there could not well be the same security as to the success of the means. Iago had to pass through a different ordeal: he had no appliances and means to boot; no royal road to the completion of his tragedy. His pretensions were not backed by authority; they were not baptized at the font; they were not holy-water proof. He had the whole to answer for in his own person, and could not shift the responsibility to the heads of others. Mr Kean's Richard was therefore, we think, deficient in something of that regal jollity and reeling triumph of success which the part would bear; but this we can easily account for, because it is the traditional common-place idea of the character, that he is to 'play the dog - to bite and snarl.'[2] The extreme unconcern and laboured levity of his Iago, on the contrary, is a refinement and original device of the actor's own mind, and deserves a distinct consideration. The character of Iago, in fact, belongs to a class of characters common to Shakespear, and at the same time peculiar to him, namely, that of great intellectual activity, accompanied with a total want of moral principle, and therefore displaying itself at the constant expense of others, making use of reason as a pander to will - employing its ingenuity and its resources to palliate its own crimes, and aggravate the faults of others, and seeking to confound the practical distinctions of right and wrong, by referring them to some overstrained standard of speculative refinement.

The tone which he adopts in the scenes with Roderigo, Desdemona, and Cassio, is only a relaxation from the more arduous business of the play. Yet there is in all his conversation, an inveterate misanthropy, a licentious keenness of perception, which is always sagacious of evil, and snuffs up the tainted scent of its quarry with rancorous delight. An exuberance of spleen is the essence of the character. The view which we have here taken of the subject, (if at all correct) will not therefore justify the extreme alteration which Mr Kean has introduced into the part.

Actors in general have been struck only with the wickedness of the character, and have exhibited an assassin going to the place of execution. Mr Kean has abstracted the wit of the character, and makes Iago appear throughout an excellent good fellow, and lively bottle-companion. But though we do not wish him to be represented as a monster, or a fiend, we see no reason why he should instantly be converted into a pattern of comic gaiety and good humour. The light which illumines the character, should rather resemble the flashes of lightning in the mirky sky, which make the darkness more terrible. Mr Kean's Iago is, we suspect, too much in the sun. His manner of acting the part would have suited better with the character of Edmund in King Lear, who, though in other respects much the same, has a spice of gallantry in his constitution, and has the favour and countenance of the ladies, which always gives a man the smug appearance of a bridegroom!

. . .

The general groundwork of the character of Iago, as it appears to us, is not absolute malignity, but a want of moral principle, or an indifference to the real consequences of the actions, which the meddling perversity of his disposition and love of immediate excitement lead him to commit. He is an amateur of tragedy in real life; and instead of exercising his ingenuity on imaginary characters, or forgotten incidents, he takes the bolder and more desperate course of getting up his plot at home, casts the principal parts among his nearest friends and connections, and rehearses it in downright earnest, with steady nerves and unabated resolution. The character is a complete abstraction of the intellectual from the moral being; or, in other words, consists in an absorption of every common feeling in the virulence of his understanding, the deliberate wilfulness of his purposes, and in his restless, untamable love of mischievous contrivance. We proceed to quote some particular passages in support of this opinion.

In the general dialogue and reflections, which are an accompaniment to the progress of the catastrophe, there is a constant overflowing of gall and bitterness. The acuteness of his malice fastens upon every thing alike, and pursues the most distant analogies of evil with a provoking sagacity. He by no means forms an exception to his own rule:-

> 'Who has that breast so pure,
>
> But some uncleanly apprehensions
>
> Keep leets and law-days, and in sessions sit
>
> With meditations lawful?'

His mirth is not natural and cheerful, but forced and extravagant, partaking of the intense activity of mind and cynical contempt of others in which it originates. Iago is not, like Candide, a believer in optimism, but seems to have a thorough hatred or distrust of every thing of the kind, and to dwell with gloating satisfaction on whatever can interrupt the enjoyment of others, and gratify his moody irritability.

52.   FROM 'MR KEAN'S IAGO' (ii)

When first published, the reviews above drew criticism from Thomas Barnes ('the Correspondent'), and Hazlitt responded in the following way in *The Examiner*, September 11, 1814.

MR EXAMINER, - I was not at all aware that in the remarks which I offered on Mr Kean's Iago my opinions would clash with those already expressed by the respectable writer of the Theatrical Examiner: for I did not mean to object to 'the gay and careless air which Mr Kean threw over his representation of that arch villain,' but to its being nothing but carelessness and gaiety; and I thought it perfectly consistent with a high degree of admiration of this extraordinary actor, to suppose that he might have carried an ingenious and original idea of the character to a paradoxical extreme. In some respects, your Correspondent seems to have mistaken what I have said; for he observes that I have entered into an analysis to shew, 'that Iago is a malignant being, who hates his fellow-creatures, and doats on mischief and crime as the best means of annoying the objects of his hate.' Now this is the very reverse of what I intended to shew; for so far from thinking that Iago is 'a ruffian or a savage, who pursues wickedness for its own sake,' I am ready to allow that he is a pleasant amusing sort of gentleman, but with an over-activity of mind that is dangerous to himself and others; that so far from hating his fellow-creatures, he is perfectly regardless of them, except as they may afford him food for the exercise of his spleen, and that 'he doats on mischief and crime,' not 'as the best means of annoying the objects of his hate,' but as necessary to keep himself in that strong state of excitement which his natural constitution requires, or, to express it proverbially, in *perpetual hot water.* Iago is a man who will not suffer himself or any one else to be at rest; he has an insatiable craving after action, and action of the most violent kind. His conduct and motives require some explanation; but they cannot be accounted for from his interest or his passions, - his love of himself, or hatred of those who are the objects of his persecution: these are both of them only the occasional pretext for his cruelty, and are in fact both of them subservient to his love of power and mischievous irritability. I repeat, that I consider this sort of unprincipled selfwill as a very different thing from common malignity; but I conceive it also just as remote from indifference or levity. In one word, the malice of Iago is not *personal*, but *intellectual.* Mr Kean very properly got rid of the brutal ferocity which had been considered as the principle of the character, and then left it without any principle at all. He has mistaken the want of moral feeling, which is inseparable from the part, for constitutional ease and general indifference, which are just as incompatible with it. Mr Kean's idea seems to have been, that the most perfect callousness ought to accompany the utmost degree of inhumanity; and so far as relates to callousness to moral considerations, this is true; but that is not the question. If our Ancient had no other object or principle of action but his indifference to the feelings of others, he gives himself a great deal of trouble to no purpose. If he has nothing else to set him in motion, he had much better remain quiet than be broken on the rack. Mere carelessness and gaiety, then, do not account for the character. But Mr Kean acted it with nearly the same easy air with which Mr Braham sings a song in an opera, or with which a comic actor delivers a side-speech in an after-piece.

But the character of Iago, says your Correspondent, has nothing to do with the manner of acting it. We are to look to the business of the play. Is this then so very pleasant, or is the part which Iago undertakes and executes the perfection of easy comedy? I should conceive quite the contrary. 'The rest of what your Correspondent says on this subject is 'ingenious, but not convincing.' It amounts to this, that Iago is a hypocrite, and that a hypocrite should always be gay. This must depend upon circumstances. Tartuffe[1] was a hypocrite, yet he was not gay: Joseph Surface[2] was a hypocrite, but grave and plausible: Blifil[3] was a hypocrite, but cold, formal and reserved. The hypocrite is naturally grave, that is, thoughtful, and dissatisfied with things as they are, plotting doubtful schemes for his own advancement and the ruin of others, studying far-fetched evasions, double-minded and double-faced. - Now all this is an effort, and one that is often attended with disagreeable consequences; and it seems more in character that a man whose invention is thus kept on the rack, and his feelings under painful restraint, should rather strive to hide the wrinkle rising on his brow, and the malice at his heart, under an honest concern for his friend, or the serene and regulated smile of steady virtue, than that he should wear the light-hearted look and easy gaiety of thoughtless constitutional good humour. The presumption therefore is not in favour of the lively, laughing, comic mien of hypocrisy. Gravity is its most obvious resource, and, with submission, it is quite as effectual a one. But it seems, that if Iago had worn this tremendous mask, 'the gay and idle world would have had nothing to do with him.' Why, indeed, if he had only intended to figure at a carnival or a ridotto, to dance with the women or drink with the men, this objection might be very true. But Iago has a different scene to act in, and has other thoughts in his contemplation. One would suppose that Othello contained no other adventures than those which are to be met with in Anstey's Bath Guide,[4] or in one of Miss Burney's novels. The smooth smiling surface of the world of fashion is not the element he delights to move in: he is the busy meddling fiend 'who rides in the whirlwind, and directs the storm,'[5] triumphing over the scattered wrecks, and listening to the shrieks of death. I cannot help thinking that Mr Kean's Iago must be wrong, for it seems to have abstracted your Correspondent entirely from the subject of the play.

.   .   .

An accomplice in knavery ought always to be a solemn rogue, and withal a casuist, for he thus becomes our better conscience, and gives a sanction to the roguery. Cassio does not invite Iago to drink with him, but is prevailed upon against his will to join him; and Othello himself owes his misfortunes, in the first instance, to his having repulsed the applications of Iago to be made his lieutenant. He himself affects to be blunt and unmannerly in his conversation with Desdemona. There is no appearance of any cordiality towards him in Othello, nor of his having been a general favourite (for such persons are not usually liked), nor of his having ever been employed but for his understanding and discretion. He every where owes his success to his intellectual superiority, and not to the pleasantness of his manners. At no time does Othello put implicit confidence in Iago's personal character, but demands his proofs; or when he founds his faith on his integrity, it is from the gravity of his manner: 'Therefore these stops of thine fright me the more,' &c.[6]

53. FROM 'MR KEAN'S RICHARD [III]'

Published in *The Champion*, October 9, 1814, reprinted in *A View of The English Stage*. Hazlitt is never sycophantic in his praise of Kean, and here he admits to being 'hypercritical' in speaking of Kean's style and '*bye-play*'.

It is almost needless to observe, that executive power in acting, as in all other arts, is only valuable as it is made subservient to truth and nature. Even some want of mechanical skill is better than the perpetual affectation of shewing it. The absence of a quality is often less provoking than its abuse, because less voluntary.

.   .   .

Mr Kean's *bye-play* is certainly one of his greatest excellences, and it might be said, that if Shakespear had written marginal directions to the players, in the manner of the German dramatists, he would often have directed them to do what Mr Kean does. Such additions to the text are, however, to be considered as lucky hits, and it is not to be supposed that an actor is to provide an endless variety of these running accompaniments, which he is not in strictness bound to provide at all. In general, we think it a rule, that an actor ought to vary his part as little as possible, unless he is convinced that his former mode of playing it is erroneous. He should make up his mind as to the best mode of representing the part, and come as near to this standard as he can, in every successive exhibition. It is absurd to object to this mechanical uniformity as studied and artificial. All acting is studied or artificial. An actor is no more called upon to vary his gestures or articulation at every new rehearsal of the character, than an author can be required to furnish various readings in every separate copy of his work. To a new audience it is quite unnecessary; to those who have seen him before in the same part, it is worse than useless. They may at least be presumed to have come to a second representation, because they approved of the first, and will be sure to be disappointed in almost every alteration. The attempt is endless, and can only produce perplexity and indecision in the actor himself. He must either return perpetually in the same narrow round, or if he is determined to be always new, he may at last fancy that he ought to perform the part standing on his head instead of his feet. Besides, Mr Kean's style of acting is not in the least of the unpremeditated, *improvisatori* kind: it is throughout elaborate and systematic, instead of being loose, off-hand, and accidental. He comes upon the stage as little unprepared as any actor we know. We object particularly to his varying the original action in the dying scene. He at first held out his hands in a way which can only be conceived by those who saw him - in motionless despair, - or as if there were some preternatural power in the mere manifestation of his will: - he now actually fights with his doubled fists, after his sword is taken from him, like some helpless infant.

.   .   .

It was our first duty to point out Mr Kean's excellences to the public, and we did so with no sparing hand; it is our second duty to him, to ourselves, and the public, to distinguish between his excellences and defects, and to prevent, if possible, his excellences from degenerating into defects.

54.   FROM 'MR KEAN'S MACBETH'

Published in *The Champion*, November 13, 1814, reprinted in *A View of the English Stage*. Most of the review is taken up with a comparison between Macbeth and Richard III as tyrants, and the analysis found its way into the essay on *Macbeth* (above, no. 15) in *Characters*. Reproduced below are the more general remarks about the representative nature of Shakespeare's art, and a passage which powerfully evokes Hazlitt's impression of one of Kean's great acting moments.

The genius of Shakespear was as much shewn in the subtlety and nice discrimination, as in the force and variety of his characters. The distinction is not preserved more completely in those which are the most opposite, than in those which in their general features and obvious appearance most nearly resemble each other. It has been observed, with very little exaggeration, that not one of his speeches could be put into the mouth of any other character than the one to which it is given, and that the transposition, if attempted, might be always detected from some circumstance in the passage itself. If *to invent according to nature*, be the true definition of genius, Shakespear had more of this quality than any other writer. He might be said to have been a joint-worker with Nature, and to have created an imaginary world of his own, which has all the appearance and the truth of reality.

His mind, while it exerted an absolute controul over the stronger workings of the passions, was exquisitely alive to the slightest impulses and most evanescent shades of character and feeling. The broad distinctions and governing principles of human nature are presented not in the abstract, but in their immediate and endless application to different persons and things. The local details, the particular accidents have the fidelity of history, without losing any thing of their general effect.

It is the business of poetry, and indeed of all works of imagination, to exhibit the species through the individual. Otherwise, there can be no opportunity for the exercise of the imagination, without which the descriptions of the painter or the poet are lifeless, unsubstantial, and vapid. If some modern critics are right, with their sweeping generalities and vague abstractions, Shakespear was quite wrong. In the French dramatists, only the class is represented, never the individual: their kings, their heroes, and their lovers are all the same, and they are all French - that is, they are nothing but the mouth-pieces of certain rhetorical common-place sentiments on the favourite topics of morality and the passions. The characters in Shakespear do not declaim like pedantic school-boys, but speak and act like men, placed in real circumstances, with 'real hearts of flesh and blood beating in their bosoms.'[1] No two of his characters are the same, more than they would be so in nature. Those that are the most alike, are distinguished by positive differences, which accompany and modify the leading principle of the character through its most obscure ramifications, embodying the habits, gestures, and almost the looks of the individual. These touches of nature are often so many, and so minute, that the poet cannot be supposed to have been distinctly aware of the operation of the springs by which his imagination was set at work: yet every one of the results is brought out with a truth and clearness, as if his whole study had been directed to that peculiar trait of character, or subordinate train of feeling.

.   .   .

The two finest things that Mr Kean has ever done, are his recitation of the passage in Othello, 'Then, oh, farewell the tranquil mind,'[2] and the scene in Macbeth after the murder. The former was the highest and most perfect effort of his art. To enquire whether his manner in the latter scene was that of a king who commits a murder, or of a man who commits a murder to become a king, would be 'to consider too curiously.'[3] But, as a lesson of common humanity, it was heart-rending. The hesitation, the bewildered look, the coming to himself when he sees his hands bloody; the manner in which his voice clung to his throat, and choaked his utterance; his agony and tears, the force of nature overcome by passion - beggered description. It was a scene, which no one who saw it can ever efface from his recollection.

55.   FROM 'MR KEAN'S ROMEO'

(The Champion, January 8, 1815)

Of the characters that Mr Kean has played, Hamlet and Romeo are the most like one another, at least in adventitious circumstances; those to which Mr Kean's powers are least adapted, and in which he has failed most in general truth of conception and continued interest. There is in both characters the same strong tincture of youthful enthusiasm, of tender melancholy, of romantic thought and sentiment; but we confess we did not see these qualities in Mr Kean's performance of either. His Romeo had nothing of the lover in it. We never saw any thing less ardent or less voluptuous.

56.   FROM 'MR KEAN'S RICHARD II'

(The Examiner, March 19, 1815, reprinted in *A View*...) Hazlitt repeats his general agreement with Lamb's opinion that the stage is an inferior vehicle for Shakespeare's poetry, but he also shows that some of his own critical insights come when he can clarify his imaginative version against the actuality of a performance by Kean.

We are not in the number of those who are anxious in recommending the getting-up of Shakespear's plays in general, as a duty which our stage-managers owe equally to the author, and the reader of those wonderful compositions. The representing the very finest of them on the stage, even by the best actors, is, we apprehend, an abuse of the genius of the poet, and even in those of a second-rate class, the quantity of sentiment and imagery greatly outweighs the immediate impression of the situation and story. Not only are the more refined poetical beauties and minuter strokes of character lost to the audience, but the most striking and impressive passages, those which having once read we can never forget, fail comparatively of their effect, except in one or two rare instances indeed. It is only the *pantomime* part of tragedy, the exhibition of immediate and physical distress, that which gives the greatest opportunity for 'inexpressible dumb-show and noise,'[1] which is sure to tell, and tell completely on the stage. All the rest, all that appeals to our profounder feelings, to reflection and imagination, all that affects us most deeply in our closets, and in fact constitutes the glory of Shakespear, is little less than an interruption and a drag on the business of the stage. *Segnius per aures demissa,* &c.[2] Those parts of the play on which the reader dwells the longest, and with the highest relish in the perusal, are hurried through in the performance, while the most trifling and exeptionable are obtruded on his notice, and occupy as much time as the most important. We do not mean to say that there is less knowledge or display of mere stage-effect in Shakespear than in other writers, but that there is a much greater knowledge and display of other things, which divide the attention with it, and to which it is not possible to give an equal force in the representation. Hence it is, that the reader of the plays of Shakespear is almost always disappointed in seeing them acted; and, for our own parts, we should never go to see them acted, if we could help it.

Shakespear has embodied his characters so very distinctly, that he stands in no need of the actor's assistance to make them more distinct; and the representation of the character on the stage almost uniformly interferes with our conception of the character itself.

.   .   .

All that we have said of acting in general applies to his Richard II. It has been supposed that this is his finest part: this is, however, a total misrepresentation. There are only one or two electrical shocks given in it; and in many of his characters he gives a much greater number. - The excellence of his acting is in proportion to the number of hits, for he has not equal truth or purity of style. Richard II was hardly given correctly as to the general outline. Mr Kean made it a character of *passion*, that is, of feeling combined with energy; whereas it is a character of *pathos*, that is to say, of feeling combined with weakness. This, we conceive, is the general fault of Mr Kean's acting, that it is always energetic or nothing. He is always on full stretch - never relaxed. He expresses all the violence, the extravagance, and fierceness of the passions, but not their misgivings, their helplessness, and sinkings into despair. He has too much of that strong nerve and fibre that is always equally elastic. We might instance to the present purpose, his dashing the glass down with all his might, in the scene with Hereford, instead of letting it fall out of his hands, as from an infant's; also, his manner of expostulating with Bolingbroke, 'Why on thy knee, thus low, &c.'[3] which was altogether fierce and heroic, instead of being sad, thoughful, and melancholy. If Mr Kean would look into some passages in this play, into that in particular, 'Oh that I were a mockery king of snow, to melt away before the sun of Bolingbroke,'[4] he would find a clue to this character, and to human nature in general, which he seems to have missed - how far feeling is connected with the sense of weakness as well as of strength, or the power of imbecility, and the force of passiveness.

57.   FROM 'MR KEAN'S OTHELLO'

(Published *The Times,* performed Drury Lane, October 27, 1817)

Mr Kean's Othello is, we suppose, the finest piece of acting in the world. It is impossible either to describe or praise it adequately. We have never seen any actor so wrought upon, so 'perplexed in the extreme.' The energy of passion, as it expresses itself in action, is not the most terrific part; it is the agony of his soul, showing itself in looks and tones of voice. In one part, where he listens in dumb despair to the fiend-like insinuations of Iago, he presented the very face, the marble aspect of Dante's Count Ugolino.[1] On his fixed eyelids 'Horror sat plumed.'[2] In another part, where a gleam of hope or of tenderness returns to subdue the tumult of his passions, his voice broke in faltering accents from his over-charged breast. His lips might be said less to utter words, than to bleed drops of blood gushing from his heart. An instance of this was in his pronunciation of the line 'Of one that loved not wisely but too well.'[3] The whole of this last speech was indeed given with exquisite force and beauty. We only object to the virulence with which he delivers the last line, and with which he stabs himself - a virulence which Othello would neither feel against himself at that moment, nor against the turbaned Turk (whom he had slain) at such a distance of time. His exclamation on seeing his wife, 'I cannot think but Desdemona's honest,'[4] was 'the glorious triumph of exceeding love;'[5] a thought flashing conviction on his mind, and irradiating his countenance with joy, like sudden sunshine. In fact, almost every scene or sentence in this extraordinary exhibition is a masterpiece of natural passion. The convulsed motion of the hands, and the involuntary swellings of the veins of the forehead in some of the most painful situations, should not only suggest topics of critical panegyric, but might furnish studies to the painter or anatomist.

58. FROM 'MR KEAN'S CORIOLANUS'

(Published in 'The Drama: No. II', *The London Magazine*, February, 1820.) Here Hazlitt reveals his political sympathy for the demotic, populist style of Kean. Hazlitt feels this style is inappropriate to Coriolanus, a role which the aristocratic Kemble, in Hazlitt's opinion, suited.

Mr Kean's acting is not of the patrician order; he is one of the people, and what might be termed a *radical* performer. He can do all that may become a man 'of our infirmity,'[1] 'to relish all as sharply, passioned as we;'[2] but he cannot play a God, or one who fancies himself a God, and who is sublime, not in the strength of his own feelings, but in his contempt for those of others, and in his imaginary superiority to them. That is, he cannot play Coriolanus so well as he plays some other characters, or as we have seen it played often. Wherever there was a struggle of feelings, a momentary ebullition of pity, or remorse, or anguish, wherever nature resumed her wonted rights, Mr Kean was equal to himself, and superior to every one else; but the prevailing characteristics of the part are inordinate self-opinion, and haughty elevation of soul, that aspire above competition or controul, as the tall rock lifts its head above the skies, and is not bent or shattered by the storm, beautiful in its unconquered strength, terrible in its unaltered repose. Mr Kean, instead of 'keeping his state,'[3] instead of remaining fixed and immoveable (for the most part) on his pedestal of pride, seemed impatient of this mock-dignity, this *still-life* assumption of superiority; burst too often from the trammels of precedent, and the *routine* of etiquette, which should have confined him; and descended into the common arena of man, to make good his pretensions by the energy with which he contended for them, and to prove the hollowness of his supposed indifference to the opinion of others by the excessive significance and studied variations of the scorn and disgust he expressed for it. The intolerable airs and aristocratical pretensions of which he is the slave, and to which he falls a victim, did not seem *legitimate* in him, but upstart, turbulent, and vulgar. Thus his haughty answer to the mob who banish him - 'I banish you'[4] - was given with all the virulence of execration, and rage of impotent despair, as if he had to strain every nerve and faculty of soul to shake off the contamination of their hated power over him, instead of being delivered with calm, majestic self-possession, as if he remained rooted to the spot, and his least motion, word, or look, must scatter them like chaff or scum from his presence! The most effective scene was that in which he stands for the Consulship, and begs for 'the most sweet voices'[5] of the people whom he loathes; and the most ineffective was that in which he is reluctantly reconciled to, and overcome by the entreaties of, his mother. This decisive and affecting interview passed off as if nothing had happened, and was conducted with diplomatic gravity and skill.

.   .   .

59.   FROM 'MR KEAN'S LEAR'

(Published in *The London Magazine*, June, 1820 as 'The Drama: No. VI.') Hazlitt was disappointed by Kean's performance in Tate's rewriting of *King Lear*. This review consists largely of particular moments when Hazlitt feels Kean made mistakes of interpretation. The excerpt printed below is the part of the essay where the comments are more generally directed to what Hazlitt sees as the true nature of Shakespeare's *Lear*, compared with *Othello*.

[Kean's performance as Lear] is altogether inferior to his Othello. Yet, if he had even played it equal to that, all we could have said of Mr Kean would have been that he was a very wonderful man; - and such we certainly think him as it is. Into the bursts, and starts, and torrent of the passion in Othello, this excellent actor appeared to have flung himself completely: there was all the fitful fever of the blood, the jealous madness of the brain: his heart seemed to bleed with anguish, while his tongue dropped broken, imperfect accents of woe; but there is something (we don't know how) in the gigantic, outspread sorrows of Lear, that seems to elude his grasp, and baffle his attempts at comprehension. The passion in Othello pours along, so to speak, like a river, torments itself in restless eddies, or is hurled from its dizzy height, like a sounding cataract. That in Lear is more like a sea, swelling, chafing, raging, without bound, without hope, without beacon, or anchor. Torn from the hold of his affections and fixed purposes, he floats a mighty wreck in the wide world of sorrows. Othello's causes of complaint are more distinct and pointed, and he has a desperate, a maddening remedy for them in his revenge. But Lear's injuries are without provocation, and admit of no alleviation or atonement. They are strange, bewildering, overwhelming: they wrench asunder, and stun the whole frame: they 'accumulate horrors on horror's head,'[1] and yet leave the mind impotent of resources, cut off, proscribed, anathematised from the common hope of good to itself, or ill to others - amazed at its own situation, but unable to avert it, scarce daring to look at, or to weep over it. The action of the mind, however, under this load of disabling circumstances, is brought out in the play in the most masterly and triumphant manner: it staggers under them, but it does not yield. The character is cemented of human strength and human weaknesses (the firmer for the mixture): - abandoned of fortune, of nature, of reason, and without any energy of purpose, or power of action left, - with the grounds of all hope and comfort failing under it, - but sustained, reared to a majestic height out of the yawning abyss, by the force of the affections, the imagination, and the cords of the human heart - it stands a proud monument, in the gap of nature, over barbarous cruelty and filial ingratitude. We had thought that Mr Kean would take possession of this time-worn, venerable figure, 'that has outlasted a thousand storms, a thousand winters,'[2] and, like the gods of old, when their oracles were about to speak, shake it with present inspiration: - that he would set up a living copy of it on the stage: but he failed, either from insurmountable difficulties, or from his own sense of the magnitude of the undertaking. There are pieces of ancient granite that turn the edge of any modern chisel: so perhaps the genius of no living actor can be expected to cope with Lear.

NOTES

3.   FROM 'ON PEOPLE OF SENSE'

1.   Hazlitt's theory is a development from Renaissance principles of literature as a vehicle for teaching and delighting through the idealizing of nature. Cf. Sidney's *Defence*: 'Nature never set forth the earth in so rich tapestry as diverse poets have done' (p.78), and '... so no doubt the philosopher with his learned definitions - be it of virtue, vices, matters of public policy or private government - replenisheth the memory with many infallible grounds of wisdom, which, notwithstanding, lie dark before the imaginative and judging power, if they be not illuminated or figured forth by the speaking picture of poesy.' (p.86)

5.   FROM 'WHETHER GENIUS IS CONSCIOUS OF ITS POWERS'

1.   *Timon of Athens*, I.i.21-5.

6.   FROM 'ON POSTHUMOUS FAME, - WHETHER SHAKSPEARE WAS INFLUENCED BY LOVE OF IT?'

1.   Howe notes that the quotation comes from Addison's *Cato*, V.i.

2.   Hazlitt has the following note to this sentence:

> 'Oh! for my sake do you with fortune chide,
>
> The guilty goddess of my harmless deeds,
>
> That did not better for my life provide,
>
> Than public means which public manners breeds.
>
> Thence comes it that my name receives a brand,
>
> And almost thence my nature is subdued
>
> To what it works in, like the dyer's hand.'

At another time, we find him 'desiring this man's art, and that man's scope': so little was Shakespeare, as far as we can learn, enamoured of himself!

7.   FROM 'SCHLEGEL ON THE DRAMA'

1.   Madame de Staël (1766-1817) was active among progressive thinkers in Paris before the French Revoltuion, introduced to French readers the German philosophic movement (of which Schlegel was a member), wrote novels, and entertained Schlegel at her house at Coppet for many years.

2.   Jean Charles Léonard Sismondi (1773-1842), French historian of Italian descent.

3.   Hazlitt wrote in his *Life of Napoleon Buonaparte* (Preface): 'It is the practice of the partisans of the old school to cry *Vive le Roi, quand meme!*'

4.   Compare pages 188 - 9 above.

5.   'Gusts' is a favourite word for Hazlitt, and it is related to his use of 'gusto' (above no. 2).

6.   Hazlitt appends a footnote:

> The universality of Shakespear's genius has, perhaps, been a disadvantage to his single works: the variety of his resources has prevented him from giving

that intense concentration of interest to some of them which they might have had. He is in earnest only in Lear and Timon. He combined the powers of Æschylus and Aristophanes, of Dante and Rabelais, in his own mind. If he had only been half what he was, he might have seemed greater.

7.   Hazlitt runs together phrases from *Paradise Lost*, II. 139 and V. 285.

8.   William Collins, 'Verses humbly address'd to Sir Thomas Hanmer on his Edition of Shakespear's Works', line 76.

8.   FROM 'SHAKESPEAR'S FEMALE CHARACTERS'

1.   *Romeo and Juliet*, III.ii.16.

9.   FROM *LECTURES ON THE ENGLISH POETS*

(i)   FROM LECTURE ONE

1.   This is one of several echoes of Sidney's theory of poetry ('Now, for the poet, he nothing affirms, and therefore never lieth', *Defence of Poetry*, p. 102), which make it likely that Hazlitt had absorbed the *Defence of Poetry*, as did Shelley.

2.   *Macbeth*, II.i.44: 'Mine eyes are made the fools o' th' other senses'.

3.   *A Midsummer Night's Dream*, V.i.19-22.

4.   *Cymbeline*, II.ii.19-21.

5.   *King Lear*, III.iv.191: 'If you yourselves are old'.

6.   *King Lear*, III.iv.70-1 misquoted.

7.   *King Lear*, III.vi.61-2.

8.   *King Lear*, IV.vii.69.

9.   *Othello*, III.iii.347-57.

10.   *Othello*, III.iii.453-60.

11.   *Othello*, IV.ii, lines 57 and 60 conflated.

12.   Again, the idea here has precedents and analogues in English theory, such as Sidney's *Defence of Poetry* and Shelley's *A Defence of Poetry*.

13.   Edward Moore was author of *The Gamester* (1753) and George Lillo wrote *The London Merchant, or the History of George Barnwell* (1731), both minor eighteenth-century dramatists popular in their age.

(ii)   FROM LECTURE THREE

1.   *Paradise Lost*, III. 44.

2.   Spenser, *The Faerie Queene*, I.iii.4, adapted.

3.   'These words occur in the first line of the laudatory poem on Shakespeare prefixed to the Second Folio (1632)' (Howe).

4.   Compare Keats's *Letters*, I.387, speaking of the 'poetical Character' which 'enjoys light and shade; it lives in gusto, be it foul or fair, high or low, rich or poor, mean or elevated - It has as much delight in conceiving an Iago as an Imogen. What shocks the virtuous philosopher, delights the camelion Poet'.

5.   *Cymbeline*, III.iv.37-8.

6.   *A Midsummer Night's Dream*, III.i.174, paraphrased.

7.   *The Tempest*, V.i.50, adapted.

8.   *Measure for Measure*, III.i.9, misquoted.

9.   Collins, 'Ode on the Poetical Character', line 66.

10.   Howe compares *Paradise Lost*, VII. 9-11.

11.   *Macbeth*, III.i.41-2.

12.   Hazlitt's target here must be primarily Wordsworth, the subtitle to whose *Poems in Two Volumes* (1807), 'Moods of My Mind', indicates the naure of Hazlitt's objection.

13.   See Mark iv.24 and Luke vi.38.

14.   *A Midsummer Night's Dream*, V.i.13.

15.   *Ibid.*, II.i.175-6.

16.   'Hieroglyphics' were topical as the Rosetta Stone was brought to France in 1798 and deciphered in 1824.

17.   *Macbeth*, III.ii.50-1.

18.   *Othello*, I.iii.91.

19.   *Othello*, IV.ii.166.

20.   *1 Henry IV*, III.i.206-8.

21.   *Two Gentlemen of Verona*, II.vii.31-2 (he *for* it).

22.   Cowley's *Translation of Horace's Ode* III.1.

23.   One of the greatest eighteenth-century satirists, Voltaire condemned Shakespeare for breaking the classical rules of drama and for lacking taste (*Lettres sur les Anglais*).

24.   Both Ben Jonson and Samuel Johnson made this accusation of Shakespeare.

25.   *Antony and Cleopatra*, V.ii.88-9 misquoted.

10.   FROM *LECTURES ON THE ENGLISH COMIC WRITERS*

(i)   LECTURE ONE

1.   *King Lear*, I.iv.173.

2.   *King Lear*, I.iv.215-6.

3.   *King Lear*, I.iv.224-5 conflated.

(ii)   FROM LECTURE TWO

1.   Hazlitt subtly distorts Johnson's view which was that '[Shakespeare's] tragedy seems to be skill, his comedy to be instinct' (Wimsatt, p.64). See also below, the essay on *Twelfth Night* in *Characters*.

2.   Compare Burke, *A Letter to a Noble Lord* (*Works*, Bohn, v.129): 'The Duke of Bedford is the leviathan among all the creatures of the Crown. He tumbles about his unwieldy bulk; he plays and frolics in the ocean of the royal bounty' (Howe). Hazlitt has clearly turned around the tone from derogatory to complimentary, but it may be the idea of 'royal bounty' that sparked off the memory, as much as 'unwieldy bulk'.

3.   *Hamlet*, III.i.62-3.

4.   *Romeo and Juliet*, I.iv.

5.   *As You Like It*, II.vii.111.

6.   *Twelfth Night*, II.iv.21-2.

7.   *Ibid.*, I.i.5-7.

8.   Steele's last play (1722), based on the *Andria* of Terence.

9.   I Peter, iv.8.

10.   Characters in the *Henry IV* plays.

11.   Hazlitt speaks of the Society for the Suppression of Vice, a Church of England society founded in 1801, in 'On the Causes of Methodism' (*The Round Table*). His contempt for its repressive attitudes is evident in the context.

12.   *2 Henry IV*, V.iii.40.

13.   *Ibid.*, III.ii.215. Falstaff says the words.

14.   *Troilus and Cressida*, III.iii.175.

15.   *2 Henry IV*, IV.iii.99-100.

16.   *Twelfth Night*, I.iii.128-9.

17.   Etherege, *The Man of Mode*, V.ii.

18.   Cf. Hazlitt's 'Character of Cobbett': 'He "lays waste" a city orator or Member of Parliament' (Howe, viii. 50).

19.   Vanbrugh, *The Relapse*, III.i.

20.   *As You Like It*, III.ii.38-52, adapted.

21.   *A Midsummer Night's Dream*, V.i.16.

22.   *Twelfth Night*, I.i.34-5, slightly misquoted.

23.   *Macbeth*, V.iii.45-6 (patient *for* mind).

24.   *Coriolanus*, IV.v.222-3 (waking *for* lively).

11.   FROM 'SIR WALTER SCOTT, RACINE AND SHAKESPEAR'

1.   Perhaps from Dryden's 'And o'er-inform'd the tenement of clay', *Absalom and Achitophel*, I.158.

2.   *Macbeth*, I.iii.79-80.

3.   *Ibid.*, I.iii.44-5 misquoted.

4.   *Ibid.*, I.iii.80-1 ('Whither are they vanish'd? / Into the air'), or *The Tempest*, IV.i.150 ('are melted into air, into thin air').

5.   Two editions of Captain Thomas Medwin's *Conversations of Lord Byron, noted during a residence with his Lordship at Pisa in the years 1821 and 1822* appeared in 1824, and editions followed in Paris, New York and Germany (Howe).

6.   *Othello*, III.iv.69.

7.   *2 Henry IV*, III.i.29.

8.   *Othello*, III.iii.302 ('It is a common thing -').

9.   *Ibid.,* III.iii.215.

10.   *Ibid.* III.iii.460.

11.   *Ibid.* III.iii.453 misquoted ('Like to the Pontic Sea...').

12.   *King John,* IV.i.

13.   *Juliua Ceasar* I.ii.

14.   Harry Bertram is a character in Scott's *Guy Mannering.*

12.   FROM 'COBBETT AND SHAKESPEAR: A POSTCRIPT'

1.   See headnote. An omitted concluding paragraph, headed 'Note Extraordinary,' from the 'Round Table' paper, 'On the Midsummer Night's Dream' (vol. iv. pp.61-4).

2.   Howe, vol. v, p.108.

3.   The Duke of Wellington's letter of 23 Septembver 1815, relative to the dispersal of the Louvre.

4.   *Morning Chronicle* during the autumn and winter of 1815, beginning 22 September.

5.   Samuel Parr (1747-1825) and Charles Burney (1757-1817) are presumably intended.

6.   *2 Henry IV,* II.iv.99-100 misquoted.

7.   *A Midsummer Night's Dream,* I.ii.81-2.

8.   A character in *Measure for Measure.*

9.   *Henry V,* IV.i.

13.   FROM *THE PLAIN SPEAKER*

1.   *Macbeth,* III.iv.21-2 adapted.

2.   Leigh Hunt, *Descent of Liberty: A Mask* (1814), written during his imprisonment for reflections on the Prince Regent (1813-15). Hunt was editor of *The Examiner.*

14.   FROM 'CYMBELINE'

1.   Johnson's *Preface to the Edition of Shakespear's Plays,* ed. Wimsatt, p.66.

2.   *Apology for the Life of Mr Colley Cibber* (1740), vol.I, ch. iv.

3.   I.vi.112-3.

4.   IV.ii.218-24.

5.   II.ii.14-39 *passim.*

6.   II.v.9-10.

7.   III.ii.107 (is up *for* a-foot) or *1 Henry IV* I.ii.278 or *Henry V* II.i.32.

8.   *As You Like It,* II.vii.111.

9.   II.iii.2-10 *passim* (Stoop *for* See).

10.   IV.ii.255-6.

11.   IV.ii.10-11.

12.   I.v.19-20.

13.   I.v.23-4.

15.   'MACBETH'

1.   *A Midsummer Night's Dream*, V.i.12-17.

2.   *Hamlet*, III.ii.125 (jig-maker).

3.   I.vi.1-6.

4.   I.iii.77.

5.   III.iv.61.

6.   IV.i.123.

7.   I.iii.39-42.

8.   I.vii.80.

9.   II.ii.10-11 (th' attempt, and not the deed, confounds us).

10.   I.iii.130 (This supernatural soliciting).

11.   I.vii.72-4.

12.   I.vii.60.

13.   II.ii.68-9.

14.   II.ii.64.

15.   I.vii.26.

16.   I.v.69-70 (misquoted).

17.   I.v.39-40.

18.   I.v.40-54.

19.   I.v.31 adapted.

20.   I.v.25-30. Hazlitt transposes events here, implying that Lady M. receives her husband's letter *after* receiving news of Duncan's impending arrival (P.J.R.).

21.   Sarah Siddons (1755-1831), the great tragic actress, who began acting as a child and retired in 1819.

22.   I.iv.11-16.

23.   II.i.1-9 *passim*.

24.   III.ii.50-1.

25.   III.iii.6-7.

26.   I.iii.38.

27.   IV.iii.138 (things at once).

28.   IV.iii.170-3 misquoted.

29.   I.v.65-6.

30.   III.iv.90-1.

31.   III.iv.92.

32.   III.iv.107 (I am a man again).

33.   IV.i.86.

34. III.ii.40-4.

35. II.ii.12-13.

36. Perhaps *Julius Caesar* III.i.114: How many times shall Caesar Bleed for sport?

37. I.iii. 45-6.

38. I.iii.126 (deepest *for* deeper).

39. IV.i.125-6.

40. The comparison between Macbeth and Richard III is a commonplace: see headnote.

41. I.v.17.

42. Perhaps alluding to *Richard III*, V.iii.182.

43. III.i.64-9 *passim*.

44. III.ii.22-3.

45. V.v.14 adapted.

46. V.iii.38-9 misquoted.

47. *Measure for Measure*, III.i.9 (servile *for* subject).

48. V.iii.22-8 misquoted.

16. FROM 'JULIUS CAESAR'

1. I.i.20-31 (with errors).

2. V.v.69-72.

3. IV.iii.150.

4. II.i.288-90.

5. II.i.97-111.

6. II.i.229-33.

17. 'OTHELLO'

1. Aristotle, *The Poetics*, description of *catharsis*.

2. Dedication to Bacon's *Essays*.

3. The preceding three sentences come from Hazlitt's 'Shakespear's Exact Discrimination of Nearly Similar Characters', *Round Table* series, May 12, 1816.

4. III.iii.453-6 misquoted.

5. I.iii.61-4 misquoted.

6. III.iii.70-83 *passim*.

7. III.iii.278-9.

8. III.iii.330.

9. III.iii.341 (found *for* felt).

10. Hazlitt has a note: 'See the passage beginning - "It is impossible you should see this, were they as prime as goats" etc.' (III.iii.403-4).

11. III.iii.444 9.

12.   IV.i.196 misquoted.

13.   V.ii.97-8.

14.   I.iii.91.

15.   III.iii183-9.

16.   III.iv.25-30.

17.   IV.iii.10-11.

18.   From I.iii.252.

19.   I.iii.94-6 misquoted.

20.   II.i68-73 *passim.*

21.   This paragraph comes from 'Shakespear's Female Characters', *The Examiner*, 28 July 1816, published anonymously (see above, no. 8).

22.   From I.iii.251-2.

23.   I.iii.253-4.

24.   Hazlitt's note reads "'*Iago.* Ay, too gentle.
                    Othello. Nay, that's certain.'" (IV.i.194-5).

25.   I.iii.155-6 misquoted.

26.   IV.ii.148-68 *passim.*

27.   IV.iii.18-21 (with errors).

28.   The next two lines come from 'On Mr Kean's Iago', below, no. 52.

29.   A reference to Coleridge's phrase, the 'motive-hunting of a motiveless malignity.'

30.   I.i.66-73.

31.   I.i.74-7.

32.   II.i.250-3. The text from here down to 'placed' comes from Hazlitt's essay in *The Examiner*, August 7, 1814.

33.   III.iii.227-30.

34.   *Macbeth*, I.v.17.

35.   *Hamlet*, III.iii.92.

36.   II.i.199-201.

37.   III.iii.92-108, with variants.

38.   III.iii.373-80.

39.   IV.i.58-60.

40.   A reference to *The Revenge*, by Edward Young, first acted 1721.

18.   'TIMON OF ATHENS'

1.   Juvenal, a Roman of the first century A.D. in his *Satires* attacked the vices, abuses and follies of Roman life.

2.   The Stoic school of philosophy was founded at Athens *c.*315 B.C. by Zeno. It involved a doctrine of detachment from the outer world, and hence became known for its self-discipline and austerity.

3. Diogenes (4th century B.C.) was the principal representative of the Cynic school of philosophy. He is reputed to have lived in a tub in the public street, and to have hurled satirical abuse at passers-by.

4. I.i.80-3 with omissions.

5. IV.iii.221-31.

6. I.i.20-5. The passage is a favourite of Hazlitt's and he quotes it often.

7. Probably quoting Wycherley's 'Ugly all over with the affectation of fine gentlemen', quoted in *The Tatler*, No. 38.

8. *De Sapientia Veterum*, published 1609, a collection of interpretations of classical myths and fables.

9. IV.iii.34-42. This was one of Karl Marx's favourite quotations from Shakespeare.

10. IV.iii.319-20.

11. I.i.59-60.

12. V.i.214-9.

13. V.iv.74-9.

19. 'CORIOLANUS'

1. *Reflections on the French Revolution* (1790), a conservative statement.

2. *The Rights of Man*, published in two parts in 1791 and 1792 was a radical answer to Burke, justifying the French Revolution.

3. *Macbeth*, I.vi.6-8.

4. This statement on the imagination was something of a Romantic commonplace. It can be compared with Coleridge's *Biographia Literaria*, Shelley's *Defence of Poetry* and Hazlitt's own 'On Imitation'.

5. II.i.158-9.

6. 'Ode: 1815' by Wordsworth.

7. I.i.249 (these rats).

8. III.i.81-2.

9. III.i.90.

10. III.i.137.

11. IV.i.13-14.

12. These sentiments echo Paine (above). See Hazlitt's defence of these statements in his letter to William Gifford (below, no. 48).

13. I.ix.13-15.

20. 'TROILUS AND CRESSIDA'

1. The phrase is from Sir John Denham's *Cooper's Hill* (line 192), describing the Thames.

2. III.ii.27 (joys *for* thoughts).

3. III.ii.28-9.

4. II.ii.194-200.

5. V.vii.1-7.

6. I.ii.235-9 misquoted.

7. III.ii.33-4.

8. Leigh Hunt, *The Story of Rimini* (1816), 111.41.

9. *All's Well That Ends Well*, IV.iii.71-2.

10. V.v.37-42.

11. I.iii.379.

12. III.ii.38-9 misquoted.

21. 'ANTONY AND CLEOPATRA'

1. III.ii.48-50.

2. I.i.13-17.

3. II.ii.191-4.

4. III.x.19.

5. I.v.24-5.

6. III.xiii.184-6.

7. III.xiii.123-6.

8. II.ii.234-7. Modern editors adopt the Folio reading of stale *for* steal.

9. II.v.28-9.

10. V.ii.309-12 *passim.*

11. III.xi.35-8.

12. IV.xiv.1-13.

13. III.xiii.31-4.

14. IV.ix.22.

22. 'HAMLET'

1. II.ii.298-303.

2. II.ii.309-10.

3. I.ii.67.

4. III.i.71-3.

5. Probably recalling I.ii.86.

6. I.ii.85, adapted. ·

7. The next section is taken from Hazlitt's review in *The Morning Chronicle*, March 14, 1814.

8. III.iii.92.

9. III.iii.72-89 with several mistakes, probably evidence that Hazlitt is quoting from memory.

10. Lamb's phrase in *Specimens of English Dramatic Poets*, on Middleton and Rowley.

11.   Anonymous pamphlet, 1659, a popular ethical treatise.

12.   *Academy of Compliments, or the whole Art of Courtship, being the rarest and most exact way of wooing a Maid or Widow, by way of Dialogue or complimental Expressions*, 1655 and 1669.

13.   Perhaps recalling *Timon of Athens*, '...fill'd the time / With all licentious measure' (V.iv.3-4).

14.   I.ii.254.

15.   V.i.269-71.

16.   V.i.243-6.

17.   IV.v.158.

18.   Hazlitt notes: 'In the account of her death, a friend has pointed out an instance of the poet's exact observation of nature:-

> "There is a willow growing o'er a brook,
>
> That shews its hoary leaves i' th' glassy stream"

The inside of the leaves of the willow, next the water, is of a whitish colour, and the reflection would therefore be "hoary".'

The (mis)quotation is from IV.vii.166-7. Howe suggests that the 'friend' is Lamb, perhaps only because Hazlitt is often assumed to have one friend. I do not find much sensitivity to colour and nature in Lamb's writings.

19.   This is Lamb's opinion, expressed in 'On the Tragedies of Shakespeare, considered with reference to their fitness for stage representation'.

20.   *The Winter's Tale*, IV.iv.141.

21.   Compare 'Mr. Kean's Hamlet' (below, no. 50).

23.   'THE TEMPEST'

1.   *Hamlet*, II.ii.396-400.

2.   *Macbeth*, IV.i.49.

3.   I.ii.298.

4.   *A Midsummer Night's Dream*, V.i.16-17.

5.   *1Henry IV*, V.iii.21.

6.   Perhaps from III.i.38-9.

7.   Sonnet 111.

8.   Perhaps Polonius, 'The law of writ and the liberty', *Hamlet*, II.ii.401.

9.   John, iii.31.

10.   Schlegel, p.395.

11.   III.ii.135-43.

12.   V.i.102.

13.   *A Midsummer Night's Dream*, II.i.175-6.

14.   V.i.17-24.

15.   IV.i.152.

16.   An allusion to the work of Godwin, on whom Hazlitt wrote in several essays, including one in *The Spirit of the Age*. Godwin's ideas can loosely be described as utopian anarchism.

24.   'THE MIDSUMMER NIGHT'S DREAM'

1.   III.ii.9-10.

2.   I.ii.70.

3.   I.ii.84.

4.   I.ii.66-69.

5.   III.i.15.

6.   III.i.17-22.

7.   IV.i.2-4 *passim*.

8.   IV.i.10-14.

9.   II.i.101. Keats, perhaps prompted by Hazlitt's emphasis, double-underlined this phrase in his two texts of Shakespeare; see White, p.103.

10.   *Paradise Lost*, II.628.

11.   Coleridge, though it is a little unfair to him.

12.   III.i.164-74.

13.   III.i.32.

25.   'ROMEO AND JULIET'

1.   Schlegel, p.400. Coleridge (notoriously) translates this passage and represents it, perhaps inadvertently, as his own; see Hawkes, pp.24-5.

2.   Compare 'cowslips wan', *Lycidas*, 147.

3.   Howe suggests the reference is to John Philpot Curran, the Irish orator, speaking at Horne Tooke's Wimbledon parties.

4.   'harsh and crude': *Lycidas*, 3.

5.   A play by A.F.F. Kotzebue (1761-1819).

6.   Matthew, vii.16.

7.   II.ii.133-4.

8.   Wordsworth's 'Ode: Intimations of Immortality', 77.

9.   *Ibid.*, 67.

10.   Gray's 'Progress of Poesy', 41.

11.   *Paradise Lost*, V.310-11 (mid-morn).

12.   Wordsworth, 'Ode: Intimations of Immortality', 64.

13.   I.v.21-5 (with omission).

14.   I.ii.24-30 (fennel *for* female).

15.   I.i.147-53.

16.   III.iii.36 (dear *for* his).

17.   I.v.41-6 (line omitted).

18.   Collins, 'Epistle to Thomas Hanmer', line 76.

19.   III.ii.16 misquoted.

20.   Thomas Bowdler's *Family Shakespeare* was published in 1818, and he has the dubious distinction of lending to the language the word 'bowdlerize'.

21.   Schlegel, p.400.

22.   II.vi.16-20.

23.   II.v.235.

24.   *Lycidas*, 153 (false *for* faint).

25.   V.i.1 (flattering truth *for* flatteries is the accepted modern reading; Hazlitt is following Pope).

26.   V.iii.76-8.

27.   V.i.1-11.

28.   Bandello popularised the story, although there were several Italian versions. The names of the lovers are first used by Luigi de Porto. The story was translated into English by Arthur Brooke (1562) and William Painter (1567).

29.   III.ii.90-99.

30.   But see below, no. 55 for Hazlitt's full comments on Kean's Romeo.

31.   *The Beauties of Shakespeare*, ed. Dr William Todd (1753).

26.   FROM 'LEAR'

1.   Compare the opening sentences in the essay on *Timon of Athens*.

2.   I.i.145-6.

3.   I.i.276.

4.   I.ii.118-33.

5.   *Comus*, 790-1.

6.   I.iv.271 (this gate).

7.   I.iv.173, rephrased.

8.   I.v.46-7.

9.   II.iv.95-7.

10.   III.vi.62-3.

11.   III.vi.76-7.

12.   III.iv. 63, 70-1, rephrased.

13.   iii.vi.10-11.

14.   IV.vi.11.

15.   V.iii.175.

16.   IV.iii.27 misquoted.

17.   IV.iv.1-2.

18.   V.iii.306-10.

19.   V.iii.314-6 (tough *for* rough: H. is following Pope's emendation).

27.   FROM 'RICHARD II'

1.   I.iii.213-5.

2.   Milton, 'L'Allegro', 119.

3.   IV.i.260.

4.   V.v.76-8.

28.   FROM 'HENRY IV IN TWO PARTS'

1.   Cf. Colossians, ii.9.

2.   *1HIV*, II.ii.109.

3   *The Tempest*, IV.i.150.

4.   *1HIV*, IV.ii.74 misquoted.

5.   *Canterbury Tales*, Prologue, 345.

6.   *2HIV*, IV.iii.97-100.

7.   *1HIV*, II.iv.448.

8.   *1HIV*, II.iv.225-6 misquoted.

9.   Perhaps a paraphrase of *2HIV*, I.ii.247-8: 'A good wit will make use of any thing. I will turn diseases to commodity.'

10.   *2HIV*, II.iv.244.

11.   *2HIV*, III.ii.309.

12.   *2HIV*, II.ii.211-5 misquoted.

13.   The remainder of this paragraph is taken from *Round Table*, 'Shakespear's Exact Discrimination of Nearly Similar Characters', where exclamation marks stand for the question marks here.

14.   *2HIV*, V.iii.112.

15.   Hazlitt is, of course, characteristically referring with irony to his own times. George III was notoriously repetitive.

16.   *2HIV*, V.iii.6-15.

17.   *King Lear*, III.iv.107-9 paraphrased.

18.   *1HIV*, I.iii.201-2, omitting 'pale-fac'd'.

19.   *2HIV*, II.iii.43-5.

29.   FROM 'HENRY V'

1.   *Othello*, I.iii.393.

2.   Pope's *Dunciad*, IV.188.

3.   I.ii.224-5, adapted.

4. I Prologue, 1-7.

5. I.ii.169-71.

6. I.ii.164-5.

30. FROM 'HENRY VI IN THREE PARTS'

1. Hazlitt in a footnote writes: 'There is another instance of the same distinction in Hamlet and Ophelia. Hamlet's pretended madness would make a very good real madness in any other author.'

31. 'RICHARD III'

1. David Garrick played Richard on 19 October, 1741.

2. Kean's first role was Shylock (26 January, 1814 at Drury Lane), and he played Richard on 12 February.

3. Unidentified.

4. I.iii.262-4.

5. Compare pp. 12, 210, 237 no. 53 fn 1.

6. A character in Massinger's *A New Way to Pay Old Debts*.

7. *Oroonoko, or The Royal Slave* by Thomas Southerne, 1696, based on Aphra Behn's novel.

8. Cibber's adaptation of *Richard III* (1700) held the stage until 1821. Its most famous line is 'Off with his head. So much for Buckingham'.

9. See I.iv.1-75.

10. IV.i.97-104.

11. A show of marionettes, puppets animated by manipulating strings.

32. FROM 'HENRY VIII'

1. Unidentified.

2. Howe mentions that the phrase is applied to Ferdinand VII of Spain in official documents, and used ironically by Hazlitt elsewhere. See *The Examiner*, 25 September, 1814.

33. FROM 'KING JOHN'

1. *Othello*, III.iii.428.

2. *Hamlet*, V.i.206.

3. 'He sometimes needed strength', from Jonson, *Discoveries*, 818, 'De Shakesepare Nostrati'.

4. II.i.573 *et seq.*

34. FROM 'TWELFTH NIGHT OR WHAT YOU WILL'

1. Dr Johnson wrote in his *Preface to Shakespeare* that 'a quibble is to Shakespeare what

luminous vapours are to the traveller... A quibble was to him the fatal Cleopatra for which he lost the world, and was content to lose it'.

2. I.i.15.

3. I.iii.125-33.

4. II.iii.58-9.

5. II.iii.114-6.

6. See headnote above.

35. FROM 'THE TWO GENTLEMEN OF VERONA'

1. Hazlitt notes this: 'The river wanders at its own sweet will - WORDSWORTH.' ('Sonnet composed upon Westminster Bridge', misquoting: glideth *for* wanders).

2. II.vii.21-38.

3. 'L'Allegro', 133-4.

36. FROM 'THE MERCHANT OF VENICE'

1. Allusion to Richard Cumberland's *The Jew* (1795).

2. *Macbeth*, V.viii.29.

3. *King Lear*, III.ii.60 adapted.

4. IV.i.60-1 adapted.

5. *Macbeth*, I.v.17.

6. I.iii.112.

7. I.iii.127-9.

8. I.iii.130-1.

9. III.i.122-3 misquoted.

10. The foregoing analysis adapts sentences from 'Mr Kean's Shylock', *The Examiner*, 7 April, 1816.

11. This sentence is taken from 'Mr Kean's Shylock', *The Morning Chronicle*, 27 January, 1814.

12. IV.i.175; Antonio *for* Bassanio.

13. *Hamlet*, I.ii.135-6 misquoted. 'Gender' is from *Othello*, IV.ii.62.

37. FROM 'THE WINTER'S TALE'

1. Malone.

2. I.ii.267-75, ending mid-sentence.

3. I.ii.284-94.

38. FROM 'ALL'S WELL THAT ENDS WELL'

1. II.v.43-4.

2.   III.vi and IV.i.

3.   IV.i.44-45.

39.   FROM 'LOVE'S LABOUR'S LOST'

1.   Pope's note to *The Two Gentlemen of Verona*.

2.   A twelfth-century professor of theology, and later bishop of Paris.

3.   V.i.13-14.

4.   *A Midsummer Night's Dream*, V.i.394, brier *for* brake.

41.   FROM 'AS YOU LIKE IT'

1.   I.i.118.

2.   II.vii.111.

3.   *Cymbeline*, III.iii.46.

4.   Cowper, *The Task*, IV, 99-100: 'I behold the tumult, and am still'.

5.   II.i.15-17, adapted.

6.   II.v.13.

7.   II.vii.29.

8.   V.iv.184-5.

9.   'L'Allegro', 141-2 misquoted.

10.   IV.i.145.

11.   I.iii.73-6.

12.   III.ii.11-21.

42.   FROM 'THE TAMING OF THE SHREW'

1.   I.i.253-4.

2.   Induction, ii.75.

3.   Induction, ii.5-12 and 17-24.

4.   Induction, i.3.

5.   Don Quixote's squire in Cervantes's novel, a favourite comic character for Hazlitt.

43.   FROM 'MEASURE FOR MEASURE'

1.   *Paradise Lost*, I.24: 'The highth of this great argument'.

2.   Howe compares Pope's 'sublimely bad' ('Epistle to Arbuthnot', 187) and 'sublimely sweet' by Beattie (*The Minstrel*, I, xlii), but the phrase may be a commonplace oxymoron.

3.   IV.ii.142-4.

4.   IV.iii.43.

5.   II.i.253.

6.   IV.ii.28-31.

7.   *Henry V*, IV.i.4.

44.   FROM 'THE MERRY WIVES OF WINDSOR'

1.   Schlegel, p.427.

2.   See above, note on *The Taming of the Shrew*.

3.   *Hamlet*, V.i.190-1 misquoted.

4.   *2 Henry IV*, II.i.93-100 *passim* ('such poor people').

46.   'DOUBTFUL PLAYS OF SHAKESPEAR'

1.   *Titus Andronicus*.

2.   *Pericles*, IV.i.20 (whirring *for* hurrying).

47.   FROM 'POEMS AND SONNETS'

1.   *Macbeth*, III.iv.22 misquoted.

2.   *Macbeth*, III.iv.23 misquoted.

3.   *A Midsummer Night's Dream*, V.i.13.

4.   Coleridge and Wordsworth were virtually the first to make a point of praising the Sonnets, and Coleridge in *Biographia Literaria* takes lines from *Venus and Adonis* as touchstones of metaphorical poetry.

48.   ADDENDUM TO *CHARACTERS*: FROM 'A LETTER TO WILLIAM GIFFORD ESQUIRE'

1.   Hazlitt's note: 'This extreme tenderness, it is to be observed, is felt by a person who in his life of Ben Jonson, hopes that God will forgive Shakspeare for having written his plays!'

2.   *Hamlet*, II.i.72 and 70.

3.   Allusion to *Measure for Measure*, II.ii.118.

4.   *Hamlet*, III.ii.61-2.

5.   Anti-populist works of Hazlitt's time.

6.   Adaptation of *Troilus and Cressida*, I.iii.109-10.

7.   Events during the French Revolution.

8.   *Othello*, III.iii.349-50 adapted.

9.   From Bishop Porteus's prize poem *Death* (1795) (Howe).

10.   *As You Like It*, III.ii.292-3.

11.   Quotation from Wordsworth's *Tintern Abbey*, 1. 91.

12.   On these political matters, Howe directs attention to *Letters on a Regicide Peace* (ed. Payne, p.50). Hazlitt's overall point is that while Gifford expresses horror of violence in the French Revolution (which Hazlitt saw as a just cause), he turns a blind eye to threats of atrocity in England perpetrated with the approval of Tory apologists such as Burke and

Southey.

13. Hazlitt's note: 'It was a phrase, (I have understood,) common in this gentleman's mouth [Southey], that Robespierre, by destroying the lives of thousands, saved the lives of millions. Or, as Mr Wordsworth has lately expressed the same thought with a different application, "Carnage is the daughter of humanity".'

14. *2 Henry IV*, III.ii.68-72.

15. A conflation of two quotations, *Measure for Measure*, IV.ii.30 and *2 Henry IV*, II.iv.254.

16. *Cymbeline*, II.ii.38-9.

17. Hazlitt's note: 'Quoted from the *Edinburgh Review*, No. 56.' The sentence was probably intended as a pastiche from Hazlitt's comments on *Romeo and Juliet* and *A Midsummer Night's Dream*.

18. *Macbeth*, IV.iii.138.

19. See above, no. 25, note 8.

20. Crepidarian: of or pertaining to a shoemaker (OED). The first use quoted in OED (indeed the only use) is Leigh Hunt in 1819, but Hazlitt here may have just preceded him. Hazlitt's exact meaning is unclear.

50. FROM 'MR KEAN'S HAMLET'

1. Pope, *Moral Essays*, II.17-20.

2. *The Winter's Tale*, IV.iv.141.

3. *Hamlet*, I.ii.85.

4. *Ibid.*, I.iv.44-5.

5. *Ibid.*, V.i.283-4.

6. *Ibid.*, II.ii.450.

7. Cf. Pope, *Moral Essays*, II.51-2: 'Touch'd the brink of all we hate'.

51. FROM 'MR KEAN'S IAGO' (i)

1. *Hamlet,* IV.v.124 adapted.

2. *3 Henry VI*, V.vi.77.

3. *Othello*, III.iii.138-41.

52. FROM 'MR KEAN'S IAGO' (ii)

1. The hypocrite in the play *Tartuffe* by Moliere.

2. In Sheridan's *School for Scandal*.

3. In Fielding's *Tom Jones*.

4. Published in 1766 as *New Bath Guide* by Christopher Anstey.

5. Addison, *The Campaign*, 292.

6. *Othello*, III.iii.120.

53. FROM 'MR KEAN'S RICHARD'

1. Compare 'the bye-play, the varying points of view, the venturous magnanimity of dramatic fiction' (Howe, xviii, 308). Hazlitt is here arguing that Wordsworth does *not* have this Shakespearean capacity.

54. FROM 'MR KEAN'S MACBETH'

1. Burke, *Reflections on the Revoltuion in France* (ed. Payne, p.101) (Howe).

2. *Othello*, III.iii.348.

3. *Hamlet*, V.i.206.

56. FROM 'MR KEAN'S RICHARD II'

1. *Hamlet*, III.ii.12 (inexplicable *for* inexpressible).

2. Horace, *ars Poetica*: '... the mind is less actively stimulated by what it takes in through the ear than by what is presented to it through the trustworthy agency of the eyes - something that the spectator can see for himself' (180).

3. *Richard II*, III.iii.190-5.

4. *Ibid.*, IV.i.260-2.

57. FROM 'MR KEAN'S OTHELLO'

1. Dante's *Inferno*, Canto xxxii,125 and xxxiii.87.

2. *Paradise Lost*, IV.989.

3. *Othello*, V.ii.344.

4. *Ibid.*, III.iii.225.

5. Perhaps from 'exceeding honesty', *Othello*, III.ii.258.

58. FROM 'MR KEAN'S CORIOLANUS'

1. *Coriolanus*, III.i.82 ('their infirmity').

2. *The Tempest*, V.i.23-4 adapted.

3. *Henry VIII*, I.iii.10: 'they keep state so'.

4. *Coriolanus*, III.iii.123.

5. *Ibid.*, II.iii.172.

59. FROM 'MR KEAN'S LEAR'

1. *Othello*, III.iii.370.

2. Beaumont and Fletcher, *Philaster*, V.iii: 'Held out a thousand storms, a thousand thunders'.

INDEX

STUDIES IN BRITISH LITERATURE